Best Hikes

CHILDREN®

in Pennsylvania

By Sally Trepanowski
Photos by Marty Trepanowski

THE
MOUNTAINEERS

Published by
The Mountaineers
1001 SW Klickitat Way
Seattle, Washington 98134

0 9 8 7 6
5 4 3 2 1

Published simultaneously in Canada by Douglas & McIntyre, Ltd., 1615 Venables Street, Vancouver, B.C. V5L 2H1

Published simultaneously in Great Britain by Cordee, 3a DeMontfort Street, Leicester, England, LE1 7HD

Manufactured in the United States of America

Edited by Kris Fulsaas
Maps by Debbie Newell
All photographs by Marty Trepanowski
Cover design by Watson Graphics
Book design by Bridget Culligan
Book layout by Virginia Hand

Cover photographs: *Fern spread and hardwoods, Allegheny National Forest, Pennsylvania* © David Muench/Tony Stone Images; inset: *A family enjoys a stroll through the forest* (Marty Trepanowski).

Library of Congress Cataloging-in-Publication Data
Trepanowski, Sally.
    Best hikes with children in Pennsylvania / by Sally Trepanowski ;
  photos by Marty Trepanowski.
        p.   cm.
    ISBN 0-89886-462-3
    1. Hiking—Pennsylvania—Guidebooks. 2. Trails—Pennsylvania—
  Guidebooks. 3. Family recreation—Pennsylvania—Guidebooks.
  4. Pennsylvania—Guidebooks. I. Title.
  GV199.42.P4T74 1996
  796.5'1'09748—dc20   96–3438
                                                          CIP

*To the memory of my mother,
Margaret Greeley Gwinner,
who helped instill in me a love
for all of God's creation.*

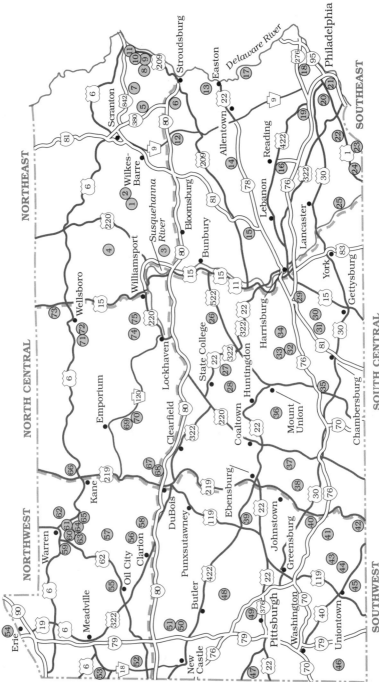

Contents

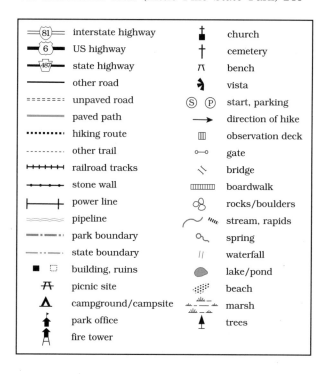

═(81)═	interstate highway	church
■(6)═	US highway	cemetery
═(487)═	state highway	bench
———	other road	vista
========	unpaved road	(S) (P) start, parking
———	paved path	→ direction of hike
··········	hiking route	observation deck
---------	other trail	○—○ gate
++++++	railroad tracks	bridge
•—•—•—	stone wall	boardwalk
├———┼	power line	rocks/boulders
≈≈≈≈	pipeline	stream, rapids
═··═··═·	park boundary	spring
——··—·	state boundary	// waterfall
■ ⬚	building, ruins	lake/pond
开	picnic site	beach
▲	campground/campsite	marsh
🏠	park office	trees
🏠	fire tower	

Acknowledgments

Thanks to the following people (in no particular order):

Rick and Kathy Baldauf, for use of the printer when ours went kaput and for company on hikes; Don and Brita Dorn, for the measuring wheel and books; Kathy Frank, for information on the Allegheny National Forest; My sister Nancy and her husband Papo Gomez, for letting me borrow the kids; the Warren Library Association reference room librarians, for being so helpful; Anne Papalia-Berardi and Gerry Berardi for encouragement; My father, Robert Gwinner, who taught me the names of all the trees in the forest (though he has forgotten some of them by now); MacQueen Photographics; folks at the Allegheny Outdoor Club; many friends and coworkers in Sugar Grove, Pittsfield, and Youngsville Elementary Schools for support; and my students at those schools who serve as a constant reminder of why I wrote this book.

Introduction

One of my earliest childhood memories is of walking along a wooded trail near our home in southeastern Pennsylvania, scrambling over rocks and roots with my mother in an eager quest to spot the first snowy petals of the bloodroot flower, a sure sign that spring had indeed arrived. Some of my happiest days as a child were spent on that trail. Initially, I toddled behind my mother when I first learned to walk; later, my sister and I raced ahead of her on our way to the wild raspberry patches. When we were grown and my mother became ill, I became the hike leader as we casually strolled along the well-worn path, pointing out the same bloodroot flowers. Those early walks instilled in me a love of the outdoors and a thirst for hiking that I hope is never fully quenched.

Going on hikes with your children is one of the best gifts you can give them. Long after the Christmas toys are broken and the Saturday morning cartoons are over, your children will cherish the memories of those hikes, when you shared with them not only your enthusiasm for nature, but, even more importantly, your time.

Hiking with children requires a little more planning and attention,

Children see the wonder in little things that adults sometimes overlook.

but their enthusiastic response to each new discovery makes the extra effort worthwhile. Though you may have seen thousands of toads in your lifetime, the sight of a fingernail-sized amphibian may be the most exciting event of the day to your toddler. Children of all ages help adults see the wonder that is right there all around us, if we would just look for it.

Getting Started

The first and most important rule for hiking with children is to have fun. Encourage your children to think of hiking as an adventure in which something new and exciting may be around every bend. Plan your hikes as a family, and allow the children to take an active part in preparing for the hike, such as looking at the maps, gathering equipment, and picking out favorite trail snacks. To heighten their anticipation, set something special aside, such as a favorite story, trail snack, or special piece of clothing, for the day of the hike. Do not forget to set a rain date, just in case the weather does not cooperate when the day comes around. Read the trail description ahead of time so you can tell your hikers what they may expect to see when you get there. Children mirror the attitudes of the adults around them; if you are excited about an upcoming hike, your children easily catch your enthusiasm.

When choosing a trail, it is important to consider the age and experience of your particular group. Although all of the hikes in this book are suitable for families or groups hiking with children, check the distance and the difficulty rating to find a trail that is best for you. In general the shortest, easy hikes are best for families with babies, toddlers and young children, pregnant mothers, older folks, and those short on time, while the longer, more challenging hikes would be suitable for families with older or more experienced children or teenagers. If you are not sure about your family's abilities, err on the side of caution and choose an easy hike your first few times out. Refer to the "How to Use This Book" section at the end of this chapter for a key to interpreting the trail symbols and descriptions.

What to Take

Even if you are only out for a day hike, there are certain items that you must not leave home without. The Mountaineers has compiled a list of Ten Essentials that should accompany every group of hikers into the woods. Though you may never have to use some of the Ten Essentials, having them gives you the peace of mind that comes with knowing you are prepared should an emergency situation arise.

The Ten Essentials

1. Extra clothing—Rain gear, knit hat, sweater, and mittens keep hikers warm should there be a drop in temperature or a sudden storm. An old pair of sneakers is useful for wading creeks, and extra dry socks can help prevent blisters.

2. Extra food—Carry plenty of high-energy snack foods, such as trail mix, candy, granola bars, nuts, and fruit chews, setting some aside to be used only in an emergency. Carry enough water for each hiker, as water sources along the trail may not be reliable.

3. Sunglasses—Glasses that screen out ultraviolet rays are best. Sunscreen and a hat with a brim are also recommended.

4. Knife—Bring a pocket knife that has two blades, scissors, a can opener, and tweezers.

5. Fire starter (candle or chemical fuel)—In case you need to build a fire.

6. First-aid kit—Do not forget to include moleskin for blisters, baking soda for bee stings, and special medication if your child is allergic to bee stings or insect bites.

7. Matches in a waterproof container—Sporting goods stores should carry this.

8. Flashlight—Check the batteries before your hike, and carry an extra set just in case.

9. Map—Look at the map before you start and check it regularly as you progress along the trail.

10. Compass—Learn how to use it, and teach your children how. It can be fun.

In addition to the Ten Essentials, the following suggestions will help make your family hike more enjoyable.

Carry a small roll of toilet paper. As any parent knows, though you may admonish children to go before you leave, the time when your child needs a toilet is most likely to be when there is not one around. Carry a small plastic trowel for such occasions. Show your child how to go off the trail 200 feet (about 100 kid steps) away from water sources, and dig a 6- to 8-inch hole in which to deposit and bury solid wastes. For liquid wastes, a distance of 100 feet from trails and water sources is sufficient, and there is no need to dig a hole. Experts now recommend carrying out toilet paper. A resealable plastic bag works well for this purpose.

Insect repellent is useful in Pennsylvania during the spring and summer, when the mosquitoes are out. Choose a brand of repellent that is recommended for children—those containing high percentages of DEET (diethyl toluamide) may be too strong. Try dabbing repellent around your ankles and socks to help ward off ticks, which are in abundance throughout the summer. Extra dabs around the ears and hat brims may help keep that annoying hum of mosquito wings out of range.

Extra items that may add interest to the hike include binoculars for bird-watching, a magnifying glass, sketch pad and colored pencils for drawing, and a camera. If you have a point and shoot camera, try letting children take pictures of each other and of their favorite sights along the trail.

Footwear. The number-one consideration when choosing appropriate footwear is comfort. Some of the trails in this book, particularly the flat, paved trails, can be hiked easily in an ordinary pair of sneakers. For these trails there is no need to go out and buy new shoes; old broken-in ones do just fine. However, unpaved trails (which account for most of the trails in this book) require that both children and adults wear some sort of hiking boot with lug soles. Boots provide the extra ankle support needed on uneven terrain and better traction on slippery slopes.

Choose children's boots the same way you choose your own. Children generally prefer lightweight fabric-and-leather boots. When shopping for boots, take along the thick socks your youngsters will be wearing on the trail. Do not pay too much attention to size—go by what feels best for your child. Have your child walk around the store in the boots and try out the elevated ramp most stores have for simulating what it feels like to go downhill in the boots. Try this test to make sure the boots are not too small: have the child push the toes all the way to the front of the boot, and then see if he or she can slide an index finger into the boot behind the heel. If one finger fits easily, the boots are probably the right fit; if not, look for a bigger size. If much more than one finger's width fits in behind the heel, look for a smaller size.

Once you have the right boots, it is essential to break them in. Have your children wear their boots around the house, to the playground, to school, to the grocery store; wearing them as much as possible will ensure that they are amply comfortable when you leave the trailhead.

Choosing the correct socks to pair with the boots is important, too. Cotton socks are not the best choice because they absorb moisture, which can cause blisters in tender young feet. Look for thick wool-blend socks or synthetic socks made of nylon, acrylic, or polypropylene blends. Many hikers also prefer to wear a thin, silky liner sock underneath the thick sock, to help prevent blisters. Admittedly, these type of socks can be difficult to find in children's sizes. If you do not have any luck with your local sporting goods store, try some of the mail-order catalogs.

Clothing. Clothing for hiking should be, above all, comfortable. No matter what season you are hiking in, take several layers of clothing, so that you can add or remove pieces as the temperature changes. Even in the middle of summer, it is possible to get chilled when you stop in a shady or breezy area and your perspiration begins to evaporate.

For hot weather, T-shirts and shorts are probably most comfortable, as long as you carry an extra long-sleeved shirt, light jacket, or synthetic sweater in case it gets cool. Lycra or spandex shorts or tights are comfortable and can help prevent chafing on the inside of the thighs. Loose gym shorts with ample leg room work well. Blue jeans, though they are popular, are usually not very comfortable to hike in. Choose a light pair of sweat pants, tights, or synthetic pants instead. Jeans are especially a no-no in cold weather. Because they are cotton, they hold moisture and can cause considerable chilling. Synthetic pants are the only way to go when the temperature drops. In cold spring, fall, and winter weather, long underwear is a particularly important layering item to wear on your hikes. Unlike cotton, synthetic thermal underwear (polypropylene and polyester blends) wicks moisture away from your skin and keeps you warm even when you sweat.

Every member of your party should have some sort of rain jacket. Coated nylon jackets with hoods are usually the best deal. You can buy high-tech waterproof/breathable-fabric rain coats for children, but they are costly, especially considering that your child will outgrow them quickly. Even if it does not rain, the jackets also double as windbreakers on breezy mountaintops.

Though not essential, bandanas are fun to wear and come in handy for mopping up sweat and mud, for nose blowing, and as makeshift belts, emergency bandages, hair bands, extra diapers, and so on. Start a collection and let your children choose their favorite color.

Packs. Even the littlest hikers seem to feel more important when they can don a small day pack that contains some item they or the group needs for the hike. For younger children, the small book-bag-style day packs do just fine for day hikes. Older children may prefer a more elaborate day pack with several pockets for water bottles and snacks.

Adults may need to carry a full-sized backpack in order to take the extra gear that the younger children may not be able to carry. Either an internal- or external-frame backpack is fine, as long as it has a well-padded hip belt. There are numerous types of child and infant carriers on the market, some designed for carrying infants close to their parent's chest and others that accommodate older babies and toddlers backpack-style. Take your child with you when you shop for one of these carriers and walk around the store with it for a while before deciding what is most comfortable. Models with a well-padded hip belt and extra storage pockets for diapers and bottles are the most practical for hiking.

Food. Eating is one of the great pleasures that accompanies hiking, and for kids the chance to eat special "trail food" can be one of the highlights of the trip. Hiking burns a lot of calories, so carry high-energy foods to snack on throughout the hike.

Kids enjoy taking an active part in preparing food for the hike. Gorp is a favorite high-energy trail food, the primary ingredients being "good old raisins and peanuts." Take your children shopping with you to help choose other nuts, dried fruits, and small candies to add to the gorp. Fruit leather is a fun trail snack. You can buy it or, better yet, make it yourself in the oven. All that is needed is a jar of applesauce and a cookie sheet. In the evening, spray a tiny bit of cooking oil on the cookie sheet and pour the applesauce onto the sheet, spreading it out evenly. Sprinkle with ground cinnamon and leave it in the oven overnight with the door open, the temperature set on the lowest possible setting. In the morning, roll the leather up in plastic wrap and it is ready to eat. Other snack foods that are popular with children include jellied fruit drops, goldfish crackers, fruit bar cookies (apple, fig, raspberry), granola bars, banana chips, dry cereal, animal crackers, string cheese, peanut butter crackers, oatmeal cookies, pretzels, and beef jerky strips.

For lunch food that will not turn to mush in your pack, make sandwiches out of bagels, pita bread, or tortillas instead of regular loaf bread. Good fillings include cheese, peanut butter with jelly or honey or bananas, cream cheese and pimientos, and slices of cheese and lunch meat. If you are just out for a day, most lunch items keep

Grapes make an excellent trailside snack for young hikers.

without spoiling; the exceptions are chicken and mayonnaise, which can be dangerous to carry in warm weather. Flavored crackers can be a nice change of pace. Apples pack well and satisfy that need to crunch; and a seedless orange never tastes so exquisite as when it is eaten on the trail on a hot sunny day. If the weather is cool, consider carrying a bottle of hot water for making hot chocolate or instant soup on the trail. To avoid fusses, stick to foods your children are already familiar with and that they enjoy.

Setting Off

It is important to allow plenty of time for your hike so your children can hike at their own pace. Kids tend to start out fast and tire more quickly than adults. They also need more bathroom and snack breaks. Let them set the pace. Allow each child a chance to be the leader for a portion of the trip—and give the leader the privilege of deciding where to take rest breaks. If you notice one of your charges lagging behind, it is a good idea to put that one up in the lead for a while. Encourage your child to bring along a friend. That is a great way to keep your own youngster from getting cranky, and it also introduces yet another child to the joys of hiking.

Take advantage of children's natural curiosity while you hike. Stop to look closely at that shiny black beetle crossing the path, or the trail of ants leading up a maple tree. Smell the flowers, and touch the plush softness of the thick moss on the sides of the boulders near the creek. Look for animal tracks and speculate about what the animal that left them behind must have been up to. See if your kids can spot all three shapes of leaves on the sassafras tree, and sniff their sweet spicy smell. Notice how tulip poplar leaves have a bright golden sheen when held up to the sunlight. Put a jewelweed leaf under a trickle of water and see how the leaf appears to magically turn into silver. Taste the wild blueberries and raspberries and chew on a birch twig to sample the root beer flavor (but also see the section on safety later in this chapter). Imitate the calls of the birds and the chipmunks. Look for salamanders under creekside logs and rocks. The forest itself offers endless sources of entertainment. The more you learn about the natural history of the area you plan to hike in, the more exciting discoveries you will be able to point out to your children.

Have Fun. Trail and camp games are another good way to have fun and learn about nature. Try some of these activities with your children the next time you need something to liven up your hikes.

Hug a tree. Pair off and have one member of the pair don a bandana blindfold. The partner carefully leads the blinded person to a nearby tree, and gives them 3 to 5 minutes to explore the tree with hands, nose, etc., trying to get to know the tree by touch. After time is up, the partners lead the blinded ones back to a central spot, where they are unblindfolded. The previously blinded person tries to locate the tree he or she had explored while sightless. The partner offers clues and help as needed.

Still hunt. Assign each person a tree to sit by with a partner or alone. Sit quietly for 15 minutes, not moving or making a sound. Come back to report what each person saw or heard. This is an excellent activity for older children—you can increase the time for those with longer attention spans.

Silent walking. Walk like the Lenni Lenape Indians did when they hunted, placing their weight on the ball of their feet first, then gently placing the heel down, carefully avoiding stepping on crackly leaves or brittle sticks. See how quietly your group can progress down the path. This is especially good to try in early morning or at dusk when there is the greatest chance of surprising a white-tailed deer, rabbit, chipmunk, or porcupine.

Calling all owls. When camping overnight, practice calling the owls. Try the barred owl by hooting "who cooks for you—who cooks for you, who?" I've seen a barred owl fly right into camp when a group of children called him in.

Swamp orchestra. Assign every member of the party a swamp noise to make, for example, "ribbit, ribbit" for a frog, the word "swamp, swamp . . ." for the bullfrog, a high-pitched "hummmmmmmm" for a mosquito, "who cooks for you . . ." for the owl, the word "garbage, garbage . . ." for the cicada bug, a repeated cluck of the tongue for the woodpecker, adding others of your own creation. Have each person practice their sound one at a time. Then, when you give the signal, every orchestra member is to repeat his or her sound simultaneously for several minutes. See how closely your orchestra resembles the real nightly summer orchestra.

Scavenger hunt. While you are walking, collect about eight to ten common natural items such as a pine cone, a pebble, a fallen colored leaf, an acorn, etc., and lay these out on a bandana. (Include items that are plentiful and do not require picking of live plant material.) Gather the kids around, and let them study your collection for 1 minute. Supply them with a small bag and let them collect as many of these items as they can recall while you all progress down the trail.

I spy. Play twenty questions, picking something that lives, grows, or is located along the trail as the subject. Begin with a clue, such as "I spy something that lives by the water . . .", and allow children to guess what it is. Take turns until everyone has had a chance to pick a subject.

Numbers walk. As your group walks along, assign each hiker a number. That hiker is to point out items along the trail that come in that number. For example, Number One may point out single flowers, Number Two might notice twin trees, Number Three might point out poison ivy leaves, Number Four may notice four-leaf clovers, and so on. Assign the lower numbers to younger hikers.

It smells like . . . use your nose on the next hike and stop frequently to smell flowers, leaves, moss, dirt, etc. After sniffing, each person must complete the sentence "It smells like . . . "

If I were . . . When the walk is getting long or you are confined to the tent or picnic pavilion because it is raining, try this: Ask each hiker to complete the following sentence "If I were an animal I would be a _____ because_____," having each hiker fill in the blanks with his or her favorite animal, and the reason why it would be fun to be that animal. You can vary the game by asking about favorite trees, flowers, and birds.

Noah's ark. If you hike with a group of children, try this during lunch: Pairs of children become animals (two bears, two bluejays, two frogs, two owls . . .) and must shut their eyes and find their partner by sound only.

Find yours. Find and distribute a blade of grass to each hiker. Hikers spend a few minutes carefully inspecting their blade, then all the blades are collected and mixed up. See how many hikers can identify which is "their" blade. Variation: do the same thing but use sticks instead.

Apartment house. Find a tree and talk about what lives in it (grubs and worms in the cellar, woodpeckers in the kitchen, raccoons in the living room, cardinals singing in the attic . . .).

Ode to a dead tree. When you come across a dead tree, take turns making up a story about the tree's life, from birth to death to rebirth (as another tree eventually grows in its place).

The coming and going of the rain. Stand in a circle and turn sideways to face your neighbor's back. Imitate the sounds of a storm by consecutively rubbing hands on the back of the person in front of you (the wind), then snapping fingers (rain drops), then gently slapping back (heavy rain), then reverse.

Hitchhikers walk. When you are hiking in the late summer or fall, give your kids an old pair of socks to put on over their shoes for a portion of the hike. After the hike, collect and examine the seed hitchhikers that have attached themselves to the socks. Plant the seeds when you get home, water them, and see which ones sprout.

Garden of Eden. Have children pretend they are walking in the Garden of Eden and it is their job to make up names for all the plants and animals they see. There are two other variations to this game. One, pretend to be Lenni Lenape Indians and name the plants and animals according to their characteristics (for example, a rabbit might henceforth be known as "furry one who hops"). Or, pretend to be pioneers discovering the area and naming the streams, mountains, waterfalls, valleys, and so on.

Trail Etiquette

For the sake of the trails and your children, teach them to hike with an attitude of respect toward the trail and those with whom they share it. When you give them a rule, explain why it exists so they understand that they are doing their part to help keep the environment healthy so that others may enjoy it after they have.

Pack It Out. The "pack it in, pack it out" ethic is easily remembered and understood: If you brought it in with you, take it back out with you when you leave. Even biodegradable items such as food scraps can take a long time to break down. An orange peel, for example, can take five years to disintegrate. Food scraps are not good for wild animals to eat, either. Children can help clean up after less thoughtful hikers by picking up candy wrappers or soda cans they find along the trail. Carry an extra garbage bag for this purpose.

Do Not Pick the Flowers. "Take only pictures, leave only footprints" is another wise saying that can help children remember not to pick the flowers, dig up the moss, squash the beetles, or cart home favorite rocks. Younger children especially need guidance in this area. Remind children that the flowers, trees, and bugs are living, too, and that picking or squishing can hurt or kill them. Using a camera or sketch pad for recording interesting finds is a good alternative.

Stay on the Trail. Children love to run ahead and get there first, but in their zeal sometimes they take shortcuts around the trail or cut across the switchbacks to skid down the hills more quickly. Teach your kids to stay on the trail. Cutting switchbacks causes erosion and makes the path ugly, and it is more difficult than using the trail itself. One way to instill appreciation for trails is to do some volunteer trail work as a family. Go out with a local hiking club when they are doing trail maintenance, or volunteer to adopt a section of a trail to maintain. Once kids see how much work there is in making and keeping a trail, they not only stick to the trail themselves but will likely tell others to do so, too.

Passing Techniques. On crowded trails it is good for children to know the etiquette for passing others and for stopping along the trail. When two parties meet on a narrow trail, the party going uphill has the right of way. Those heading downhill should step aside and let the others pass. When stopping for a break, try to choose a spot beside the trail where the group is not obstructing the path.

Walk and Speak Softly. Children may be loud in their exuberance about nature; do not squash their enthusiasm, but remind them the group has a much better chance of seeing animals if they use quiet voices. Try silent walking or still hunts (see the Have Fun section earlier in this chapter) for fun. Other hikers appreciate your efforts in this respect.

Selecting a Campsite. When camping, choose designated sites, or locate a camp at least 200 feet away from the trail or water sources. When washing, do not use soap directly in a stream or body of water; take water from the source and wash and rinse at least 200 feet away from the water, even if using biodegradable soap. Children can think about it this way: you do not want your bath water to be someone else's drinking water!

Practice what you preach when it comes to taking care of the environment. Make the motto "leave nothing but footprints" a family challenge. See if you can leave a campsite not only looking the same as when you left it, but better. If you had a fire, drown it and dismantle any fire rings. Make it a contest to see who can pick up the most litter. Have children fluff up the leaves, and throw a few pine cones back over the campsite. Before you leave, play detective and ask, "Will anyone be able to tell that we have been here?"

Safety

Pennsylvania is generally a safe place to hike. Still, any activity in the outdoors carries some element of risk. The best protection is some knowledge of what the possible hazards are.

Hypothermia. Hypothermia is the biggest threat to hikers anywhere, though it is entirely preventable. This life-threatening condition comes about when a hiker becomes chilled and the body temperature drops to a dangerously low level if the hiker is not warmed up sufficiently. Hypothermia can occur any time of the year, and at surprisingly high temperatures (into the 50s), but is most commonly a threat in spring, fall, and winter.

Children are susceptible to hypothermia because they are typically small and lean, they tend to deny discomfort if they are having a good time, and they love to get wet. Watch your kids to see that they are warm enough. Blue-tinged lips, goose bumps, shivering, crankiness, or excessive stumbling help clue you in to discomfort. Dress them in layers of synthetic or wool clothing, which hold in warmth even when wet. Keep in mind that exposed ridges or deep stream valleys are usually much cooler than home. In cool or cold weather, discourage water play. See that kids drink plenty of fluids, as a well-hydrated body is less vulnerable to hypothermia. Frequent high-energy snacks help, too. If your charges begin to shiver, remove wet clothing and warm them with a good body-surrounding embrace so your body heat is conducted to them. Add a hat and additional warm layers of clothing. If shivering continues, head back to your vehicle.

Rabies. Another issue to be aware of is rabies. In the past few years, Pennsylvania and other Middle Atlantic states have had an increasing number of rabies cases in certain animal species. Though contact with a rabid animal is still uncommon, here is what to watch for. The most commonly afflicted animals are raccoons and skunks, but foxes, coyotes, and others can also have the disease. This viral disease can be transmitted to humans through a bite from an infected animal or contamination of an open wound by saliva. Do not approach, touch, or feed raccoons, skunks, other wild creatures, or stray pets. Do not touch any dead animal. If you do find a dead animal or see an animal behaving strangely, steer clear of it and notify the land manager. If you do receive a bite or a scratch from a wild animal, clean the area with soap and water and allow it to bleed. Go to the nearest physician's office or hospital for treatment and report the incident to the land managers.

Ticks. Ticks are common in Pennsylvania, especially in spring or early summer. Wearing long pants or gaiters helps keep ticks away. All ticks are dark brown. Wood ticks are about the size and shape of a dill seed. They can carry Rocky Mountain spotted fever. More of a concern, however, are the tiny deer ticks, which are about the size of a sesame seed or smaller. They can carry Lyme disease, which has been on the rise in Pennsylvania. Check for ticks at the end of each hike, looking especially at the ankles, shins, back, chest, head, and ears. Wood ticks can usually be removed carefully by hand if they have not burrowed their head under the skin. Deer ticks may require tweezers. If you cannot remove it easily or if a portion of the tick remains embedded, see a doctor. Afterward, watch for any unusual symptoms. If a tick bite becomes inflamed and develops a large circular rash around it, or if you develop flulike symptoms, see your doctor.

Bee Stings. Bee stings are a concern mainly for those who are allergic to them. If your children are allergic to bees, carry an epinephrine kit with you when you hike and know how to use it. Avoid bee hives and poking around in rotting logs. Yellow jackets, which are crankiest in the late summer and fall, like to build hives in the ground, so steer clear of tiny holes in the trail if you see a bee emerging. If someone gets stung, encourage him or her to run away from the nest, but to take his or her pack so you do not have to go back amongst angry bees to retrieve it.

Snakes. Pennsylvania has twenty-two species of snakes, only three of which are poisonous: the copperhead, and timber and Massasuaga rattlesnakes. All three species have triangular-shaped heads, fangs, and vertical pupils. The timber rattler has dark diamond shapes on a lighter background, with rattles at the end of the tail, one "button" for each time it has shed its skin. This snake species usually shakes its rattles when it feels the vibrations of approaching hikers. The

Massasauga rattler is a threatened species in Pennsylvania, and there is only one hike in this book located in its territory: hike 50, Jennings Environmental Education Center. Both species of rattlers prefer sunny rocky areas, particularly along the band of Appalachian Mountains that stretches from the southcentral to northeast region of the state. The copperhead has irregularly shaped copper-colored patches on its back and blends in well with dead leaves. It is shy—in decades of hiking in the state, I have seen about a dozen timber rattlers, but only two copperheads.

A harmless water snake suns himself amidst the poison ivy vines—which he can touch but hikers should not.

To avoid snake encounters, it is best to avoid reaching hands or feet in between boulders. All snakes are shy and typically flee if a human approaches. They generally will not bite unless provoked or injured. If you see a snake, give it a wide berth and move past it quietly. Children need not fear snakes but can learn about their benefits. For example, the black rat snake keeps farmers' barns free from rodents and is considered a better mouser than a cat.

Drinking Water. Drinking water can be an unnoticed hazard if it is polluted. *Giardia* cysts can be present in any water source and cause unpleasant symptoms of nausea, vomiting, and diarrhea. Carry in your own water, or carry a water filter.

Poisonous Plants. Numerous poisonous plants should be avoided. The most common, poison ivy, has three leaves which may or may not be shiny. All parts of this plant can cause itchy rashes, even in people who have not been susceptible in the past. Poison sumac, which grows near swamps and has white berries, has a similar irritating effect on the skin. Staghorn sumac with its red berries is safe to touch. Do not allow children to pick or eat any species of fungus or mushroom, as it takes an expert to identify these plants and many species are poisonous. Teach children not to eat anything at all unless an adult identifies the plant first. Generally only raspberries, blackberries, blueberries, huckleberries, black raspberries, and wine berries are edible. Learn to identify these berries, which can be a delight on a summer hike. Do not allow children to eat other types of berries. Oak acorns are not safe to eat. Other poisonous plants common to Pennsylvania include jack in the pulpit, may apple, buttercups, and pokeweed. All of these can have bad effects if eaten. In addition, when camping, do not burn rhododendron or mountain laurel branches, which have toxic smoke, and do not use the branches of these plants or of any cherry trees for marshmallow or hot dog sticks.

Lost-Proofing Kids. Getting lost is probably every child's biggest fear about being in the woods. If children stay within sight of the adults and stick to the trail, this most likely will not be a problem. Teach your children that if they do become lost to stay put. Some parents tell their kids to find a tree and hug it. It is a good idea to equip children with a whistle to wear around their necks. If they become lost, three short blasts on the whistle help searchers locate them. Three is the distress signal, so children should be told to blow three short blasts only in an emergency.

Water Safety. Swimming is great fun, but do use common sense about where children swim. State parks do not allow swimming except at lifeguarded beaches and pools. Sometimes wading is permitted in portions of the state parks. Children should wear an old pair of sneakers for swimming or wading to protect feet from sharp objects. When swimming is permitted, it is a good idea to have children wear life preservers. Do not allow children to swim upstream from waterfalls or dangerous rapids.

Hunting Season. Hunting is a very popular outdoor activity in Pennsylvania. Many of the hiking trails in this book are on property that is open to hunters in the fall and winter hunting seasons. Buck and doe deer seasons are probably the most popular, with opening days the most hazardous time for hikers. There are also archery seasons, fall and spring turkey seasons, small game season, muzzle loaders' dates, and a limited bear season. Avoid hiking on the opening day of any hunting season. Opening dates vary, so check with your local Game Commission office for the exact dates. Even hiking in a wildlife sanctuary can be hazardous, as many of them border areas popular with hunters. If hiking during hunting season, the best bet is to hike on Sunday, when hunting is prohibited throughout the state. Next best is to hike wearing hunters' blaze orange clothing; avoid wearing any white clothing.

Why Pennsylvania?

Pennsylvania is an ideal place to hike with children. With literally thousands of miles of hiking trails, "Penn's Woods" is rich in beauty and wildlife as well as history. Children love to see how many bodies it takes to encircle a 300-year-old hemlock in one of the state's virgin forests, or how many times a rock can skip across a meandering creek, and they enjoy making up stories about how it must have felt to be a Lenni Lenape Indian walking through these same vast woods. Whether your family prefers spring wildflower walks, summer saunters along cool forest paths, autumn adventures amidst the blazing maples, or tromps in the snow, there is a trail for you in Pennsylvania, not far from where you live. From the Allegheny National Forest to the paths through Philadelphia's John Heinz Wildlife Preserve at Tinicum, there is plenty in Pennsylvania for both children and their parents to enjoy. This book is intended to help you to scratch the surface.

Geology. Do not let the seemingly small size of the mountains in Pennsylvania fool you; these were once high and mighty peaks that have worn down over the eons. Geologically, Pennsylvania has undergone many changes over the millennia and knowing about these changes helps hikers appreciate the scenery a bit more.

In prehistoric times the state was on the edge of a huge inland sea that covered most of the interior of what is now the United States. Pennsylvania was a vast swamp, rich in vegetation. Eventually, the decaying vegetation and animals were pressed together under pressure to form the famous Pennsylvania coal beds in the central part of the state and oil reserves in the northwest (thus the term "fossil fuels"). Later, the southern reaches of the Jerseyan Glacier in the northeast, and the Wisconsin Glacier in the northwest, brought an icy climate in which the force of melting and thawing, and the grinding power of the moving ice, scoured the landscape of these areas. The remains of the glacier can be seen here in the form of long moraines (ridges of rocks marking the end of the glacier).

The rest of the state was subject to forces that uplifted the Appalachian and Allegheny Mountains. The Appalachians arc across the state from the southcentral to the northeast, part of a chain of mountains that runs from Georgia to Maine. Long rows of low ridges and valleys characterize these mountains. Most of the state is in this region, termed the Appalachian Highlands.

The plateaus are found on both sides of the Appalachians. The Pocono plateau is probably the most famous. Though the Poconos are called mountains, technically they are not. Mountains are rocks that were uplifted; a plateau is a high plain through which water cuts deep valleys. The effect looks very similar. In the southwest is the pretty Appalachian plateau. Northward the Allegheny plateau consists of river and stream ridges and valleys. In the southwest and southeast corner of the state, the Piedmont dominates, with gently rolling hills and streams in mixed forest and fields. Erie and Philadelphia are on narrow strips of coastal plain, a decidedly flat contour with plenty of wetlands.

Trees. Pennsylvania's name—Penn's Woods—characterizes what the state is best known for, and Pennsylvania is still a heavily forested state, though the character of the forest has changed over the years. Once the state had abundant forests of virgin eastern hemlock and white pine. These forests were vast and majestic. Other forests contained millions of American chestnut trees, so many that it was said that every other tree was a chestnut.

The ancient forests have all but disappeared; only 1 percent of the virgin forests remain. Hemlock was logged for its bark, which is rich in tannic acid, needed by leather tanneries. Pine was lumbered for growing construction needs, as were many of the other hardwood trees. Lumbering gave way to forest fires, then reforestation. The American chestnut species was destroyed in a blight in the early part of this century. Forest was cleared for farming. Today, most of the state is once again forested, with hardwood species such as oak dominating. Beech, hickory, tulip poplar, maple, cherry, and yellow birch are common. Pockets of virgin forest are preserved throughout the state, and this book includes hikes in these areas so hikers can enjoy the majesty of the ancient trees. Learning the names of the many tree species is an interesting and fun activity for children. Try making a collection of tree leaves—gather fall leaves, press them, and mount in a photo album with a label of their names underneath. Or, take along butcher's paper and wide crayons and make rubbings of the leaves and collect the samples in a scrapbook.

Wildlife. Besides the trees, the wildlife was different hundreds of years ago, too. Elk roamed the state, especially in the Allegheny plateau. Bison were common, and the gray wolf was an important predator. A few moose and wolverines lived in the state as well. White-

Hikers never know what surprises may await them along the trail.

tailed deer were actually less plentiful then, due to higher mortality rates and less suitable habitat. The elk are gone except for a small, well-protected herd in northcentral Pennsylvania. Bison, wolves, moose, and wolverines are also gone. The white-tailed deer is more abundant than ever before. The farmlands mixed with patches of forest are perfect habitat for them and predators are few. The deer are shaping the way the future forests are growing; they are eating up all the young trees in many areas. Black bears enjoy a healthy population in the state. Coyotes are becoming more plentiful; abundant ground hog populations are sure to help encourage their stay. Many mammals make their home here, including opossums, shrews, moles, bats, rabbits, hares, porcupines, chipmunks, squirrels, rats, muskrats, beavers, foxes, raccoons, weasels, skunks, otters, minks, ermines, and occasionally bobcats.

Kids may enjoy making a wildlife sighting calendar. Designate a calendar for this purpose and when you sight an animal, note the location and time of day on the calendar. At year's end you will have a complete list of all the animals your family has seen. Another option is to put your wildlife log in a blank book, with room for pictures.

Birds. Much of Pennsylvania is in the path of the Eastern Flyway, a general route that migratory birds take as they head toward (or away from) the Great Lakes or the eastern coastal waters. Hikers may spot all kinds of raptors such as eagles, ospreys, and hawks, many of which can be seen during the fall migration at Hawk Mountain. Waterbirds of all kinds, including ducks, Canada geese, great blue herons, green herons, egrets, and bitterns, are found on the ponds, lakes, and rivers. The John Heinz Wildlife Preserve is one of the best places to view these birds. Songbirds of every variety are found throughout the state. Many of the trails in this book follow edges of fields and hedgerows where songbirds prefer to nest. Owls, such as the great horned, barred, screech, barn, and long-eared, live in the state year-round. It is a very lucky hiker who sees one of these. Woodpeckers can be heard on almost any hike, hammering away in search of insects and grubs. Look for the large pileated woodpecker, which is not common but exciting to find because of its impressive size and loud drilling. Consider starting a family bird list. Many state parks and bird guidebooks have lists you can use to check off the birds you have spotted on your family hikes.

Wildflowers. One of the treats of hiking in the warmer seasons in Pennsylvania is the show of wildflowers that graces the woodlands throughout the state. Hundreds of species of wildflowers are native to Pennsylvania. Children enjoy learning the names of things and flowers are easy to teach, as their colors and shapes are usually pretty distinctive. Get a wildflower guide and start with the easy, more common flowers in each season. For example, in the spring children may look for spring beauties, violets, bloodroot, trillium, trout lily, jack-in-the-pulpit, mayapples, wild roses, and dogwood. In the summer children may recognize day lilies, Indian pipes, wild berry blossoms, thistles, clovers, forget-me-nots, buttercups, Queen Anne's lace, rhododendron, mountain laurel, milkweed, phlox, jewelweed, daisies, black-eyed Susans, and butter and eggs. Fall brings more colors as the various asters and goldenrods come into full bloom. Even as late as November, hikers find flowers on the witch hazel plant, which blooms around Halloween. Children may enjoy drawing or painting the scenes they have encountered following a hike. Taking photos of the various flowers may also become a family hobby.

How to Use This Book

This book covers the entire state of Pennsylvania, which is divided into six regions, starting in the northeast and circling clockwise through the state: northeast, southeast, southcentral, southwest, northwest, and northcentral. Interstate 80 divides the north and south regions; US 15 and the Susquehanna River divide the east and central regions; US 219 divides the central and west regions. Each region contains hikes that vary according to type of scenery, difficulty, and location. Read the hike description and look at the map before hiking the trail so that you make the best choice for your group.

Each hike has a number that corresponds with the trail's location on the state map at the beginning of this book. Each hike's name includes the name of the trail(s), if there is one, and the name of the park, natural area, or other designated area in which it is located, as it appears on most maps. Pennsylvania has several state parks that are officially designated Environmental Education Center rather than State Park; this book contains hikes in four of these types of state parks.

Each hike begins with an information block that contains a short summary to assist your selection. These are the headings:

Type: Most of the hikes in this book are *day hikes*, a designation that means the trail is short enough that the average group with children can complete the hike within a day or less (in most cases, just a few hours). There are some hikes that are designated *overnight*, which indicates a longer hike that is suitable for an overnight trip. Some groups may be able to hike these trails on a day hike, but the possibility for an overnight exists. The average group on one of these trails will probably want to make these hikes into a backpacking outing. The location of possible campsites is noted.

Difficulty: Trails are rated easy, moderate, or challenging. Ratings take into consideration the distance, hiking time, difficulty of terrain, and elevation gain. *Easy* trails are usually 0.25 to 3 miles long, with gentle terrain and an elevation gain of less than 200 feet. *Moderate* trails may be from 1 to 4 miles long, and may have less even footing. *Challenging* trails may be 1 to 6 miles long, and usually involve elevation gain of more than 200 feet, rougher footing, or somewhat brushy conditions.

Distance: The length of the trail is given in miles, with an indication of whether the distance is one way or round trip. Most of the trails in this book are loop trails, and distance for these is for one entire circuit, from start to finish.

Hiking time: An estimated amount of time is given for the average family to hike this trail, with short rest stops and snack stops. This does not include lunch stops or side trips. Generally, a pace of about 1 mile per hour is assumed.

Elevation gain: The increase in elevation from the low point on the trail to the high point is given in feet. Hikes with higher elevation gains tend to be more difficult.

Hikable: The seasons that are best for hiking the trail are listed.

Maps: The most commonly available map for each hike is in many cases a state park map, national forest map, or state forest public use map. Many of these can be picked up at the area's land management office. In some cases, U.S. Geological Survey maps (topographical) are listed when there is no more readily available map. Most topos do not have the trail outline on them, though they do show the lay of the land.

Rest rooms: The locations of the closest rest rooms and drinking water are listed.

Fees: A few hikes require fees; in cases where they are required, an explanation of what the fee is used for is given. Fee hikes are included only in areas that use the fees to further the protection of the land or animals in the area. The listed fees are current as of the summer of 1995.

The description of each hike begins with an overview of the area and highlights of the hike. Notes of particular interest about the area— how to obtain brochures, any special attractions, etc.—are included where pertinent. Next, driving directions to the trailhead are given. In addition to interstates and US highways, there are state highways (designated PA) and state routes (designated SR), as well as secondary roads. Notes about any access difficulties are included in this paragraph.

A summary of the trail, with mileages and points of interest, gives the reader a sense of what may be encountered on the hike. Possible turnaround points, when feasible, are mentioned.

Other trails of interest: At the end of some of the hikes, trails in the area that may be of interest are briefly described, with their length and access point given. These trails have not been hiked by the author, but are generally considered popular family trails, based on recommendations by the various land managers.

Key to Symbols

 Day hikes. These are hikes that can be completed in a single day. While some trips allow camping, only a few require it.

 Backpack trips. These are hikes whose length or difficulty makes camping out either necessary or recommended for most families.

 Easy trails. These are relatively short, smooth, gentle trails suitable for small children or first-time hikers.

 Moderate trails. Most of these are 2 to 4 miles total distance and feature more than 500 feet of elevation gain. The trail may be rough and uneven. Hikers should wear lug-soled boots and be sure to carry the Ten Essentials.

 Difficult trails. These are often rough, with considerable elevation gain or distance to travel. They are suitable for older or experienced children. Lug-soled boots and the Ten Essentials are standard equipment.

 Hikable. The best times of year to hike each trail are indicated by the following symbols: flower—spring; sun—summer; leaf—fall; snowflake—winter.

A Note About Safety

Safety is an important concern in all activities. No guidebook can alert you to every hazard or anticipate the limitations of every reader. Therefore, the descriptions of roads, trails, routes, and natural features in this book are not representations that a particular excursion will be safe for your party. When you follow any of the routes described in this book, you assume responsibility for your own safety. Under normal conditions, such excursions require the usual attention to traffic, road and trail conditions, weather, terrain, the capabilities of your party, and other factors. Keeping informed on current conditions and exercising common sense are the keys to a safe, enjoyable outing.

The Mountaineers

Northeast Pennsylvania

Deer Leap Falls is just one of the many beautiful falls in the northeast.

1. Ganoga Glen, Glen Leigh, and Highland Trails

Type:	Day hike
Difficulty:	Challenging (elevation gain)
Distance:	3-mile loop
Hiking time:	5–6 hours
Elevation gain:	1,000 feet
Hikable:	Spring–fall
Map:	Falls trail map
Rest rooms:	Toilets, water at state park campground
Fee:	None

This is a truly spectacular hike through the Glens Natural Area that is well worth the effort for the chance to be transported into a world of waterfalls—nineteen along the route described here—each one exquisitely beautiful in its own way. In the summer the pools at Waters Meet, about halfway, make an excellent place to stop for lunch. Big hemlocks, mossy rock ledges, and water, water, everywhere are the highlights of this hike. Bring a camera with plenty of film. A shorter hike can be made by turning around at the base of Ganoga Falls, the highest in the park at 94 feet, making a round trip of about 1 mile.

Hikers descending by one of the nineteen waterfalls in the Glens Natural Area

Take your time on this trail. The path can be very slippery when wet, which is often. Children need to be well supervised on this trail, to keep them on the trail and prevent them from playing in the water above falls. Fall is the driest time of the year to hike.

To reach the trailhead, take PA 309 north from Wilkes-Barre and turn left on PA 118 west. At Red Rock turn right onto PA 487 north. Climb the twisting road to reach a junction with Main Park Road on the right, with a sign pointing to Ricketts Glen State Park; turn right onto Main Park Road. Just past the park office, turn right onto a dirt road and follow it 0.7 mile to its end at the Lake Rose parking area and trailhead sign. Please note: if you plan to visit the Ricketts Glen area with a camper or trailer in tow, it is best to approach the park from the north to avoid the 18 percent grade on PA 487 south of the park. Take PA 220 north from the Williamsport area and turn right on PA 487 south at Dushore.

The trail begins from the Lake Rose parking lot and heads downhill. In less than 0.2 mile, bear right on the Ganoga Glen Trail. Passing through hemlocks and beeches, the trail begins its long descent to Waters Meet, with ten major waterfalls along the way.

Cross Kitchen Creek, which the trail follows all the way down to Waters Meet. The trail is lined with magnificent hemlocks. Some of the hemlocks in the park are over 500 years old. Rangers have found

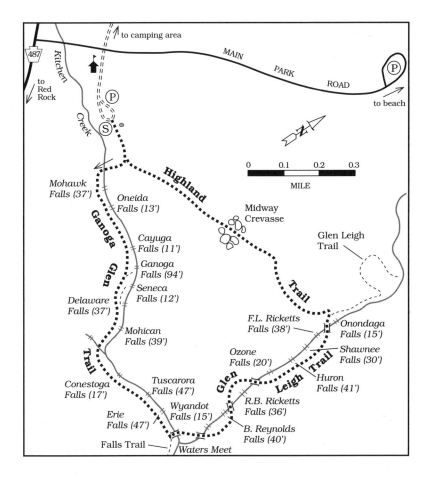

trees 5 feet in diameter, with 900-year-old growth rings. It is fun to speculate with children what the world was like when some of these old trees first sprouted 100, 200, 300, 400 years ago. Soon Mohawk Falls is on the left shoulder and immediately the trail descends steeply with rock steps. Many ledges line the edges of the path from now on. Look at the mosses, liverworts (can children figure out why they might be called that?), and ferns that grow on these moist ledges. A magnifying glass is helpful in examining some of these tiny plants.

Drop to Oneida Falls, then Cayuga Falls. The falls on this trail are named after tribes of the Iroquois Nation, which inhabited Pennsylvania long before Columbus set foot on the continent. Gently descend for a brief time at the top of Ganoga Falls. Notice the terraces of rocks at the top, like a thousand tiny steps for the water to march down. A guard wire begins on the left—keep kids strictly on the trail in this area. The trail switchbacks once and bears right again. Take the side trail to the left for a better view of this spectacular falls. Just over 0.5 mile from the trailhead, this is a possible turnaround point.

Returning to the trail, continue descending along the creek's edge. Feel the coolness of the rocks by Seneca Falls. Delaware and Mohican Falls come quickly as you cross a tributary creek with a falls all its own on the right. This is a good place to rest before reaching Waters Meet. Notice how tall the trees are—some at least 100 feet. Seedlings have a long way to grow up to meet the sun. Wood sorrel is abundant here—its leaves look like clover and taste tangy.

Pass Conestoga and Tuscarora Falls, noticing the smoothness of the rocks along the creek's edge. Do children know why they are so smooth? Erie Falls may show off "rainbows" if the morning sun hits the water mist just right. Soon you reach the junction of the two branches of Kitchen Creek at Waters Meet, 1 mile from the trailhead. This is a nice place to stop and gather strength for the climb back up. Colonel Ricketts, who used to own this land, had these trails built for his fishing pals. They took four years to complete.

At the bridge at Waters Meet, the Falls Trail takes off to the right; take the trail to the left to cross the bridge and begin the climb up on the Glen Leigh Trail. Cross another bridge by Wyandot Falls. The colonel named the falls on this branch of the creek after friends and family. Climbing steadily, cross a bridge by B. Reynolds Falls, then soon reach R. B. Ricketts Falls. The ascent becomes steeper here. The trail switchbacks and goes up rock steps. Cross a bridge by narrow Ozone Falls. Steps lead up to gorgeous Huron Falls, which looks like a natural amphitheater carved into the rock ledges.

The trail levels somewhat, and you can catch your breath. It is not long to the top of the steep climbs now. Up past the last three falls—Shawnee, F. L. Ricketts, and Onondaga—cross another bridge and reach a trail junction at 1.9 miles where the Glen Leigh Trail continues off to the right. Go left on the Highland Trail by a signed trail map. Cross a creeklet and ascend gently now through mixed forest. Have kids watch for Midway Crevasse. At 2.5 miles the trail passes through this jumble of boulders.

Continuing on the rocky but moderately graded trail, reach the trail junction where you began and bear right to the parking lot.

Other trails of interest: Across the street from the picnic area on PA 118 is the other end of the Falls Trail along Kitchen Creek. This area is famous for its virgin hemlock and pines. There are three waterfalls—Murray Reynolds, Sheldon Reynolds, and Harrison Wright Falls—at the top portion of this trail, near where it joins with the loop described here at Waters Meet.

The Evergreen Trail, which was closed during the summer of 1995 for bridge repair, is a short, pretty, self-guiding trail through ancient hemlocks. It is a great place to get a feel for what the forest in this area once was. The trail is accessed from the picnic area on the left on PA 118, just east of Red Rock.

---

2. Grand View Trail

Type:	Day hike
Difficulty:	Moderate (some rocks on way down)
Distance:	2.5-mile loop
Hiking time:	1.5 hours
Elevation gain:	150 feet
Hikable:	Spring–fall
Map:	Ricketts Glen State Park map
Rest rooms:	Toilets, water at state park campground
Fee:	None

There are not many places in Pennsylvania to get a mountaintop view, and far fewer that require so little climbing. At 2,449 feet, Grand View Mountain summit is one of the highest points in this part of the state and it does indeed have a great view of the Poconos. In early summer when the mountain laurel is in bloom, this is a particularly picturesque walk.

To reach Grand View Trail, take PA 309 north from Wilkes-Barre and turn left on PA 118 west. In Red Rock turn right onto PA 487 north. Go up the steep hill past a quarry area on the left, and watch for a gated grassy road on the left (1.5 miles south of the Main Park Road intersection described in hike 1, Ganoga Glen, Glen Leigh, and Highland Trails). Pull off the road on the wide shoulder by the gate, but do not block the gate. If you are traveling with a trailer or camper in tow, see the note in the directions for hike 1, Ganoga Glen, Glen Leigh, and Highland Trails, for the best route into the area.

The hike begins as you pass by the gate and take the grassy road to the left. Mountain laurel, the state flower, lines the road, which climbs gently and easily. Look for animal tracks in the dirt. Animals like to use the same trails we do. Can children tell the difference between a walking white-tailed deer track and a running one? A running deer's two-toed tracks are spread widely apart at the front of the toes as it runs, and sometimes the two imprints of the "knobs" on its lower leg touch down behind the toe prints. A walking deer's prints are heart-shaped, with the narrow end pointing in the direction it was walking.

Sweet fern grows here, as does sheep laurel, a pretty pink flowering cousin of the mountain laurel. Children may enjoy looking for sassafras trees, which sprout along the trail, best recognized by the three different shapes of leaves. Notice that the trees get shorter and sparser as the trail climbs. The poor soil and higher elevation here does not allow trees to grow very tall.

In about 0.7 mile the fire tower comes into view directly ahead. It is gated and locked to the public, but the view from the barren

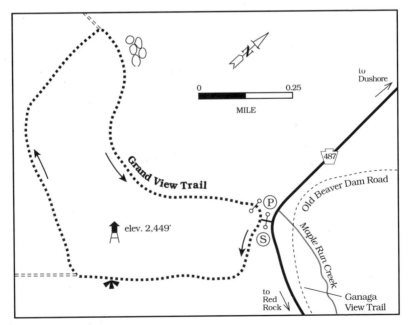

summit (2,449 feet) on which it stands is very good on a clear day. To the southeast you can look at the dropoff of the ridges that creates the terrific waterfalls in the Glens Natural Area (see hike 1, Ganoga Glen, Glen Leigh, and Highland Trails). This park lies on the Allegheny Front, a transition zone between the Allegheny plateau, which covers all of northcentral and northwestern Pennsylvania, and the Appalachian Mountains, which stretch from the southcentral to northeast corner of the state. Turn around for the northwest view of the Allegheny plateau.

Fire tower on the summit of lofty Grand View Mountain

Spend some time on the summit looking around and perhaps munching on wild strawberries. Some families with young children may want to turn around here and go back to the parking area on the road, because the trail ahead is rougher and rockier than the road.

The trail continues briefly on a grassy road on the opposite side of the tower. By a large old oak tree where the grassy road continues straight, take the trail that bears right and enters a blueberry patch, which makes for good trailside munching. Watch as the trees get taller as you descend, entering the woods again, along the edge of a private property boundary.

Head downhill now through the ever-present ferns, very thick here, so thick you cannot see your feet at times. Look for ground pine by the trail. Can children figure out why it is called that?

Continue through the ferns on the rocky trail to a junction with a woods road at about 1.5 miles. Turn right on the woods road, noting the rocky ledges to the left. Kids may enjoy looking in the grass for spit bugs, which nestle inside a bubbly mass that resembles, well, spit. The road curves left and goes uphill ever so slightly, then downhill again. Children may also enjoy looking out for bird feathers—guessing what kind of bird lost them. As the trail winds up, it passes through a large wooden gate to rejoin the road you came in on.

35

3. Chilisuagi Trail

Type: Day hike
Difficulty: Easy–moderate (distance)
Distance: 4.25-mile loop
Hiking time: 4 hours
Elevation gain: 50 feet
Hikable: Spring–fall
Map: Montour Preserve map
Rest rooms: Toilets, water at visitor center, fishing pier
Fee: None

Montour Preserve, whose centerpiece is man-made Lake Chillisquaque, is a pleasant walk through country woodlands and wetlands around the perimeter of the lake. Many species of songbirds and waterbirds reside in the wildlife sanctuary. Children may also observe evidence of beavers along the shore. The preserve is run by the Pennsylvania Power and Light Company and has an interesting child-oriented nature center. Interpretive signposts are spread out along the length of the trail.

To get to the preserve, take Interstate 80 west from Bloomsburg, exiting onto PA 54 north toward Williamsport. Take a right on PA 44 south to the village of Exchange. After 1.9 miles turn right on SR 1003 in Exchange. Stay on SR 1003 (passing two small roads, PP&L Farm Road and T380, on the left) and make a left at the intersection of SR 1003 and SR 1006. Go 0.5 mile on SR 1006 and turn left into the preserve. Pick up a map and visit the nature center on the right. If you plan to take any of the side trails to the blinds, secure a permit at the office, because access to these areas is limited. Then proceed straight on the preserve road past the dam to the Goose Cove overlook. Park here.

Begin the Chilisuagi Trail at the corner of the parking lot, walking up the grass along the edge of the park road, past Goose Cove picnic area, to the large sign and trail map at the top of the hill. The trail is then an easy-to-follow wide path.

Lake Chillisquaque's name comes from a Native American word that means "song of the wild goose." You should see wild geese and other creatures along this trail. As the mowed trail passes a field on the left, do not be surprised to see deer munching at the edges of the field. Throughout this preserve, meadows and farmland are left open for the benefit of the animals, who like to browse here.

Canada geese goslings race toward the safety of Lake Chillisquaque.

At 0.25 mile pass a 0.3-mile side trail to Muskrat Blind, where folks can peek at the waterfowl undetected. Chilisuagi Trail goes straight, crossing a gravel driveway and continuing into the woods. Cross a creek that flows into Muskrat Cove. For about 0.5 mile the trail is a woodland corridor between a paved road on the left and fields on the right. A bench begs you to pause by a fine old white oak tree, which is probably at least two centuries old. How may kids does it take to encircle this tree?

Cross another gravel drive and notice the numerous walnut trees. Look for deer and other animal pathways from this trail up into the fields and thickets. Animals make and like to use trails, too. Why do you think they do? Cross a small wooden bridge, then at 0.85 mile pass a 0.3-mile side trail to Smokehouse Blind, another chance to observe wildlife while remaining unobserved. Soon you see the lake as Chilisuagi Trail curves toward it. Cross a small creek and notice the many wildflowers here. Someday, if left alone, the fields will turn into forest again.

Bear right at a junction with the West Branch Trail at 1.25 miles, and stop to see the remains of an old farmstead. You can also see a power plant in the distance. Listen for the meowing call of the catbird as you head downhill easily. Soon cross the Middle Branch Chillisquaque Creek at 1.6 miles, the headwaters of the dammed Lake Chillisquaque. Stop for a while to watch the water striders skate on the surface tension of the water.

Head uphill now toward a plantation of larch and pine. Larch is the only deciduous softwood, which means it loses all its needles each fall after they turn bright yellow. Head downhill now, halfway along the hike, through a stand of hickory trees. At about 2.1 miles, pass both ends of the Ridgefield Point Trail on the right, by another old white oak, which is tired and twisted. How much longer do the children suppose it will be here?

The trail now follows closely along the edge of Jellyfish and Heron Coves. Watch for signs of old and new beaver activity here. Cross a bridge with a good view of the cove, then at 2.7 miles pass by the side trail to the left leading to Fossil Pit and, shortly after, the Bluebird Trail on the left. (Fossil Pit is an entertaining 0.2-mile side trip—children and adults can forage for fossils on the shale pile and keep the fossils they find. To reach Fossil Pit, follow the trail left and cross the road to the pit.)

With about 1 mile to go, pass by the fishing pier on the right. At Heron Cove picnic area on the left, stop to eat or visit with the Canada geese, who make themselves at home here. Refreshed, continue past the boat ramp, around a gate, and up to the dam at 3.7 miles. Cross the dam to end at the Goose Cove overlook.

Other trails of interest: The Wildlife Management Trail is a 0.75-mile loop that leaves from the parking area at the nature center. It passes two small ponds and follows fencerows where birds and small mammals may be observed.

The Braille Trail is a 0.3-mile loop trail that leaves from the nature center and offers a multisensory experience. Interpretive signs in braille and printed text assist hikers in taking in the sounds, smells, and textures of the forest.

The Bluebird Trail is a 0.7-mile loop trail that features bluebird boxes and viewing opportunities. Access is from the Fossil Pit parking area.

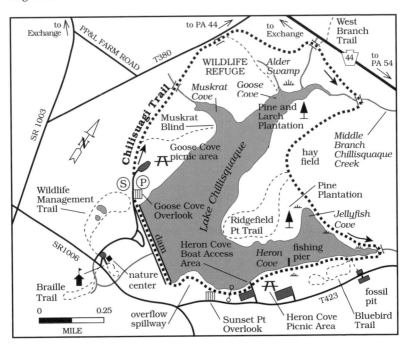

4. Loyalsock and Canyon Vista Trails

Type: Day hike
Difficulty: Challenging (steep, rocky)
Distance: 0.9-mile loop
Hiking time: 1 hour
Elevation gain: 200 feet
Hikable: Spring–fall
Map: Worlds End State Park map
Rest rooms: Toilets at trailhead; water at state park campground
Fee: None

Hiking at Canyon Vista in Worlds End State Park is like being transported to a wild, remote place. This trail hugs the edge of the dramatic Loyalsock Canyon, then loops through the rocks to give hikers a flavor of the rugged but beautiful landscape. Of particular interest is the Rock Garden, across from the parking area, where a tumble of ledges and boulders makes for excellent exploring. The state park has camping, and camping is also allowed on the adjacent state forest land in the woods off the dirt roads.

To get here, take Interstate 180 east from the Williamsport area. Near Montoursville, head north on US 220. In Muncy Valley take PA 42 north and turn left onto SR 3009. Go 3.2 miles and turn right on (dirt) Shaneburg Road. Turn left on (dirt) Mineral Spring Road after 2.4 miles. Turn right onto (dirt) Cold Run Road and go 0.7 mile to the Canyon Vista parking lot on the left.

Look for Indian Pipes growing in moist areas like Canyon Vista.

Start the hike at the vista to the left of the parking lot. The view into Loyalsock Canyon is gorgeous on a clear day, and a bit eerie on an overcast, misty day. Loyalsock Creek, which runs through the canyon, is popular for white-water kayaking. Follow the trail (three trails in one, at this point—the Canyon Vista is blue blazed, the Link is red x blazed, and the 59-mile Loyalsock Trail is LT blazed)

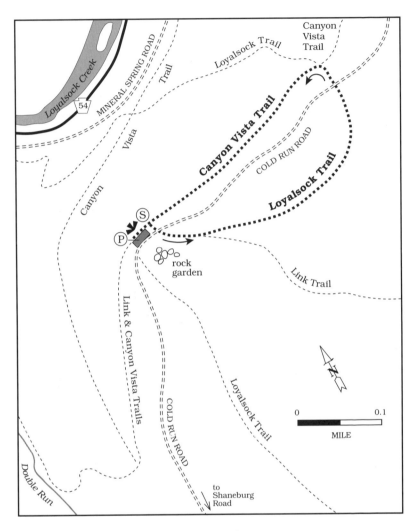

along the split rail fence. Bear right, back up toward the road. The Canyon Vista Trail goes left—you will return to this point. Cross Cold Run Road, and head uphill through grasses and a thick blanket of hay-scented ferns. Soon see ledges on your right. Notice the ragged-looking lichen on the rocks, known as black lichen. Though the top side is green, the underside is noticeably black.

The treadway is rocky as you carefully step over some rock fissures. At the upcoming junction, where the Link Trail goes off to the right, bear left on the Loyalsock Trail. The ruggedness and lushness of this area is reminiscent of northern Washington State or New England. Watch for red efts, which are bright orange with red spots;

they come out from under rocks in the spring or after a rainstorm. A red eft is one stage in the life of a newt. The Loyalsock Trail leads back to Cold Run Road and crosses it just before 0.4 mile. Those who are tiring at this point might head left on the road back to the parking lot for a trip of about 0.65 mile. Those with energy can continue, heading steeply downhill on the Loyalsock Trail. Listen for a rushing creek off to the right. At 0.5 mile, 0.1 mile from the road, turn left on the blue-blazed Canyon Vista Trail. (The Loyalsock Trail continues downhill steeply to the canyon bottom.) Climb steeply for 0.1 on the Canyon Vista Trail, then traverse on rolling terrain. The many red maples here are pretty in the fall.

The trail tunnels through a corridor of striped maples on an old road, then quickly bears right off the old road and climbs on a narrower trail. You will start to hear the far-off roar of Loyalsock Creek. Continuing uphill, break out into the open again, bearing right, back along the split-rail fence to where you began.

5. Lakeside Trail

Type: Day hike
Difficulty: Easy–moderate (distance)
Distance: 5.5-mile loop
Hiking time: 4–5 hours
Elevation gain: 50 feet
Hikable: Spring–fall
Map: Gouldsboro and Tobyhanna State Park map
Rest rooms: Toilets, water available at trailhead
Fee: None

Tobyhanna is a Native American word that means "a stream whose banks are fringed with alder." The Tobyhanna is just one of the many creeks that flow into pleasant Tobyhanna Lake. The Lakeside Trail starts at the lifeguarded beach area and leads hikers around its breezy and lush shores. With several places to stop for water and play, this is an appealing hike on a hot summer day. The wide, smooth path, almost completely flat, adds to its appeal for families. During the drier summer and fall months, the trail is suitable for baby strollers. Note: Bicycles and snowmobiles are permitted on this trail. The trail is also suitable for cross-country skiing in the winter. Tobyhanna State Park has a campground.

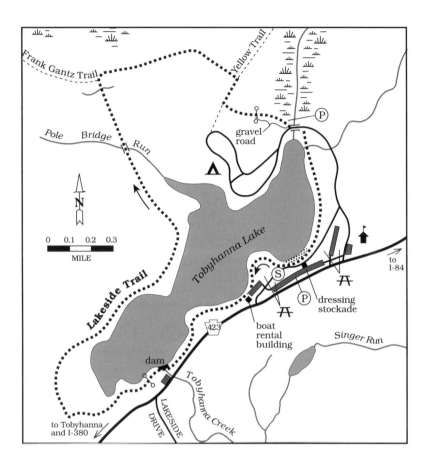

To reach the state park, take Interstate 80 west from Stroudsburg to Interstate 380 west, taking that to the Tobyhanna exit (exit 7). Take PA 423 north 2.4 miles past the military reservation to Tobyhanna State Park. Enter the day-use area on the left and park in front of the dressing stockade in the picnic area.

Begin the hike at the dressing stockade, heading southwest along the lakeshore, following blue blazes. Bug stuff might be needed here during the summer to ward off the deer flies, which can be annoying on still days. Passing by some birches, you soon reach a small, rocky beach. This is a good place to see what is swimming around in the water. As the trail continues, the breeze picks up, cooling hikers as they travel past the boat building on the left where canoes and rowboats can be rented. Heading into the woods again, late-summer hikers might be stopped by the sight of ripe high-bush blueberries. This is the first of several good blueberry picking areas along the trail.

At 0.9 mile, the trail leaves the woods briefly to cross Tobyhanna Creek, where there is a dam. There are cement "stones" for long-legged hikers to hop across the stream on—shorter folk will want to cross the stream on the bridge on PA 423 to the left of the trail. Canada geese congregate in this area and they have left many of their calling cards behind. Do your charges know that there is a branch of science that is devoted to studying animal excrement? It is called scatology. Can they imagine what a scientist might learn from this kind of study?

The trail goes through a gravel parking area, past a gate on an old road, and into the woods again. From this point to the end of the trail, the vegetation is lush green and thick with moisture-loving plants. Ferns and rhododendrons line the smooth pathway. Through the branches an observant hiker can catch glimpses of the wetland. The trail dips down to water level, though it keeps its distance from the edge. Close your eyes—can you smell the water?

If hiking in summer, children may notice the bright green new growth on the tips of the spruces. Ask your children how much they have grown this year.

Strolling comfortably now on level terrain, note the huge interrupted ferns trailside. At the halfway point at 2.75 miles, cross over Pole Bridge Run on a bridge and get set for a leisurely walk in the deep woods as the trail veers west, away from the lake. Notice the smooth gray bark of the beeches. Many of the beeches and maples have twin or triplet trunks—two or three trunks rising from a single root system. Make a game out of seeing who can locate the tree with the most "siblings." Are there quads or quints? Sextuplets?

To keep your charges interested along this portion of the walk, tell them about the history of Tobyhanna Lake. This lake and Gouldsboro Lake supplied places as far away as Florida with ice in the early 1900s. The ice was cut in big blocks in the winter when the lake was frozen. The ice was stored in barns insulated with straw or sawdust. During the warm months the ice was sent to Philadelphia and other distant cities and states via railcars for use in home iceboxes and hospitals, and for preserving fresh meat during delivery. If your children have ever wondered why some older people still call refrigerators "ice boxes," it is because that is exactly what they were.

This stretch among the tall trees

Boys practice skipping stones into Tobyhanna Lake.

is also a good place to try a blindfold walk. Put a bandana blindfold on one person and have the sighted partner guide him or her by the arm. Then switch places. What did they hear? What did they smell? What did it feel like to use a sense other than eyes to experience the trail?

Cross another small creek and at about 3.3 miles reach a junction with the Frank Gantz Trail, which leads a rugged several miles to Gouldsboro Lake. Bear right to stay on the Lakeside Trail, now going gently downhill. Soon the trees thin and hikers can snack on blackberries and blueberries in season. The trail continues gently downhill before reaching a junction with the Yellow Trail at 4 miles. Bear right on the Lakeside Trail and then left again at the next junction, reached momentarily. The trail jogs downhill toward a gate and a parking area. Past the gate, follow the gravel road 100 yards right to the paved campground road. Turn left and cross the bridge. Weary hikers will want to pause here to gaze north into the wetlands. In early morning or at dusk, waterbirds can be spotted here.

Almost done now, the trail enters the woods again and hugs the lake. Listen for cicadas, which become adults only after seventeen years of life as a grub. Then they die! Cross another small creek and at 5.4 miles from the trailhead reach the beach, where all hikers will want to head for a well-deserved frolic in the lifeguarded swimming area.

6. Monroe County Environmental Education Center Trails

Type: Day hike
Difficulty: Easy; Black Bear Trail is handicapped-accessible
Distance: 0.25 mile one way (Black Bear Trail); 1.1-mile loop (Deer, Songbird, and Woodchuck Trails)
Hiking time: 15 minutes (Black Bear Trail); 45 minutes (Deer, Songbird, and Woodchuck Trails)
Elevation gain: Negligible (Black Bear Trail); 100 feet (Deer, Songbird, and Woodchuck Trails)
Hikable: Spring–fall
Map: Kettle Creek Wildlife Sanctuary map
Rest rooms: Toilets, water at visitor center
Fee: None

Black Bear Trail and the Deer, Songbird, and Woodchuck Trails loop are just a few of a number of pleasant trails at the Kettle Creek

Wildlife Sanctuary, a child-oriented place with displays and activities at the visitor center and many environmental programs and guided hikes offered throughout the year. The Black Bear Trail is a new handicapped-accessible trail, suitable for virtually anyone, that ends by a handicapped-only fishing pier on a pond. The Deer Trail is a self-guided trail with a wide variety of young trees growing on an old homestead. Traces of human as well as natural history are seen along the trail. Pick up a brochure at the visitor center.

To reach the sanctuary, take Interstate 80 west from the Pennsylvania–New Jersey border to exit 46B, the Bartonsville exit; turn left at the light onto PA 611 north. Go 0.5 mile and turn left onto RimRock road. Go under the I-80 overpass, and after 0.3 mile bear right onto North Easton Belmont Pike. Go another 0.3 mile, bearing right at the Y intersection onto Running Valley Road (there is no sign). Monroe County Environmental Education Center (Kettle Creek Wildlife Sanctuary) is 1 mile further on the left. Parking is at the building.

The Black Bear Trail begins at the end of the lower overflow parking area. Enter the paved trail and quickly look to the right, where the remains of an old cold cellar can be clearly seen across the road. The cold cellar was part of Clayton Swink's 120-acre farmstead, which he donated to the county. Evidence of his farm is abundant, though nature is reclaiming the land. The trail parallels a small stream as it heads east.

Wildflowers are plentiful along this short trail. Hikers may see the yellow-flowered common mullein, which grows on a tall stalk that flowers only after its first year. Black walnut trees shed their fruit in the fall—the nuts are encased in a green pod with a sticky black tar-like substance covering the nut.

As the trail heads into the woods, its temperature drops noticeably. On the left is a connecting trail to Woodchuck Path and Weasel

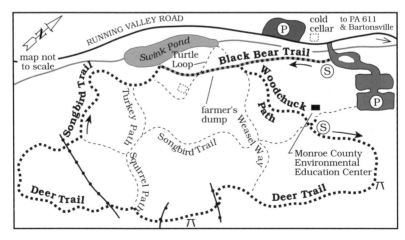

Listen for the singing of the birdhouse occupants along the Songbird Trail.

Way, and on the right shortly after is Turtle Loop, a side trip to the edge of Swink Pond. A farmer's dump on the north side of the trail is purposely left to demonstrate the futility of landfills. See how long the old cans last? Bottles last forever. The trail continues straight ahead through the forest. Red maple, black gum, shagbark hickory, pitch pine, and various oaks grow here. When the other end of Turtle Loop comes in from the right, the Songbird Trail takes off to the left; Black Bear Trail continues straight ahead.

As the trail descends gently, reach the north shore of Swink Pond, whose surface is almost covered with water plants. A fishing pier is currently being built here for handicapped hikers. This is a fun place to listen to the bullfrogs' throaty gulps. Return via the same route. On the way back, notice the remains of a chimney in the woods to the right, where a homestead once stood.

For the longer loop, begin on the Deer Trail, which leaves from behind the environmental education center building, following the same route as the Songbird Trail for a very short way. Where the two trails part company, take the Deer Trail to the left. The trail climbs steadily uphill past an open browse area, through tall grasses. Deer particularly enjoy the open areas, where they can flee quickly into the woods if danger approaches. Continue uphill into the woods. Several witch hazel trees grow on the right side of the trail. The bark, leaves, and twigs of this tree are sometimes used to make a soothing skin lotion.

Soon the climbing levels off and the path follows a ridge. Just before the first resting bench at 0.1 mile, look for a 12-foot-high dead tree on the south (right) side of the trail. This was an American chestnut. If you look closely, you will see new young shoots clustered at the base of the deceased tree. American chestnut was once the most common tree in the Pennsylvania forest. Fungi caused a blight that killed the American chestnut in the early 1900s. Since then, young shoots have been trying to reestablish themselves, and sometimes they grow to 15 feet and bear fruit before finally succumbing to the blight. Eventually these shoots will die, as have all the others. Moving on, pass by many low-bush blueberries. Continuing along the ridge, just before 0.3 mile, pass Weasel Way on the right (this is a possible turnaround point; for a shorter loop of about 0.5 mile, take Weasel Way, which connects with the Black Bear Trail in 0.15 mile). Notice the remains of an old stone wall that the trail passes through. As the trail reaches the top of the ridge, you will see another stone wall. These were common when the land was being farmed. The soil was rocky and the farmers needed fences, so stone walls were the logical solution.

A second bench invites hikers to rest a few minutes, perhaps listening for the blue jays calling raucously to each other in the trees. Next pass the Squirrel Path as it departs from the right at 0.4 mile (this is another possible turnaround point; take Squirrel Path as it descends to join the Songbird Trail, and follow it back to the starting point). The Deer Trail descends through an opening in what was once a very large stone wall. Dropping in elevation now, the trail switchbacks south again. Notice how little grows under the white pines along the trail here. Deep shade prevents any seedlings from surviving. A small meadow on the east (left) side of the trail is a great place to watch butterflies as they flit among the wildflowers. Bird boxes throughout the area make this a good bird-watching vantage.

Recross through the large stone wall and, at a τ intersection at 0.6 mile where the Deer Trail ends and the Songbird Trail heads to the left and to the right, take the left fork. Continue to the south on the Songbird Trail; soon the Turkey Path comes in from the right. Shortly after, leave the Songbird Trail for a connecting path that ends at the Black Bear Trail by Swink Pond. Follow the paved Black Bear Trail past the pond and the farmer's dump. At the edge of the woods at 0.9 mile, bear right on Woodchuck Path through tall grasses. In a short distance, Weasel Way branches off to the right. Stay left, with the environmental education center building in sight until you reach the trail's end.

Other trails of interest: If you have time or live locally, arrange to join the environmental education center on one of its guided hikes to Tannersville Cranberry Bog. This bog is one of the best examples of a northern bog in Pennsylvania and is a designated Natural Landmark. The property is owned by The Nature Conservancy and access is restricted to guided hikes. A 1,450-foot floating boardwalk gives hikers a close-up look at the bog. For information call Monroe County Environmental Education Center at (717) 629-3061.

7. Conservation Island Nature Trail

Type: Day hike
Difficulty: Easy
Distance: 1.1-mile loop
Hiking time: 1 hour
Elevation gain: 25 feet
Hikable: Spring–fall
Map: Conservation Island Nature Trail map
Rest rooms: Toilets, water at state park campground
Fee: None

The kids can pretend they are Tom Sawyer while exploring the gentle terrain on Conservation Island. This picturesque island surrounded by Promised Land Lake is a prime wildlife viewing area, with resident white-tailed deer, beaver, chipmunks, turtles, and other forest and water creatures. Go first thing in the morning for the best chance of seeing animals. Located in Promised Land State Park, the self-guiding nature trail is near the state park campground, where there is a nature center and seasonal environmental programs are offered. The island is a nice area for beginner cross-country skiing.

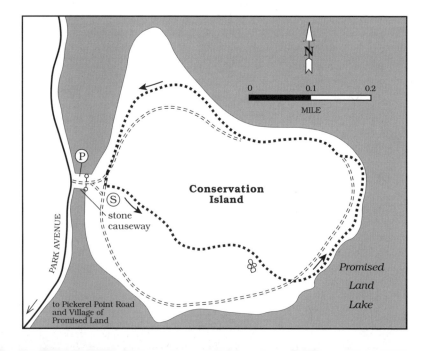

To reach the park, take Interstate 84 east from the Scranton area, exiting onto PA 390 south. Go several miles through the village of Promised Land and turn left on Pickerel Point Road, just past the park office, which has interpretive brochures for the trail. Go 0.5 mile and turn left again on Park Avenue. In 0.7 mile turn right into a dirt driveway with a small parking area by a gate.

This blue-blazed trail starts across the stone causeway, which is a good place to get out the binoculars and look at the lake. Lily pads bloom in summer and Canada geese like to swim nearby. On the island, pass under a canopy of rhododendrons and in 50 yards leave the service road and bear left on the beginning of the nature trail by marker number 1. Notice that the dead trees on the left have many woodpecker holes. Do children know what the woodpeckers are looking for in the dead trees? Woodpeckers of all varieties have especially thick skulls to withstand the hard drilling, and long, sticky, pointed tongues to reach into the holes and pluck out wood-boring insects.

Descend briefly past a beech tree whose bark is marred with carvings. People do not do this anymore, as it hurts the tree and is ugly, but it used to be a common practice. Notice how the rocks are covered with lichens and moss. The lichens grow very slowly outward in a ring; these rings are decades old. Watch your footing here; the moss makes the rocks slick when wet.

Continue ahead through a carpet of ferns. Chipmunks go scur-

Beavers live in lodges such as this one along the shore of Promised Land Lake.

rying as you march ahead through a stand of beeches. Beechnuts are a particular favorite fall munching food of the 'munks. Watch for "twin" trees on the right. One maple along this trail has six trunks coming out of one root system. Passing plenty of striped maples (look at their trunks to see how they got their name), the trail descends gently into deeper shade. Take note of the rock ledges on the right.

The trail crosses a grassy woods road and reaches the shoreline at 0.4 mile. Notice how warm it is by the sunny water's edge. If you stand still, a dragonfly might alight on your shoulder. Watch for bullfrogs and turtles, or look closer at the lily pads. Why do you suppose they float so well?

There is plenty of evidence of beaver activity on the island. Watch for an old lodge near the shore and the characteristic chiseled stumps of beaver-felled trees. It is easy to tell an active beaver lodge from an inactive one. Look for fresh mud and "whitewood," fresh white or yellow sticks whose bark has been stripped by hungry beavers.

The trail passes another column of rhododendron and joins the woods road. At just over 0.6 mile, the nature trail markers end, but turn right and follow the road. If your charges are tempted to run ahead, encourage a quiet pace while watching for white-tailed deer fawns, which, in late spring and early summer, hunker down and remain motionless among the ferns while humans and other animals pass them by, never noticing them. Look for the wide, pointed tips of ears sticking up above the hollows amongst the ferns. When we walked this trail we spotted several fawns, and even had two run right past us. If you do spot one hiding, just watch or take a few pictures. Do not worry, it is probably not abandoned. Fawns are only visited by their mothers a few times each day so the mother's scent will not give the fawn's hiding place away to predators.

On the walk back, tell how the Shakers (a communal religious sect) named this place the Promised Land in 1878 when they moved here, thinking they would profit from the riches of the wilderness. The rocky soil prevented them from even gardening, so they left, but the name remains. At 0.8 mile the trail veers to the right, off the service road, to give hikers a closer view of the water's edge. The path rejoins the service road at about 1 mile; turn right. One-tenth mile farther, reach the beginning of the nature trail, and then turn right to reach the parking area.

Other trails of interest: The Egypt Meadows Road, a 0.75-mile (one way) trail on an old road, ends at the Egypt Meadows Lake Spillway. Before the 1930s this area was covered in soft meadow grass that was harvested for use as packing material for a nearby glassworks company. Access is 4.5 miles north of the Promised Land State Park office on the east side of PA 390.

The Little Falls Trail is a 1-mile trail that follows Wallenpaupak

Creek, then returns on the opposite side, passing waterfalls. Access is at the Lower Lake dam, about 2 miles from the park office on Lower Lake Road, northwest of PA 390.

8. Thunder Swamp Trail

Type: Day hike
Difficulty: Moderate (rocks and bushes)
Distance: 1.5-mile loop
Hiking time: 1.5 hours
Elevation gain: 40 feet
Hikable: Spring–fall
Map: Thunder Swamp trail system map
Rest rooms: Nearest facilities at Peck's Pond State Forest Picnic Area, on PA 402 en route to trailhead
Fee: None

Be sure to bring binoculars on this short but rocky hike, well worth the effort for its close-up view of a typical Pocono wetland. Some interesting flowers and shrubs are seen in the spring and summer. Fall is pleasant here, perhaps the best time to hike, when the high-bush blueberries are ripe and the mosquitoes mostly gone. Long pants and bug stuff are advised for this hike, because the trail is narrow and brushy. Do not be surprised to see deer, wild turkeys, or even a black bear along the trail.

Lily pads seem to float almost magically on the surface of Thunder Swamp.

To reach the trailhead, take Interstate 84 east from the Scranton area, exiting at PA 402. Go south for 10 miles. Make a left on Old Bushkill Road (SR 2003) and go 1.4 miles, turning left onto (dirt) Flat Ridge Road. Go 2.2 miles to reach the parking lot on the right.

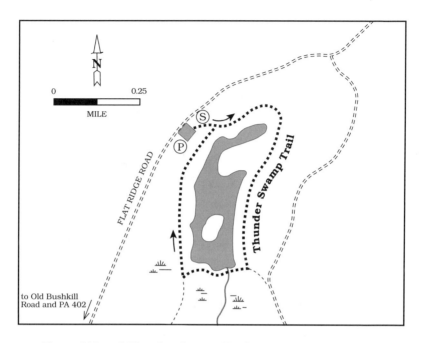

The red-blazed Thunder Swamp Trail enters the woods and after 0.1 mile reaches a junction. Bear left as the sounds of the wetland reach your ears. In the spring, fly poison and yellow eyed grass, as well as low- and high-bush blueberries, line the path. Soon the swamp comes into view through the trees on the right. Listen for bullfrogs "sawing" away, often croaking in tandem.

Practice noticing the difference between the oaks; oaks in the black oak family have pointed leaves, while those in the white oak family have the same basic shape but have rounded leaves. As you pass many oak seedlings, quiz each other on which is which.

Pause momentarily at an opening for a view of the swamp, then head downhill to the water's edge for a better look. Beavers have been busy recently; look for a dam with fresh mud on it and use binoculars to see if you can find a lodge in the water. Frogs, turtles, minnows, and other fun creatures can be found at the water's edge. At 0.7 mile, a short trail to the left goes to a woods road; stay to the right to follow the main path across the small outlet creek, being careful on the slippery rocks. The trail stays close to the shore for a short while, then heads into the blueberries again before reaching a junction at 0.9 mile where a side trail to the left goes out to eventually reach a dirt road.

Bear right at the junction as the main trail rounds the wetland. The trail can be brushy through here. Watch for more evidence of the beavers: whitewood or felled trees. Sheep laurel can be seen in this stretch in the late spring. Its magenta flower is very appealing.

A nice large rock on the right gives hikers a good excuse to sit for a spell. Get out the binoculars again and watch for red-winged blackbirds. Duck boxes provide homes to numerous species of ducks. The woodpeckers have done well here, judging from all the holes in the dead snags.

Refreshed, soon return to the junction at the beginning of the trail loop and turn left, returning to the parking lot.

9. Tumbling Waters Trail

Type: Day hike
Difficulty: Moderate (distance, some climbing)
Distance: 3-mile loop
Hiking time: 3 hours
Elevation gain: 300 feet
Hikable: Year-round (unless snowy)
Map: Pocono Environmental Education Center trail map
Rest rooms: Toilets, water at environmental education center
Fee: None

The Tumbling Waters Trail has a little bit of everything that makes a trail fun. It has two ponds, a bird blind, a waterfall with a cooling pool beneath, and scenic vistas of the Kittatinny Ridge. If you want to capture the flavor of the Poconos in one hike, this may be the best choice. The trail is just one of many that leave from the Pocono Environmental Education Center, which has educational displays and year-round environmental education programs for children and adults. Note: For information on programs, call PEEC at (717) 828-2319.

To reach the trail, take Interstate 80 east from Stroudsburg and exit at US 209 north to Marshalls Creek. Continue on US 209 into Delaware Water Gap National Recreation Area, where there is a commercial toll booth on the right. Drive 8 miles further north on US 209. Make a left on Briscoe Mountain Road and go 0.8 mile, bearing right at the Y intersection, and in 0.1 mile see the environmental education center building and parking lot on the right. Park in front of the building.

This orange-blazed trail starts across the street from the environmental education center building. The Tumbling Waters Trail follows the white-blazed Two Ponds Trail initially. Cross a small bridge on a boardwalk and peek at the birds from the bird blind. Early morning or dusk is the best time to observe great blue herons, Canada geese, and beavers on Front Pond. Bear right on the boardwalk to a small clearing where a "trash cemetery" displays the futility of landfilling garbage. Continue into the thickets where grapes and wild roses abound. Songbirds find shelter in the thickets even in the middle of the day. Listen particularly for the rufus-sided towhee, whose call is easy for children to identify, sounding like a call to "drink your tea, drink your tea...."

After crossing a creeklet, the trail reaches a paved road at about 0.2 mile. Cross the road diagonally and continue into the woods again on the left. Soon the trail widens and passes through red pines into deep shade. An unofficial trail branches off to the left, but the main trail bears right, along the northwest shore of lively Pickerel Pond, which is teeming with amphibians. Watch for bullfrogs that float with their eyes just above the surface of the water, then leap deeper if you get too close. An observant hiker might catch a glimpse of a turtle or a dragonfly.

As the trail leaves the shore of Pickerel Pond, the path heads through a patch of Virginia creeper, which is frequently confused with poison ivy. It has five leaves, rather than poison ivy's three leaves, and is not poisonous to touch. The wide, smooth path curves left through stately conifers. At nearly 0.7 mile, the white-blazed Two Ponds Trail departs on the left. From now on, follow the orange blazes only. The trail descends, then briefly sidehills on the edge of a ravine. Continue on hilly terrain. At about 1.5 miles the sound of running water can be heard. The trail heads steeply downhill to a junction with a short, steep trail that leads to the falls.

'Ribit!' You never know what surprises await hikers by the shore of Pickerel Pond.

Take the side trail, down eight switchbacks to the bottom of the falls. This is a perfect place for a picnic under the hemlocks, or to soak hot feet. Keep kids from straying too far left, downstream from the falls; another falls drops off steeply there. Notice how cool this area is compared to the trail you were just on. Do children know why?

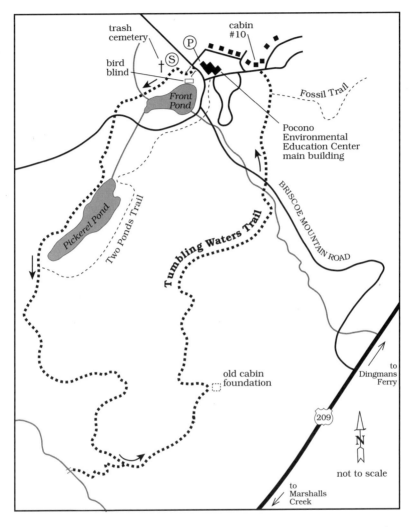

Once you have had a nice rest, go back up the side trail to rejoin the Tumbling Waters Trail and continue uphill to the right, fairly steeply.

Your efforts will be rewarded with views of the Kittatinny Ridge (Kittatinny means "endless mountains" in the language of the Lenni Lenape Indians, who used to reside here). The first view is of the New Jersey side of the ridge. As the trail continues to climb, it reaches an outcropping from which there is a good view of a farm below. The park service leases the land to farmers. Continue along the ridge to the high point of the trail, an outcropping by an old cabin foundation at about 1.8 miles. The fireplace is still visible. What a view these folks must have had!

The trail continues downhill through mixed deciduous forest. Pass a stand of tall staghorn sumac—so named for the velvety branches of new growth. Listen for woodpeckers in the old snags nearby. This is also a good place to see wild turkeys. The trail goes onward past numerous large grapevines. Notice an old fence to the left that trees have grown around.

At just over 2.6 miles, watch for poison ivy as the trail parallels a road briefly, crosses a creeklet, then crosses Briscoe Mountain Road. Go uphill through a field in which cedars grow. At 2.8 miles, watch for a junction with the blue-blazed Fossil Trail, which joins the main trail from the right. Continue straight until you come out at cabin 10. Follow the road 100 yards left to the environmental education center building.

Other trails of interest: The Two Ponds Trail is a shorter alternative. You can follow this 1.5-mile loop trail partway, by taking it to the left from its intersection with the Tumbling Waters Trail. It goes back to the environmental education center along the southeast shore of Pickerel Pond.

There are four other loop trails in the area, of varying length and difficulty, including the Fossil Trail (1.25 miles), which leads down an escarpment to an outcrop rich in fossils. The environmental education center has maps and descriptions of these other trails.

---

10. George W. Childs Recreation Site

Type:	Day hike
Difficulty:	Easy
Distance:	1.8-mile loop
Hiking time:	1.5 hours
Elevation gain:	200 feet
Hikable:	Spring–fall
Map:	Delaware Water Gap Selected Hiking Trail map
Rest rooms:	Toilets, water at trailhead in summer
Fee:	None

The Poconos are renowned for waterfalls, which cut through the ancient plateau in their rush to reach the Delaware River. A hike in George W. Childs Recreation Site offers three cascading waterfalls in a short distance, as well as several places to explore the creekside and to relax and picnic under the hemlocks.

Near the Pennsylvania–New Jersey border on Interstate 80, from either direction exit onto US 209 north, toward Marshalls Creek. At the commercial toll booth where US 209 enters the park, pick up a free map of Delaware Water Gap National Recreation Area. Stay on US 209 north for 12 miles past the toll booth. Turn left onto PA 739 north at Dingmans Ferry. Go 1.1 miles and turn left on Silver Lake Road. Go 1.7 miles and turn left onto Park Road. The parking area is 100 yards to the left off Park Road.

The trail leaves from the north end of the parking lot by the rest rooms. Head immediately into the cooling canopy of hemlocks. The trail leads gently downhill to the first of six wooden bridges, each of which crosses Dingmans Creek. (At any point where there is a bridge, it is possible to cross over for a shortened return to the parking lot.) Do not cross the bridge, but continue past several picnic tables to the second bridge; again, do not cross yet unless you wish to shorten your hike. At 0.25 mile, a side trail goes off to the right, while the main trail meanders through the hemlocks as it begins a descent to the falls.

At the third bridge (do not cross it), about 0.5 mile from the trailhead, the trail heads downhill on wooden steps. Factory Falls is visible on the left. Like the next two falls, it has a pretty pool at its base. Factory Falls is named for the woolen mill that used to be located across the creek. The remains of the mill are seen on the way back.

Exploring Dingmans Creek

The trail descends more steeply now past Factory Falls, switchbacking down a series of steps. Fulmer Falls comes into view on the left. If it is a hot day, the fourth bridge, at about 0.7 mile, is a nice place to stop. Two pools, one on either side of the bridge, offer many opportunities for exploring alongside the water. (Swimming is not permitted.) Watch for trout darting quickly among the pools. Continue on the trail along the south side of Dingmans Creek.

The trail is now guarded with wooden railings that keep hikers away from the steep ledges. Deer Leap Falls comes into view at the fifth bridge,

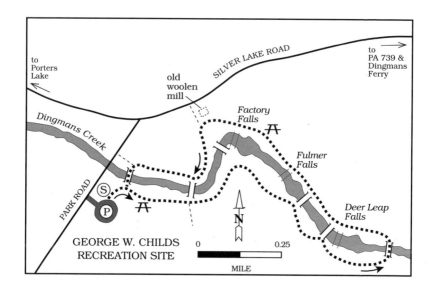

GEORGE W. CHILDS RECREATION SITE

where hikers can peer right over the edge of the sharp falls from the vantage of the bridge. Stay on the south side of the creek to the last bridge.

Continue on to the final bridge, which offers a good view back at Deer Leap Falls and the large pool beneath it. At 1 mile, cross the bridge. The trail circles back around the opposite side of Dingmans Creek now. Wooden steps lead up to the top of Deer Leap Falls. Bear left toward the fifth bridge, going down two flights of steps. At the bridge, climb some more steps.

The trail hugs the rocks on one side. Notice the ever slow-growing lichens on the rocks, whose rings expand outward as they grow. Reach the fourth bridge at Fulmer Falls again and go up the next flight of wooden steps. Notice how the trees cling to the rocks as they grow out over the cliffs. How do they manage to hang on?

Pass an overlook that gives a good view of Fulmer Falls. See how mossy the rocks are here. Do children know why? The trail continues uphill, passing through a picnic pavilion at 1.5 miles. A pool at the base of Factory Falls is visible. From this viewpoint hikers can see that the falls is actually a series of multitiered cascades.

In a short distance, come upon the remains of an old woolen mill, where a short side trail connects to Silver Lake Road. The mill was operated by Joseph Brooks of Yorkshire, England, from 1825 to 1832. Domestic sheep roamed the area then, supplying the wool for the waterwheel-powered mill.

Pass the second bridge, nearing the end of the trail. At the first bridge, just a few hundred yards further, a short side trail continues straight ahead to connect with the Park Road; however, you cross over the bridge and rejoin the trail you came in on. Bear right to reach the parking area where you began.

Other trails of interest: The Dingmans Falls Trail is a 0.5-mile loop trail that passes Silver Thread and Dingmans Falls as it passes through a hemlock ravine. Access this trail from the Dingmans Falls visitors center, located on a side road just south of the PA 739 intersection off PA 209.

---

11. The Trees of Grey Towers Trail

Type: Day hike
Difficulty: Easy
Distance: 0.5-mile loop
Hiking time: 30 minutes
Elevation gain: 50 feet
Hikable: Year-round
Map: The Trees of Grey Towers map
Rest rooms: Toilets, water available in "letter box" building at end of hike
Fee: None

Grey Towers, the homestead of Gifford Pinchot, the first head of the United States Forest Service, is a nice stop with something for both parents and children to enjoy. Parents will enjoy the tour of the unique Victorian mansion, home of one of Pennsylvania's most famous citizens. Children can romp freely along the self-guided tree tour. There is not a path here, just numbered trees, so kids can play scavenger hunt along the trail, locating the tree markers. There is even a quiz at the end to see what they have learned.

To reach Grey Towers, take Interstate 84 east from Scranton and get off at the Milford exit, taking US 6 east. Make a sharp right turn 0.1 mile after entering Milford. Go up the road 0.1 mile and turn left into the driveway. The homestead and parking lot are up at the top of the hill. From the parking lot, walk down the stairs toward the house and find a box with an interpretive brochure in it, opposite the house, on the right. The trail begins here at the black locust tree.

Gifford Pinchot collected species of trees from all over North America, Asia, and Europe. When his father had the home built, the land had been clear-cut and was highly visible on the open hillside, very different from what we see today. Pinchot (the "t" is silent) planted the trees for the future, and once remarked that "I'd like to come back in 100 years and see my trees." Undoubtedly he would be delighted.

Trees 1 through 8 are on the right side of the driveway. Have kids look for various seeds of the trees along the route. Shortly after Tree 1, cross a stone walkway to the garden. Past Tree 3, the wall ahead is the border of the large garden. Tree 3, the sweet gum, has prickly, sticky seed pods, while Tree 6, the black walnut, has seeds that resemble green golf balls.

You might send a groundhog scampering under the fruit trees as you cross the driveway after almost 0.2 mile. The trees are a favorite nesting site for songbirds in the spring. You might even surprise a fledgling baby robin, as we did. Pause to take in the view from the front lawn. The monument on the ridge in the distance is High Point State Park in New Jersey, the highest point in that state, atop the Kittatinny Ridge. The town hall of Milford peeks above the treetops in the valley below.

Continuing on to the edge of the grass at Tree 9, find the trembling aspen. Tree 10, the white pine, is easy to remember: its long needles come in clusters of five, and there are five letters in the word

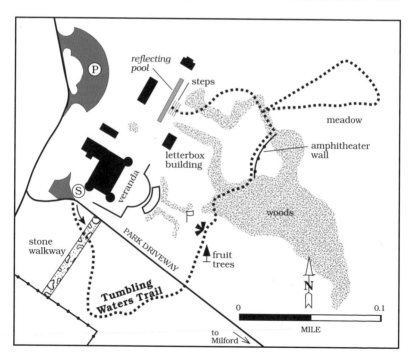

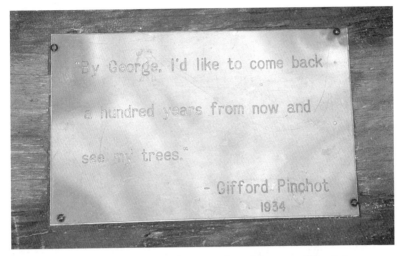

"By George, I'd like to come back a hundred years from now and see my trees."

 – Gifford Pinchot
1934

Mr. Pinchot would be pleased to see how his magnificent trees have turned out.

"white." Past these two trees, the path leads through a wooded area.

The hemlocks and hickory lead down to the edge of the amphitheater, where Pinchot, who was a two-time governor, invited as many as 4,000 citizens at a time to be entertained by everything from orchestral quartets to boxing kangaroos. Walk across the amphitheater wall and notice the metallic color of the copper beech.

After locating Tree 14, the kids can take a romp off the trail through the high grass to look for trees A through E, guessing what they are. In case you did not get a brochure: A is a Norway maple, B is a white fir, C is a white ash, D is a grey birch, and E is a Sakhalin spruce. Kids and adults who can just remember the difference between maple, ash, birch, etc., are doing well!

Once you have finished the quiz, return to the trail, cross a gravel path, and pass the sweet cherry and European linden. Head uphill via the steps straight ahead to the reflecting pool. From here, you can wander the grounds back to the parking lot.

Southeast Pennsylvania

Paved paths offer access to people of all ages and abilities.

12. Hawk Falls Trail

Type:	Day hike
Difficulty:	Easy
Distance:	0.75 mile one way
Hiking time:	30 minutes one way
Elevation gain:	120 feet
Hikable:	Spring–fall
Maps:	Hickory Run State Park map, USGS Hickory Run Quadrangle
Rest rooms:	Toilets, water in campground and picnic area
Fee:	None

Hawk Falls is an easy hike for families and those short on time but wanting a cool escape from the highway. This trail leads through the rhododendrons to 25-foot Hawk Falls, then continues to Mud Creek where there is said to be good fishing. Hikers return by the same path. Try this hike in July when the rhododendrons are in bloom. Hickory Run State Park has many hiking trails, and a family camping area.

To reach the trail, take Interstate 80 west from Stroudsburg,

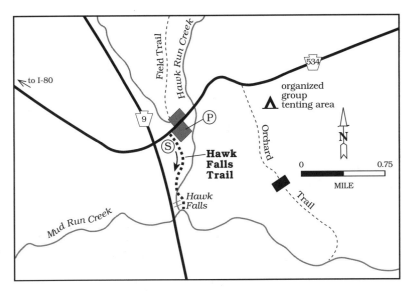

A family enjoys a Sunday stroll to Hawk Falls.

exiting onto PA 534. Head east on PA 534, which runs through the state park. Pass the park office on the right, and soon after pass the road on the right that leads to the family camping area. Go 3.4 miles past the camping area road, under the Northeast Extension (PA 9) overpass, and turn right about 100 yards past the overpass into the dirt parking lot on the right.

The Hawk Falls Trail begins 50 feet north of the parking lot at the road's edge, just past a large cement culvert. Hikers duck down quickly into a world of green. Hay-scented ferns carpet the forest floor, rhododendrons line the path, and feathery eastern hemlocks tower above.

The trail descends gently on a wide and somewhat rocky path. Soon you can hear the sound of Hawk Run Creek tumbling on your left. Continue downhill. Notice the ledges on the right that have a distinctly diagonal orientation, as if they were pushed and squeezed right up out of the ground—which they were.

Pass some larger trees; look for a grand old white pine. Can children guess how old it must be? Come to Hawk Run Creek, and cross by hopping from rock or rock. Just upstream from this crossing is a nice pool, just about the right size for cooling off feet. Continue downhill past the stream. Come to a side trail on the right that leads momentarily to a view of the falls, which you see from near the top. This is the best view of the falls along the trail, so stop and take a look.

Past the side trail to the falls, the main trail continues downhill a short while longer, flanked on both sides by rhododendrons. The trail ends at Mud Run Creek. You can soak your feet in the creek, and kids can play here. Return the way you came.

Other trails of interest: Self-Guiding Nature Trail is a 0.75-mile trail through the forest along pretty Hickory Run. The trailhead is located about 0.1 mile up the park road that heads north directly across from the park office.

Shades of Death Trail is a 1-mile trail that begins from behind the park office and follows Sand Spring Run, ending at the small Sand Spring Lake, passing several dams on the creek along the way.

---

13. Henry's Woods Nature Trail and Jacobsburg Trail

Type:	Day hike
Difficulty:	Easy
Distance:	2-mile loop
Hiking time:	2 hours
Elevation gain:	50 feet
Hikable:	Spring–fall
Map:	Jacobsburg Environmental Education Center map
Rest rooms:	Toilets at trailhead; no water
Fee:	None

The village of Jacobsburg once had a very important function in this part of Pennsylvania, but you would not know it was even there but for the remains that have been preserved in this state park. A now-vanished gun factory and iron forge helped supply guns for the War of 1812, though few structures remain intact. A hike on the wide, relaxing trails here takes hikers by dramatic slate outcroppings and through a mature woodland by the slow-moving Bushkill Creek, into the nearby meadows, and back again. A short side trip to the Benade House, open on weekends, makes for a pleasant stroll.

Take Interstate 78 east from Harrisburg, exiting onto US 22 east at Allentown. Turn onto PA 33 north before reaching Easton and take it to the Belfast exit. Get off the exit, turn right, go 0.1 mile, and turn left onto Belfast Road. Go 0.6 mile and turn left into the parking lot for Jacobsburg Environmental Education Center.

This walk follows Henry's Woods Nature Trail and joins with the Jacobsburg Trail to make a loop, which begins at the lower corner of the parking lot. At the bulletin board, cross the stone bridge over Bushkill Creek. The orange-blazed Henry's Woods Nature Trail turns

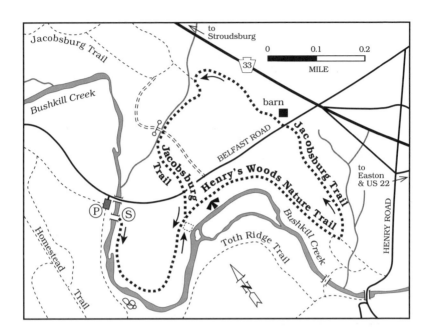

right in 50 yards into the woods. The trail is named for the family who built the gun-manufacturing plant and iron forge.

The trail soon enters a quiet grove of mature hemlocks on a very wide, easy path. The creek is easily accessible on the right. Though swimming is not permitted, wading (with shoes) is and children are encouraged to explore the water, which is only about 12 to 18 inches deep in most places. Check under the many flat rocks for crawfish, which look like miniature lobsters. A small fishnet is a useful tool for running through the water to see what creatures might be scooped up. How many different critters can kids find here?

The trail soon bears left up a short hillside away from the creek bank. In spring, mayapples line the pathway, looking like a thousand green umbrellas. In about 0.3 mile you come to the remains of a chimney on your right. Can children imagine why the chimney is the only old part of the building still standing? Shortly after, the trail comes to an intersection with the Jacobsburg Trail. You will connect with this trail later. Bear right, through a stand of tulip (poplar) trees. In the spring these trees actually do have flowers, with green and orange petals, which are tulip shaped. After a spring rain, tulips litter the ground. The inside part of the flower normally remains on the tree and matures into seeds that flutter to the ground in the fall.

Above the creek level now, the trail soon comes to an overlook on the right. The creek is split here; you can see the north branch from here. The Henry's once had a dam on the creek near here that helped power the gun factory. Head down a gentle hill and when you meet with the red-blazed Jacobsburg Trail at 0.8 mile, turn left onto it, heading uphill into a grove of younger trees. This area used to be an open field not so long ago.

At just over 1 mile, head out into the sun and cross Belfast Road and walk up to a red barn. Look for cottontail rabbits munching on the clover here. Cedars dot the pathway, which is lined with wildflowers, wild roses, and blackberry bushes. Still ascending, pass an unmarked trail to the left and follow along the side of unseen (but not unheard) PA 33. Just

The chimney is all that remains of this old homestead in Jacobsburg.

after reaching some walnut trees (check out how the fruits smell), at a trail junction, turn left, heading downhill for 100 yards, then turn right into the woods again. Continue down a gentle hill through young trees. Cross a dirt road with a gate on it at 1.4 miles and continue out into the sun on the path, which is now lined with wild roses. A horse path leads right, but go straight, crossing Belfast Road for a second time. In deep woods now, notice the two different types of vines hanging from the trees. Poison ivy vine hugs the tree and has clinging, hairy roots. Even the vines can make you itch. Grapes, on the other hand, hang loosely from the branches. Both vines can harm a tree by robbing it of sunlight.

At 1.7 miles bear right at the next intersection, back onto the Henry's Woods Nature Trail again, which you follow back to the parking lot the way you came in.

Other trails of interest: Homestead Trail (2.1 miles) offers a panoramic view of the environmental education center and the Blue Mountains beyond. There is excellent birding in the fields. Access is at the parking area on Belfast Road.

Sobers Run Trail is a multipurpose trail that loops through a 500-acre undeveloped portion of the park, along the secluded floodplain of Sober's Run. The 2.4-mile loop is accessible from either Belfast Road 2 miles west of the main parking lot, or off Douglassville Road, by the crossing of Bushkill Creek.

14. Lookout Trail

Type: Day hike
Difficulty: Moderate (rocks)
Distance: 1.5 miles round trip
Hiking time: 2 hours
Elevation gain: 221 feet
Hikable: Spring–fall
Maps: Hawk Mountain Sanctuary map
Rest rooms: Toilets, water at visitor center
Fee: $2 children 6–12, $3 seniors, $4 adults

Everyone enjoys the sight of a soaring hawk, and what better place to see these graceful birds of prey than at Hawk Mountain, a sanctuary set aside for the preservation of hawks and other great birds of prey? This short but intriguing hike is best done during the fall migration when 20,000 hawks, eagles, and falcons migrate over the north lookout. The sanctuary says that the best time to see the most birds is between August and December, particularly following the passing of a cold front on strong Northwest winds in October and November. There are rocks to climb, birds to watch, and views to see. The first viewpoint is barely 0.2 mile up the trail, so children get instant gratification for their hiking efforts. Take binoculars, or rent a pair at the visitor center and plan to take plenty of time to explore this area. The fee revenue goes to support the sanctuary and its conservation efforts on behalf of the birds.

To reach the sanctuary, take Interstate 78 west from Allentown, exiting onto PA 61 north. Pass through Port Clinton and Molino and turn right onto PA 895 east. After 2.5 miles turn right onto SR 2018 (roads are well marked with signs). Bear left at the ʏ intersection and continue ahead to the parking lot on the right. The total distance is 4.5 miles from PA 895.

Stop at the visitor center, which has maps, interesting displays, and a list of the birds that migrate through here regularly. Pay the fee here. From the visitor center, follow the orange-blazed Lookout Trail past the Habitat Garden, across the road, and through the entrance gate to the trails. Pass Laurelwood Niche, a small amphitheater. In about 200 yards, stop at South Lookout, which offers a great view of the Appalachian Mountains. From here you can see the River of Rocks, a jumble of boulders that broke off from the mountains around the time of the most recent glacier, whose furthest reach was just north of here in the Poconos. The constant freeze/thaw climate at that time caused the rocks to weather and crack, eventually tumbling together in this low part. (The trail to the River of Rocks begins to the right of the South Lookout.) Continue ahead on the Lookout Trail, passing two rock outcroppings on the right, which the kids may run to see.

If you want to tire your older kids out a little and if they like to climb on rocks, take them on an alternate route up the Escarpment Trail, which heads off to the right at about 0.4 mile, up and over piles of rocks, with two or three decent lookout points. It is a short but rugged trail that at its midway point intersects the River of Rocks Trail, then meets back with the Lookout Trail. From there you can take the Lookout Trail to the right for 0.1 mile to North Lookout and head back when you are done via the main hike on the Lookout Trail.

At the Escarpment Trail cutoff, the main hike continues straight on the Lookout Trail. The trail becomes quite rocky. Cross a wooden footbridge, then pass the other end of the River of Rocks Trail. Shortly thereafter, pass the Express Trail, which cuts up to the Escarpment Trail.

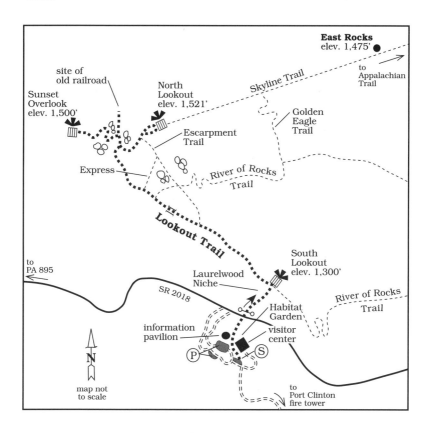

The Lookout Trail curves uphill through an area where sand was once excavated. The sand was loaded into a railroad car and sent down the mountain on a single-track gravity rail to the valley. At 0.6 mile go straight ahead for a 0.1-mile side trip to see the site of the old railroad and look at the disturbing photographs of the hawk slaughters that were routine when hawks were considered "bad." Thankfully, more enlightened wildlife management policies are now in effect to see that this kind of slaughter never happens again.

Also take time to follow the side trail that branches off to the left in this area to Sunset Overlook, a 0.2-mile side trip. Not as many poeple go to this overlook, as it is a rocky climb up through boulders, but the excellent view of picturesque farmland is well worth it. I surprised a black vulture sunning himself on the rocks here.

After exploring the side trails, continue on to the right toward the North Lookout. Pass the other end of the Escarpment Trail on the right and at 0.75 mile reach a large bouldery area at North Lookout, from which you can view many kinds of raptors. In addition to broad-winged, sharp-shinned, and red-tailed hawks, you might get lucky and see a golden or bald eagle, or an osprey, among others. Some small trees offer shade where hikers can relax and snack while taking in the views. (From the North Lookout, the Skyline Trail heads east to East Rocks and on toward the Appalachian Trail.) Backtrack along the Lookout Trail to the trailhead.

---

15. Old Railroad Grade and Appalachian Trails

Type: Day hike or overnight
Difficulty: Easy–moderate (length)
Distance: 3.4 miles one way
Hiking time: 3.5 hours one way
Elevation gain: 50 feet
Hikable: Spring–fall
Map: Weiser State Forest Public Use Map
Rest rooms: Toilets, water at Rausch Gap shelter
Fee: None

Introduce your kids to backpacking on this almost completely flat trail, which follows an old railroad bed through a quiet hemlock forest on state game lands into St. Anthony's Wilderness, the largest roadless area in this part of the state. Also a very nice day hike, the trail affords hikers a good chance of spotting some wildlife on your way to Rausch Gap, former site of an old coal mining village. Visit an old cemetery and hike the famous Appalachian Trail to Rausch Gap shelter, where there is good camping and water.

To reach the trailhead, take Interstate 78 east from Harrisburg, exiting onto Interstate 81 north. Get off at exit 30, the PA 72/Lebanon exit. Turn left off the exit ramp and left again at the stoplight onto PA 72 north. Take PA 72 north 3.5 miles to PA 443 east. Follow PA 443 east for 2.1 miles and make a left onto Gold Mine Road, which winds up on a ridge. On the way down, turn left at 2.8 miles onto an old railroad grade. Parking is on the right before the gate.

The Old Railroad Grade Trail begins at the gate on state game lands. Go around the gate and begin an easy stroll along the railroad bed. Over 100 years ago a branch of the Reading Railroad serviced this area, with stations at former Rausch Gap Village, Cold Springs, and Yellow Springs. Hemlocks line the trail all the way along this path. The trail is actually climbing, but so imperceptibly you will not notice it. The trail is very straight and clear all the way to the junction with the Appalachian Trail, nearly 3 miles west. So this is a trail to relax on and to notice what is around you—it is almost impossible to get lost as long as you stay on the railroad grade.

Children may notice that butterflies seem to love this trail; they congregate around moist patches. Another constant, especially in the early morning or early evening, is the sound of the wood thrush, whose flute-like call is most pleasant.

At about 0.8 mile, pass Sand Spring, a clear, cold spring bubbling up from the base of the trees into a sandy-bottomed pool. This is a good spot to get water if you need it, but do not wade or swim here, because it is also a source of water for other people and animals. Have a snack and explore the spring a bit, watching as it bubbles up from the ground.

Watch for wildlife along the trail. Because there is such a good view ahead, you may see animals before they see you. I have seen small creatures such

A box turtle creeps along the Old Railroad Grade in Rausch Gap.

as rabbits, turtles, frogs, and grouse, as well as many white-tailed deer and even a black bear here. Keep in mind that when seen from a distance, a deer resembles a golden retriever, and a black bear looks much like a black Newfoundland dog. Proceed quietly and bring binoculars.

At numerous spots along the railroad grade, you will notice side paths to the left. Most of these are access trails for hunters or to small open areas for browsing animals. If you hear helicopters, it is probably Fort Indiantown Gap, the National Guard base directly south of this ridge.

About 2.25 miles up the trail a gas pipeline bisects the path. Not long after, you pass a grassy road to the left that leads to a large browse area. About 0.5 mile further you come to an intersection with the Appalachian Trail, a 2,164-mile footpath that stretches from Maine to Georgia. The Appalachian Trail joins the railroad bed from the left, crossing an arched stone bridge over a branch of rushing Stony Creek.

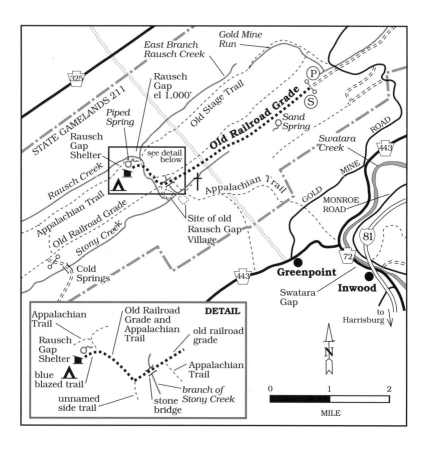

If you are day hiking, this is a good turnaround point (for a 5.5-mile round trip).

Before you do, explore the area a little. Near the intersection is the site of the ruins of the turntable pit and the Rausch Gap passenger station. Turn left on the Appalachian Trail for a short side trip past the remains of the old Rausch Gap Village, 0.2 mile down the trail. A fairly open area on the right is where it was located. Explore this side of the trail and look for the old stone well, which can still be seen amongst the hemlocks. Watch that children do not climb into the well, though it is mostly filled in now. Remains of old buildings can be seen among the trees. Rausch Gap Village was a coal mining community that thrived around the 1850s. Apparently the town was big enough to support a Catholic mission. Two miles further west on the Old Railroad Grade is the site of Cold Springs, a resort area that once was a summer school for Jesuit priests and a summer hotel offering mineral baths to tourists. In the summer months be alert for snakes sunning themselves on the rocks of the village ruins.

Walk about 0.1 mile further and watch for a narrow path on the left (which usually has a small wooden sign) heading about 200 feet to the old cemetery that contains several gravestones of the John Proud family, dated 1853. Backtrack to the railroad bridge from here. Note that there is no camping here except at the Rausch Gap shelter area.

Back at the bridge, the Appalachian Trail and the Old Railroad Grade coincide for the next 0.2 mile. Cross the stone bridge and follow the white-blazed Appalachian Trail to an intersection at 3 miles where an orange-blazed side trail leads left, and the Appalachian Trail bears right on an old mining road. Children may find huge ant mounds here. The ants are fun to watch, but do not get the ants riled up unless you want ants in your pants. If you want to explore the village area more, turn left on the orange-blazed side trail and walk about 0.1 mile, where you will notice many old stone foundations.

Leaving the Old Railroad Grade, turn right and follow the Appalachian Trail uphill, watching for Indian pipes in the leaf litter. These are actually flowers that do not have any chlorophyll. Watch for the white blazes as the trail bears left off the old mining road and continues uphill to a junction with a blue-blazed trail on the left. Follow the blue-blazed trail uphill, past an old wall on the right, till it joins with an old road. The Rausch Gap shelter is directly in front of you, with a nice piped spring and an outhouse. Note that long-distance backpackers have first dibs on the shelter, but others may stay in the shelter if there is room. Take a tent in case the shelter is full. There are several very nice flat tent sites along the old road in front and in back of the shelter.

To return, take the blue-blazed trail back to the Appalachian Trail, and retrace your steps on the Appalachian Trail and railroad grade back to Gold Mine Road.

16. Watershed and Boulevard Trails

Type: Day hike
Difficulty: Easy–moderate (ascents)
Distance: 2.7-mile loop
Hiking time: 2.5 hours
Elevation gain: 325 feet
Hikable: Year-round
Map: Nolde Forest Environmental Education Center map
Rest rooms: Toilets, water at center office
Fee: None

Nolde Forest is a real kids' place. Throughout the school year the place is normally teeming with children who participate in the many environmental education programs offered here. Any time of the year is a good time to explore the 665 acres of forest on this former estate. The property is laced with trails of varying length, most of which are appropriate for children. The trails are wide and gently graded. This pleasing loop trail on an old road is a gradual climb through the forest to a high point, then a gentle walk back down. A short 10-minute loop around the old mansion tells the story of Jacob Nolde, a hosiery baron who had thousands of trees planted when he bought the land in the early 1900s. A mixture of second-growth hardwoods and farmland existed at the site then, but Nolde was able to find only one white pine on the property. This pine inspired him to cover the property with evergreens in an effort to create the most beautiful pine forest in Pennsylvania.

To reach Nolde Forest, take Interstate 76 west from Philadelphia to the PA 222 exit. Take PA 222 north about 3 miles, and turn right onto PA 568 to the village of Knauers. Turn left onto PA 625 north, going about 5 miles. Turn left into the Sawmill parking lot.

Note: Trails are open sunrise to sunset daily, though the Sawmill and North Pond parking lots are the only lots open on weekends. The environmental education center office is open 8:00 A.M. to 4:00 P.M. Monday through Friday. For program information call the center at (610) 775-1411.

Begin the hike at the north corner of the parking lot. Go up the steps by the old sawmill building and cross a bridge, bearing left as the Watershed Trail follows along Punches Run. Before Nolde bought the land, the sawmill had been busy cutting trees, and downstream from the creek stood two iron forges. Charcoal was also made on the property to fuel the forges. On the right of the trail is the single white pine that Nolde was inspired by. Soon cross the creek again and bear right to stay on the now-gravel Watershed Trail (a park road goes to the left and the Squirrel Run Trail goes straight ahead here).

Take the Watershed Trail uphill, to the Y intersection with the Boulevard Trail at about 0.3 mile. This is a good time to take a 0.6-mile side trip to the mansion, which is a pretty English Tudor style stone home with a slate roof.

Nolde's mansion, as viewed from the short interpretive trail

To make the side trip, take the gravel Watershed Trail left to the environmental education center office. A 10-minute interpretive trail leads to the garden with blue-tiled fountains, through the butterfly garden, and under the mansion's arches. The signs tell how Nolde had 500,000 evergreen trees planted, at a rate of about 100,000 per year, hoping to create a forest similar to the Black Forest in Germany. When you are done exploring, head back down the Watershed Trail to the intersection with the Boulevard Trail.

Make a hairpin left turn near the bottom of the hill onto the Boulevard Trail, which follows an old road its entire length. Almost immediately cross another bridge and begin the gradual climb uphill. In this area are mostly beech and tulip poplar trees. Look for beechnuts, which the squirrels love. If there has been a storm recently, tulip seed pods litter the ground. If you find what look like tiny spears lying on the ground, you are looking at the core of last year's seed pods. The seeds dry out and fall off the central core.

The Boulevard Trail follows Punches Run, as does the Watershed Trail; there are a couple of short connecting trails between the two. At 0.5 mile a gas pipeline crosses the trail. At a trail junction at 0.7 mile, where Cabin Hollow Road goes left, bear right. In a few yards come to a Y where the two loops of the Boulevard Trail come together, and to which you will return later. For now, take the left fork and stay on the main trail, though a small unmarked trail goes right.

The trail switchbacks uphill past Christmas and hay-scented ferns. Look under the leaves for the spores, which look like dusty brown spots. This is how the ferns spread so extensively. The spores create clones of the parent fern. Blue jays may call raucously to each other.

They are beautiful birds, but they prey upon smaller birds, eating them and pecking their eggs. Watch for vines that wrap themselves around the tree trunks, sometimes creating permanently rippled grooves into the trunks as the tree expands around the vines.

As you near the top of the hill, smell the piney scent of the many evergreens that are mixed in with the hardwoods. Look for white pine (five needles), red pine (two long needles), Norway spruce (many short needles), Japanese larch, and Douglas-fir trees. In order to pay for all the trees that were planted, Nolde's forester sold Christmas trees (50 cents apiece), ornamental trees from the nursery, and willow boughs (to basket making companies in Philadelphia). The trail curves right after 1 mile as it come to a junction with a fire road on the left. Have the kids look for large anthills on the left.

As you reach the top of the knoll, the path becomes flat and grassy. Start downhill shortly, passing a double row of young spruces and the natural gas pipeline again. You will be heading downhill all the way back now. Look for wineberries along the trail. They resemble red raspberries and are orange-red when ripe. They taste tangy-sweet, but do not last long, because the birds often beat the people to them.

Look for pine cones from the Douglas-firs that are interspersed along this section of trail. Douglas-fir cones have feathery little tufts

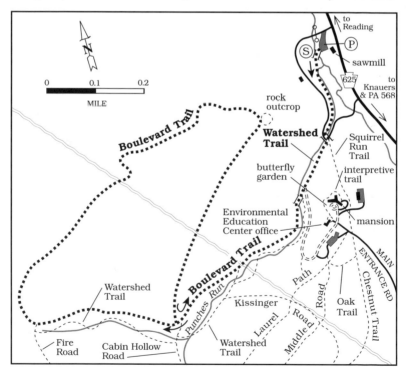

on them that look like little mouse paws reaching out of the cone. Kids might also enjoy looking for sassafras saplings, which cannot be confused with any other tree because it has three separate leaf shapes. Rub the surface of a sassafras leaf—the smell is spicy and sweet. At about 1.7 miles the Boulevard Trail curves right. Look for an unmarked trail on the left (hard to spot in the spring and summer), which leads to a rock outcrop. In the winter and fall there are limited views from this point.

As you pass the double row of spruces and the gas pipeline again, hikers might notice what appear to be 4-inch pieces of healthy evergreen tips littering the ground. Can kids guess how and why this happened? Give up? The squirrels and chipmunks chewed them off and then sat on the ground nibbling on the cones that grew on the tips.

At the Y trail junction, bear left after 2.0 miles and follow the Boulevard Trail back down the hill to the Watershed Trail and the parking lot.

Other trails of interest: The property is laced with trails of varying length, most of which are appropriate for children. The Watershed Trail is particularly recommended; a portion of it is described in this hike. Try the western portion of the trail, which departs from the Boulevard Trail near the stone bridge, and crisscrosses Punches Run for about 0.7 mile more, ending at the Fire Road.

17. Delaware Canal National Heritage Trail

Type:	Day hike
Difficulty:	Easy
Distance:	2 miles one way
Hiking time:	2 hours one way
Elevation gain:	25 feet
Hikable:	Spring–fall
Maps:	Delaware Canal State Park map; Washington Crossing Historic Park map
Rest rooms:	Pay toilets (25 cents), water at parking area and picnic pavilions
Fee:	None; $3/day parking fee

A walk along the towpath of the Delaware Canal is a stroll into American history. This National Heritage Trail follows the

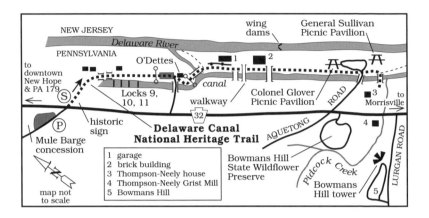

well-preserved Delaware Canal, which was one of the primary routes for transporting anthracite coal to Philadelphia, New York, and the Eastern seaboard in the early to mid-nineteenth century. This walk begins in the artsy town of New Hope, where antiques, craft shops, and restaurants draw many visitors. It takes us south to the northern end of Washington Crossing Historic Park, which commemorates Washington's crossing of the Delaware on Christmas Day, 1776, an event which helped bring renewed hope to the Revolutionary War effort. Numerous attractions in this area include a house and farm tour, grist mill, tower, and wildflower preserve. If you call ahead of time, you may be able to plan your hike to coincide with one of the numerous historic reenactments. (Note: To find out the reenactment schedule, call (215) 493-4076.) Pack lunches, and make a day of this one.

To reach Delaware Canal State Park, follow Interstate 276 from Philadelphia, exiting at the Willow Grove exit onto PA 611 north. Take PA 611 north to Doylestown and turn onto PA 202 north. Follow PA 202 north to New Hope, bearing right on PA 179 at the y inter-section where PA 202 goes across the river to Lambertville, New Jersey. Follow PA 179 downhill a few blocks to PA 32 in downtown New Hope. Turn right (south) and go about two blocks, looking for signs for the Delaware Canal State Park mule barge concession. Make a hairpin right into the parking lot and park here—there is about a $3 fee to park all day.

The Delaware Canal National Heritage Trail begins across the street from the mule barge parking lot, by a roadside historical sign. Take the gravel path, which looks very much like someone's driveway here, down a short hill past two houses on the left, crossing two wooden footbridges. As you pass another house on the left, you see locks 9, 10, and 11 on the canal, which is just a trickle now, on your right. Come to a gate and walk through a gravel parking lot past O'Dette's restaurant on the left. Bear left at the corner of the building through another gate, and over a footbridge. The canal is now filled with water, because the inlet from the Delaware River is 0.1 mile to the left. At 0.75 mile, at a junction with a side trail to the left to the Delaware River, follow the canal trail to the right along a wall and past a parking garage. Pass by a bridge on your right and go under a walkway where the trail is a narrow path. Pass an empty brick building on the left and cross under another bridge.

The trail begins to look more like a towpath, wide and grassy. This trail is shared with bicycles, so watch out for them. As the trail heads out of town, grapevines hang from the trees. Have kids look for an unusual pair of trees that grew together to form a wide x, on the left.

Sycamore trees, with their patchy calico bark, line the pathway. In the fall children enjoy finding their yellowish brown seed balls on the ground and pulling them apart to watch the seeds fly away. On the right the banks of the canal grow jewelweed. The juice of the stalk of this plant is soothing on bug bites and burns.

Tell children how the locks on the canal worked—adjusting the height of the water to safely lower heavy boats down the canal. The canal helped make it easier to use coal for households and industries, thus relieving the demand for wood and charcoal fuel, which required incredible amounts of trees. The iron industries also benefitted by having an easier means to transport cargo. In its operating lifetime, the canal transported 33 million tons of coal and 6 million tons of other goods, much of it food for local communities. The canal was like an interstate highway.

Pass numerous old sycamores and tulip trees, many too big to get your arms around. Some of these trees were here when the canal was operating. Look for rounded depressions in the creek bottom along the edges. Fish lay their eggs here. If you look in the shady, deeper

Volunteers reenact Revolutionary War days when the Minutemen had to be ready at a minute's notice to defend against British attacks.

sections of the canal, you may spot some large suckers, bottom-dwelling fish that seem to congregate together.

At about 1.7 miles, Colonel Glover picnic pavilion is on the left; at 1.9 miles, come to a park road and a stone bridge. Cross this road and continue along the canal another 0.1 mile to the next bridge; at 2 miles leave the Delaware Canal trail and turn right to cross the bridge over the canal to Washington Crossing Historical Park.

This is a fun area to explore. To the immediate right is the Thompson-Neely House, where General George Stirling stayed in the winter of 1776. He was in charge of the troops stationed along the Delaware to prevent a British crossing. The park offers tours of the Thompson-Neely House. Across the street (PA 32) is the Thompson-Neely Grist Mill, which still operates. On numerous weekends throughout the year, a military reenactment group stages encampments at this site. Children and adults find this fascinating, as the soldiers have a mock skirmish and craftspeople display their costumes and wares. If you have the time and energy, head uphill from the grist mill to the Bowman's Hill State Wildflower Preserve, whose 100 acres are dedicated to preserving native plants of Pennsylvania. There are some short trails here. Of particular interest is the 110-foot-high Bowman's Hill Tower. When you have had your fill of sights, head back to the Delaware Canal trail and return along it to New Hope.

18. Meadow Crossing, Rosebush, and Creek Road Trails

Type:	Day hike
Difficulty:	Easy
Distance:	1.5-mile loop
Hiking time:	1.5 hours
Elevation gain:	100 feet
Hikable:	Spring–fall
Map:	Pennypack Ecological Restoration Trust map
Rest rooms:	Toilets, water beneath environmental management center building
Fee:	None

Just north of Philadelphia is a cool, shady place for kids and parents to explore the forests and meadows along the banks of Pennypack Creek. This child-oriented place has a nature center with displays, two greenhouses, a bird blind, a wildflower meadow, and plenty of trails. The urban wildlife sanctuary also has a mission: the nonprofit organization is a private trust dedicated to restoring the natural habitat of the forests in this region that have suffered from overgrazing by deer, development, and invasion by nonnative species. The trails are open Monday through Saturday 9:00 A.M. to 5:00 P.M. and Sunday 1:00 to 5:00 P.M.

A cottontail rabbit is ready to run for cover along the Meadow Crossing Trail.

To reach Pennypack Ecological Restoration Trust, take the Pennsylvania Turnpike (Interstate 276) east from Philadelphia to the Willow Grove exit, PA 611, and turn south on PA 611. At the third stop light, turn left onto Fitzwatertown Road. As the road crosses PA 263, its name changes to Terwood Road. Follow Terwood across Davisville Road, bearing right where Huntington Road bears left. At the stop sign, turn left onto Edge Hill Road. Go 0.3 mile; see a driveway on the right marked by a large sign.

The hike begins at the nature center, which is at the end of the parking lot. Stop here first to look around at the exhibits. Behind the center are the greenhouses and flower and herb gardens, which are fun to explore. Solar panels help heat the enclosed areas here. Rub the herb leaves lightly with your fingers and then sniff them—some tantalizing smells!

Begin the hike at the greenhouses. Head downhill a short distance to a T junction and turn left at a persimmon tree. In about 25 feet, turn right, onto the Meadow Crossing Trail. As you cross the meadow, notice what grows here. Grass as tall as most children lines the path. Look for wild chives with their spiky purple head and blackberries, which ripen in late July or early August.

Soon enter a cherry-lined woods. Pennsylvania is known for having the most beautiful black cherry wood in the country. At nearly 0.4 mile, as you bear left onto the Rosebush Trail, a sign reminds you that this woods is being restored. Declining trees, deer browsing, and competition from exotic plants have damaged these forests. As you walk, look for saplings and flowers with protective fencing around them—these are transplants.

Head down a gentle hill on the Rosebush Trail. Some huge old tulip poplars line the path to your right. Pass the Lookout Trail on the right and continue downhill along a fence. Notice a few waterbars here—logs and stones cut into the trail at an angle to channel water off the path when it rains. This helps control erosion.

Cross a small wooden footbridge and follow along the edge of a tree farm. Saplings are growing up in plastic tubing, in order to be protected from deer browsing. Hear a stream and come to a junction with the Creek Road Trail at 0.5 mile. Turn right and follow the Creek Road Trail along the banks of Pennypack Creek. Take time to visit the creek bank to see who has been there.

Pass daylilies and walnut trees, then come to a junction at Paper Mill Road at 0.7 mile. A short side trip left on Paper Mill Road brings you to the ruins of an old water-powered paper mill and the second oldest bridge in Montgomery County (built in 1840), from which there are excellent views of the rushing creek. Return to the trail junction and go uphill (straight ahead) on Paper Mill Road past a small marsh. Bullfrogs can be heard harumphing here. Further along, notice the extensive roots of some of the larger trees, which are exposed along the trail's bank. Where the Management Trail comes in from the left, continue straight on Paper Mill Road.

Almost at the top of the hill, after 1.1 miles, bear right onto a

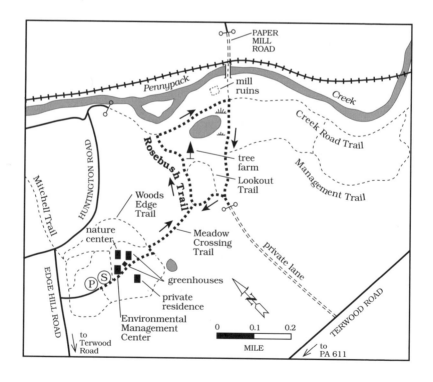

narrow path. Beautiful dogwood trees thrive here amidst the cherry and tulip. Shortly after you enter this trail, at another trail junction, stay left as the other end of the Lookout Trail goes to the right. At 1.2 miles, you come back to the beginning of the Rosebush Trail, where you began this loop; stay to the left to continue back across the Meadow Crossing Trail toward the visitor center. On the way back, keep your eyes open for rabbits and groundhogs that live in the undergrowth.

Other trails of interest: This hike can be extended by continuing on Creek Road Trail past Paper Mill Road, and then looping back on the Management Trail, which connects with the Paper Mill Road.

For shorter options, families with toddlers may want to stick to some of the short loops that encircle the nature center.

19. Historic Trace Road

Type: Day hike
Difficulty: Easy
Distance: 2.1-mile loop
Hiking time: 2 hours
Elevation gain: 100 feet
Hikable: Spring–fall
Map: Valley Forge Hiking Trail Map
Rest rooms: Toilets, water along trail
Fee: None

Valley Forge is perhaps the most widely recognized historic site associated with the American Revolutionary War, and it is also a great place to take a hike. Kids enjoy a walk along this loop trail lined with grand old trees where they can explore the reconstructed huts showing how George Washington's soldiers lived in cramped quarters during the winter of 1777–78. The hike follows the paved multipurpose hike/bike trail halfway, then returns along the Historic Trace Road, which was used to transport supplies to the troops during the encampment. Cannons are lined up at the artillery park and numerous interpretive signs are located along the route. There are limitless grassy open spaces to stop and picnic, play frisbee, fly a kite, or just sit under a tree and relax.

To reach Valley Forge National Historic Park, take the turnpike

(Interstate 76) west from Philadelphia to exit 26B/PA 202 south. Stay in the left lane and take the next exit for PA 422 west, then almost immediately take the PA 23 west exit for Valley Forge. Come off the exit and at the stoplight go straight across North Gulph Road into the park entrance. The visitor center has a film about the park that is well worth seeing. To reach the trailhead, go back out the driveway and turn left at the light onto PA 23. Pass Washington's Memorial Chapel and at 1.5 miles turn left into the parking area across the street from Varnum's Picnic Area and just past General Varnum's Quarters.

The trail begins at the corner of the parking lot by the statue of General Von Steuben, a Prussian whose efforts at retraining and constant drilling during the winter turned the ragtag army into an efficient fighting force. Next to the statue is a path leading to General Varnum's Quarters; tours are periodically offered—check at the visitor center for the current schedule.

Take the multipurpose trail downhill, where you pass by a gate to the Historic Trace Road—this is where you will end up. Inner Line Drive, the park road, is on the right—take the hike/bike path in the middle. The reconstructed Conway huts are 50 yards below the trail, and children will want to romp down the hillside and peek into them. A thousand of these huts provided shelter for the army during the winter. The single fireplace was the only source of heat and blankets were few.

Back on the trail, the path parallels the park road along rolling green hills. Though this is not a wilderness, there is still plenty of wildlife. Deer browse by the edge of the woods to your right, as do woodchucks and rabbits. Another name for groundhogs is whistle pigs because when you whistle they usually stand up on their hind legs and look around. Soon pass several cannons on your left, perched atop an earthen embankment known as a redan, which was constructed to make the area's defenses more formidable. Walking down a gentle hill, cross Gulph Road after 0.5 mile and notice numerous grand white oaks, over 100 years old. A monument on the right marks where General Washington erected his headquarters tent when the troops first

There is plenty of room for a leisurely picnic at Valley Forge.

arrived in December 1777. Next pass a parking lot with rest rooms on the left.

Continue uphill briefly and meet with the Historic Trace Road at nearly 1 mile. Turn left onto the Historic Trace Road, which you follow back to the trailhead. This road was used to haul supplies and was a muddy mess when the soldiers were here. The road leads north to the Schuylkill River, a major supply point for the troops. Heading down a gentle hill on the gravel road, pass some young maples that

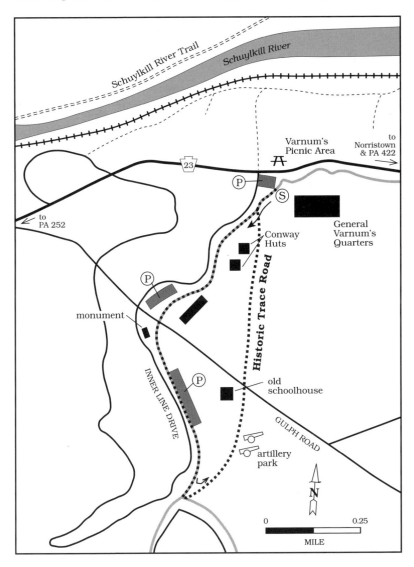

were planted by the survivors of Pearl Harbor in honor of the troops who suffered here 200 years ago. As many as 2,000 men perished here due to disease.

Soon come to a row of cannons known as artillery park. Though no battle was ever fought here, the troops had to be prepared for attacks from the British, who occupied the patriot capitol of Philadelphia, 18 miles away. Also notice an old stone structure on the right just past the artillery park. To the left is a tiny schoolhouse that was built 35 years after the encampment when the village of Valley Forge was expanding with industry. Kids can peek through the window and see the teacher's platform. How would they like to go to a school like this?

Cross Gulph Road again at 1.3 miles and pause to look uphill toward the cannons above. The view from here led the British spies to conclude that the Continental Army's position was too strong to be attacked with a clear chance of success. Little did they know that disease, cold, and filth threatened the army's very existence. Nevertheless, at the end of the 6-month encampment, Washington had a formidable fighting force under his command that was well trained and provisioned, ready to secure America's independence. Return to the Conway huts and from here head up to the gate where you began.

Other trails of interest: The Schuylkill River Trail is a 3-mile-long trail that contains a 2.3-mile loop which runs along the river. An interpretive guide for the loop is available at the trailhead, on Pawling Road at the Pawling Parking Area.

---

20. Multi-Use Trail

Type:	Day hike
Difficulty:	Easy; handicapped-accessible most of the length
Distance:	4.3-mile loop
Hiking time:	3.5 hours
Elevation gain:	220 feet
Hikable:	Year-round (plowed in winter)
Map:	Ridley Creek State Park trail map
Rest rooms:	Toilets, water at parking lot at picnic area 15 April–November and at park office year-round; portable potty at 0.6-mile marker year-round
Fee:	None

Only 16 miles from city-center Philadelphia is this gem of a park, whose 2,606 acres encompass woodlands and meadows along Ridley

Creek. The area was once a small village that grew up around a mill. Some buildings still remain and are scattered throughout the park. The Multi-Use Trail has a tree identification course; pick up a quiz and answer sheet at the front office and see how you do in identifying the forty-eight species of trees along the route. Dogs, strollers, bikes, and wheelchairs are all permitted, and you will most likely meet folks engaging in all these activities (the steep grade from picnic area 17 to the Sycamore Mills and Forge Road intersection exceeds standards for ADA accessibility). Hike the whole loop if you have time, or just a portion. Mileage is marked every 0.1 mile (starting at the Sycamore Mills and Forge Road intersection, going counterclockwise), so you always know how far you have gone.

A special attraction in the northwest part of the park is the Colonial Pennsylvania Plantation, which has living history demonstrations of life on a pre-Revolutionary Quaker farm. On weekends from April to October, the plantation is open for visitors and during the week, group tours can be arranged. The fee is $3 per adult, $1.50 for children ages four to twelve, and free for ages three and under.

To reach Ridley Creek State Park, take US 1 south from Philadelphia to PA 352 north near Lima. Take PA 352 north to Gradyville. In Gradyville turn right on Gradyville Road, bearing right at a fork. At 1.3 miles from Gradyville, turn right into the park on Sandy Flash Drive South. If you would like to stop at the park office, turn right into the second drive to the office, located in a thirty-eight-room English Tudor mansion. Then continue down Sandy Flash Drive South; at a Y intersection after two creek crossings, stay to the right, and then turn right, into the fifth drive on the right. Turn right again immediately and go 0.1 to the parking lot at picnic area 15.

To start the hike, pass by the gate at the end of the parking lot onto a paved road and in 100 yards turn left onto the Multi-Use Trail. The trail is on two old roads, Forge Road and Sycamore Mills Road. Begin on Forge Road, and return to this point at the end of the hike. Hikers are encouraged to stay to the left and bicycles to the right. Pass a side trail to the rest rooms.

The numbers on posted trees correspond to the tree identification course. Fine old oaks line the trail and soon you pass a meadow on the left where butterflies feast on milkweed plants. Pass a couple of small trails off to the left and listen to a whole host of birds. (A bird identification checklist is also available from the park office.) On the right you can see the crumbling remains of an old house. Not far past that, the White Trail crosses the path at 0.6 mile, the first of many crossings, and soon after that a trail on the left leads to the exercise court and picnic area 17. Just ahead on the right is a trail that leads to trails in Tyler Arboretum, which is adjacent to Ridley Creek State Park.

The trail heads downhill now, past a private drive on the left.

You can see an old stone house on the hill. This park was once the huge estate of a wealthy family that had bought many acres and farms; some of the farmhouses are still occupied. At the bottom of the hill, at the junction with Sycamore Mills Road near Ridley Creek at 1.3 miles, turn left onto Sycamore Mills Road and continue on its mostly flat trail now, which follows the slow-moving creek. Maple viburnum, a shrub with berries that wildlife enjoy, grows in the understory. Its berries, which are not edible to humans, turn dark purple in the fall as do the leaves. Notice the rippled trunk of the American hornbeam, also known as ironwood or musclewood, which is an extremely dense wood sometimes used for carving.

Continue upstream past some riffles in the creek. Many folks enjoy fishing here; it is one of the few streams in Delaware County that is stocked with trout. Anywhere along here is a possible turnaround point, if your children are tiring. Soon the trail begins a gentle ascent. Pass

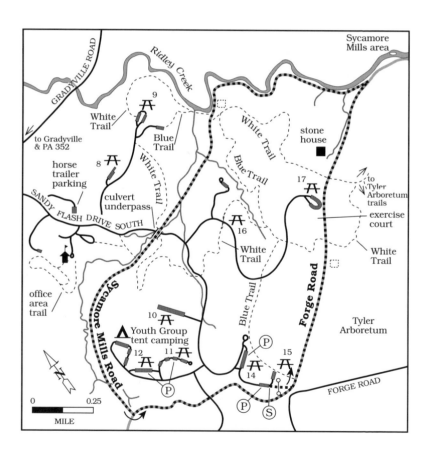

another old stone structure on the left; this is the halfway point at 2.1 miles. There are many trail crossings in this area, but other trails are not paved; you should have no difficulty staying on the paved Multi-Use Trail. Notice some more big oaks as you turn away from the creek. Wild roses line the path here—they smell terrific in the spring. Pass a private driveway and continue uphill, crossing two small creeks. At the second creek, stop to look for garter and water snakes, which drape themselves on the bushes by the creek to soak up the sun. They are not poisonous but can get cranky if provoked.

At 2.7 miles, the trail goes under Sandy Flash Drive South through a culvert underpass, and also intersects the White Trail again. Rhododendrons here are in bloom in July. Pass a sheltered bench on the left. Reach a road on the right that crosses a bridge that was the entrance to the Jeffords family estate. (A short walk across that bridge and then on the path to the left leads to the mansion housing the park office.) Note the mossy remains of an old horse watering trough on the side of the trail.

Ascend a gentle hill, soon crossing a small creek. Notice another old building on the left. At the next trail junction, a ⊤ intersection where the paved road turns into a narrower paved path at 3.6 miles, turn left and follow the trail as it heads up through the fields. Pass a private drive, and listen to the crickets. The trail flattens as it passes between two hedgerows, ideal habitat for rabbits and ground-hogs. Ascend a gentle hill and pass a paved road at an intersection— go straight. At the next junction, turn left onto Forge Road and head uphill back to the gate and the parking lot.

Other trails of interest: Several unpaved trails in the park are suitable for hiking with children. The White Trail is a 3-mile loop trail that winds through the forest most of its length, and offers hikers a quiet stroll away from the more crowded Multi-Use Trail. The White Trail is accessed from picnic area 9 or 16.

The Blue Trail is 1.5 miles long and is also mostly in the forest. It bisects the Multi-Use Trail, so could be used as an alternate return route at the halfway point. The Blue Trail begins at picnic area 9 or 15.

The park office area trail is about 0.5 mile long and encircles the park office building. This is a paved, handicapped-accessible trail that makes for a pleasant hike on the grounds of the former estate.

The trails in Tyler Arboretum, next door to the state park, are well worth a visit. There is a fee for the arboretum, and maps of the trail system are available there. Access is from the Forge Road path near picnic area 17, or from the arboretum. To get to the arboretum, follow the directions to Ridley Creek State Park via US 1 to PA 352 north, but turn right on Forge Road, before reaching Gradyville, then turn right again on Painter Road. The Tyler Arboretum is on the left.

21. Impoundment Trail

Type: Day hike
Difficulty: Easy (short loop); moderate (long loop) (distance)
Distance: 0.5 mile (short loop); 3.3 miles (long loop)
Hiking time: 25 minutes (short loop); 2.5 hours (long loop)
Elevation gain: None
Hikable: Spring–fall
Map: Impoundment Trail map of John Heinz National Wildlife Refuge at Tinicum
Rest rooms: Toilets, water at visitor contact station
Fee: None

Show your kids what a freshwater marsh looks like in this 1,200-acre wildlife preserve located within the Philadelphia city limits. The trails are easy and wide, the birds plentiful, and it is uncrowded, considering its location in the fourth-largest city in the United States. An observation platform overlooking the freshwater tidal marsh and a bird blind facilitate wildlife-watching. Over 280 species of birds have been spotted here, 85 of which nest here. Many of the species pass through here during spring and fall migrations. This area was almost obliterated by development and pollution and is still in the process of recovery and rehabilitation. Walk along a dike separating the freshwater marsh from the freshwater tidal marsh. Nature programs are offered on the weekends. Trails are open sunrise to sunset daily.

To reach the refuge take Interstate 95 south from Philadelphia to the PA 291/airport exit. Continue west on PA 291 to Bartram Avenue, turn right, and go 1.6 miles to 86th Street, then turn left. In 0.5 mile turn left on Lindbergh Boulevard. Go 0.2 mile and turn right into the refuge driveway and follow it to the left to the visitor contact station and parking area. Note: A new visitor center will be built in two to three years and the entrance may be slightly changed.

For the short loop, from behind the visitor contact station pass through the gate and go straight on the wide path, the Impoundment Trail, not the two paths to the left. Tea-colored Darby Creek rises and falls with the tides on the west side of the trail. Catch-and-release fishing is allowed in Darby Creek. Lining the pathway are a variety of trees, some of which were introduced by early settlers. These settlers diked and drained parts of the marsh, which once encompassed 5,700 acres. Wild honey locust, a native tree, is recognizable by its distinctive long seed pods that look like giant peas and its large, branching thorns. Wildflowers, cattails, and phragmites (a tall grass) line the path.

In 0.25 mile come to a boardwalk that cuts across the middle of the marsh. Turn left and walk across on it, noticing the thousands of splatterdock plants. They have yellow flowers in summer. Smaller birds make their way underneath the canopy of splatterdock and larger wading birds walk through them. About two-thirds of the way across the boardwalk is a bench and a platform for closer observation of the wetland. Look for minnows, waterbugs, frogs, and other creatures here. Take the boardwalk to its end and turn left on the trail into the woods. Pass the thicket of grapevines and watch for poison ivy. Pass a few side trails on the right and a few leading to the water's edge on the left. At the trail junction, bear left and head back to the parking lot.

For the long loop, at the trailhead behind the visitor contact station, pass through the gate and go left downhill to a trail junction (not the old road). Take the righthand trail into the woods. This trail follows the edge of the marsh, and is the latter half of the short loop, followed in reverse. Pass a few unofficial side trails heading left and right, and go through a vine-entangled area, watching for poison ivy. Just ahead, turn right onto the boardwalk that crosses the marsh at 0.2 mile. The

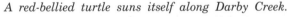

A red-bellied turtle suns itself along Darby Creek.

boardwalk offers a close-up view of the plants and animals of the marsh. (For further description of the boardwalk see the description of the short loop.) At the end of the boardwalk, turn left onto the old road (the Impoundment Trail), which you follow for the remainder of the hike. Look for the state endangered red-bellied turtle (dark color with red underparts, 10 to 12 inches long) sunning on rocks or a log, or the painted turtle, which looks similar but is much smaller. Tall phragmites rustle in the breeze along the creek and staghorn sumac lines the impoundment.

Cross an old water control structure and take time to stop at the observation platform on the left at 0.7 mile. Interpretive information here changes seasonally. In the summer we visited, the display told about splatterdock, which covers most of the watery areas of the impoundment. It is considered a weed and efforts are being made to

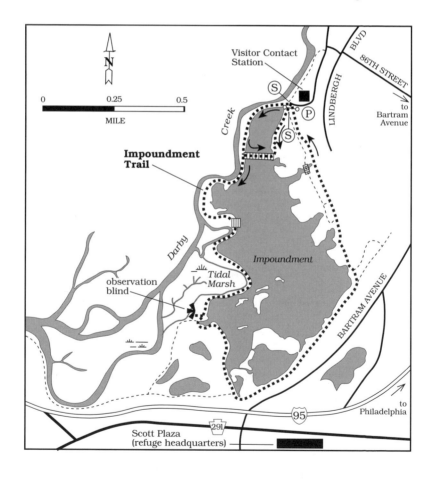

find a safe way to get rid of it so more open water will be available for birds and other creatures.

Boxelders, with their maple-type seeds, line the bank now and lush green grass fills in the edges of the marsh. Children are likely to notice what look like brown kidney beans littering the ground—these are seeds from the locust trees. Blackberries grow well on the banks and provide a nice snack in mid- to late July when they ripen.

You also pass rows of mulberry trees, whose berries look like blackberries and ripen in early July. Their berries are favored by songbirds. At 1.2 miles, take the short side trail to the right to look through the observation blind. This view of the tidal marsh is the best view on the trail. Hikers may spot Canada geese or a great blue heron from this vantage point. All the tall wading birds that frequent here are carnivores, feasting on frogs, toads, insects, and other small creatures that they find.

Just after the blind, at a Y intersection, the Impoundment Trail turns left and continues along the edge of the impoundment, right next to I-95. The history of this area is a long one of adverse human intervention. In the seventeenth century Swedish, Dutch, and English settlers diked and drained portions of the marsh for farming and grazing livestock. Industry cut into the marsh later until there were as few as 200 acres of original marsh remaining. From the 1950s until the 1970s the Folcroft landfill, the construction of I-95, and the dumping of dredgings from the Delaware River threatened the area even more. A public outcry resulted in Gulf Oil donating 145 acres to the city. In 1972 the U.S. Fish and Wildlife Service took over management of the land and added more holdings—it now protects 1,200 acres, including the last remaining large freshwater tidal marsh in the state. The refuge is named for the late Senator John Heinz, who was instrumental in the establishment of the refuge.

After 1.5 miles, a side trail heads west to another portion of the refuge. Bear left, staying on the Impoundment Trail as it parallels Bartram Avenue.

The trail passes a lush willow grove on the right and soon reaches another Y trail junction at 2.2 miles. Turn left again and head up the east side of the impoundment. Soon pass a short side trail that bears to the right off the Impoundment Trail. The grassy trail runs between tall hedgerows of honeysuckle and viburnum, shaded by mulberries and oaks. On the right come to a break where you may surprise a great blue heron.

Continuing on, notice the aspen trees, whose leaves tremble in the breeze. Kids enjoy finding the spiky sweet gum seedpods that fall to the ground in the late summer and fall. A few side trails go off to the left, but continue straight ahead on the wide Impoundment Trail to the trailhead.

22. Longwood Gardens

Type: Day hike
Difficulty: Easy
Distance: 1.5-mile loop
Hiking time: 1.5 hours or more
Elevation gain: 20 feet
Hikable: Year-round
Map: Longwood Gardens map
Rest rooms: Toilets, water at visitor center, beneath conservatory
Fee: Free for children under age 6, $2 children ages 6–15, $6 ages 16–20, $10 adults

Longwood Gardens is one of the finest botanical gardens in the country, if not the world, and people from all over the world come to see this former estate. Many hikes with endless appeal for young children are possible in this 1,050-acre park, with easy-to-follow walkways, many fountains, goldfish ponds, an arboretum, a conservatory with a special children's garden, and a bell tower to climb. This is a place I have been to hundreds of times, because I grew up 1 mile from the gardens. My mother took me here in a stroller when I was a baby, and countless times afterward when my sister and I could walk. The place still holds my interest as an adult. It is almost impossible to get lost here. The hike described here incorporates elements that are most interesting to children. Fees pay for the upkeep of the gardens by a nonprofit organization that employs 400 people.

An old boot is put to a new use as a bird house in the children's garden.

To reach Longwood Gardens, take US 1 south from Philadelphia and exit at the Longwood Gardens exit just before Kennett Square. Bear right 0.1 mile to the main entrance gate. Park in the large lot and enter the gardens through the visitor center building.

This hike begins at the visitor center, taking you through the topiary garden, conservatories, fountains, and chimes tower. At the T intersection at the starting point, turn left onto the paved path and go straight when you pass a tree-lined walkway on the right, reaching the entrance to the rose and topiary gardens on the right in about 0.1 mile. Enter the rose garden and take time to smell the flowers here. Kids enjoy trying to identify the different species of trees and examining the garden's huge sundial.

At the far left of the topiary garden, exit and make a right onto a paved path. Make a left at a four-way intersection and shortly after, at a Y intersection, again bear left uphill to the conservatories. Enter the conservatories at the east entrance at 0.3 mile. At the fountain turn left and go diagonally left into the children's garden. This fun room has fountains at touchable height for youngsters and a "kids-only" maze to run through. Exit by going left back out to the fountain and out of the conservatories. Go right, onto the paved path that runs along the front of the building, and at the far west end bear left, then left again to the lower level of the conservatories.

Continue straight ahead a short way to the entrance to the main fountain garden at 0.7 mile, a fun place for kids to run around in and

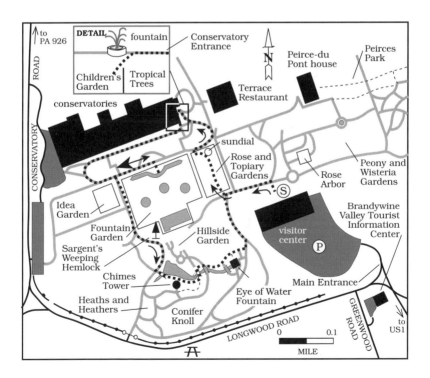

between the fountains. In the summer evenings there are colored light shows here that kids really enjoy.

When you are finished at the fountains, go back to the paved path and turn left, then proceed to a T intersection; take the path to the left, heading downhill along a tree-lined path. Reach a Sargent's weeping hemlock on the left—a fun tree we used to call the "kissing tree" because couples used to go under its roomy branches to smooch. Children enjoy playing house under the branches here. At the path around the tree, go straight ahead. Pass the Hillside Garden on the left as the path bears right, then turn left by the southwest corner of the pool by the chimes tower and waterfall. Follow the path along the water's edge, getting a good view of the waterfall ahead. Turn right at the next intersection and head uphill to the bottom of the tower at 1 mile. Steps lead up to the top of the tower, from which there is a great view.

Go back down the tower, exiting out its south side, then turn left and cross over a small bridge just above the waterfall. Turn right and then go straight ahead and then right on the path to the Eye of Water Fountain, where massive amounts of water that feed the falls well up out of an eye-like structure. Take a right and head east out of the Eye of Water Fountain area and follow the paved pathway as it curves north (left) back to the rose and topiary gardens at 1.4 miles. Return to the main entrance by turning right.

---

23. White Clay Creek Preserve

Type:	Day hike
Difficulty:	Easy
Distance:	2.8 miles round trip
Hiking time:	2–3 hours round trip
Elevation gain:	20 feet
Hikable:	Spring–fall
Map:	White Clay Creek Preserve map
Rest rooms:	Toilets, water at London Tract Baptist Meetinghouse
Fee:	None

White Clay Creek is currently being studied for possible inclusion into the National Wild and Scenic Rivers system. After walking along

Exploring White Clay Creek is always an adventure.

its banks, you will understand why. This 1,253-acre preserve, shared by Pennsylvania and Delaware, was sold to William Penn in 1683 by Lenni Lenape Indian Chief Kekelappen, who is believed to have lived in the large Indian village that once stood where the east and middle branches of the creek come together, about 1 mile north of this hike. The hike, which actually begins just over the border in Delaware, takes you on an old road upstream, passing several fun places to explore the creek and ending at South Bank Road, where hikers can explore the old Baptist meetinghouse and cemetery before heading back. Environmental education programs are held regularly at the meetinghouse. There are plenty of opportunities to turn around if your charges get weary. Those with lots of energy can continue along the east branch of the creek to where the trail ends on London Tract Road, a distance of about 4 miles one way. (It is best not to go on this hike during the opening of fishing season, when a portion of the trail is open to vehicles and gets very muddy.)

To reach the White Clay Creek Preserve, take the US 1 bypass south from Kennett Square and get off at the PA 896 exit. Go south on PA 896 through New London, Kemblesville, and the tiny crossroads that is Strickersville. Go 0.3 mile past Strickersville and turn left onto Chambers Rock Road. Go 1.5 miles to a parking lot on the left, which is just across the state line into Delaware.

The trail begins at the northeast corner of the parking lot and proceeds through a field, where tall grasses are festooned with crickets.

Kids notice mouse and chipmunk holes along the trail, as well as shiny bits of mica (schist), which make the dirt appear to sparkle in the sunlight.

Enter the woods shortly. Pass numerous unmarked paths that lead to the creek; up ahead there are better places to access the creek. The trail soon curves left up a small hill where you begin to hear water. An old bridge abutment is visible on the right, which is a good vantage point from which to view the creek. (Watch for holes in the side trail here.) Soon after you pass the bridge abutment, at 0.5 mile the trail joins with an old road, known as Peltier Road, at which you bear right and follow the rest of the way to South Bank Road. You have also crossed into Pennsylvania and will stay in state the remainder of the hike. As you walk along, children may enjoy guessing what lives in the various hollow trees along the shaded path. Inspections under rocks may reveal crickets, millipedes, or salamanders.

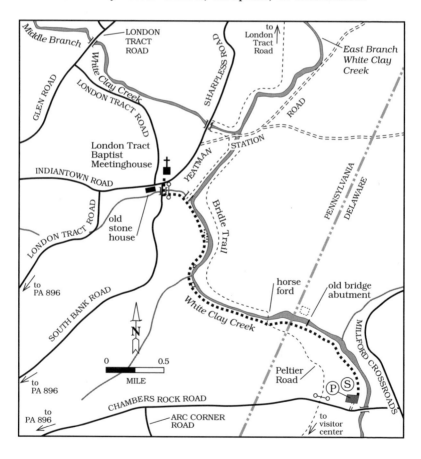

It is hard to imagine that this pretty area almost got drowned. In the early 1980s the DuPont Company owned the land and had plans to construct a reservoir here. Resistance from the community proved strong and the company relinquished the reservoir plans and turned the land over to the two states for recreational purposes. The White Clay Creek is still an important watershed for the area.

The trail is wide and level, but somewhat rocky in places. Follow the creek closely, with many opportunities to watch for waterbirds like the great blue heron, or some mallard ducks. At 1 mile, come to a fairly flat, sloping rock that leads right to the water's edge. The edges of the rock on the right side make a good bench to sit on and dangle little feet into the water. Kids enjoy looking for minnows here and watching water striders skate on the surface tension. If you are with tiring toddlers, this is a good place to turn around.

Continue ahead about 0.2 mile to a wide area on the right where anglers like to try their luck. At the northern end of this area, go to the creek's edge where there is a sandy, pebbly beach. The water is usually shallow here and good for wading. When it is really hot, this is a fun place to go tubing and float down the creek to the flat rock you just passed. (Swimming is not permitted, but tubing and wading are.) Try your hand at rock skipping on the beach. Look for small, flat pebbles and sidearm them horizontally.

Past the beach, the trail climbs briefly and you can see a tributary meet the main creek on the right. A side trail crosses the tributary. (To take an extended hike along the whole length of the creek, take this side trail about 2 miles further to London Tract Road.) The main trail on Peltier Road bears left away from the main creek, past thousands of daylilies, ending at a gate on South Bank Road. If you would like to explore a bit, turn right on lightly traveled South Bank Road, cross the bridge, and in 100 yards reach the ʏ intersection with Yeatman Station Road. On the left is an old stone farmhouse, and across the street is the London Tract Baptist Meetinghouse, built in 1729. A naturalist is sometimes in the church building. Check out the old cemetery in the churchyard. A local legend has it that one of the tombs emits a ticking sound, like the sound of a watch, because the person buried there swallowed the watch before he died. Some local residents claim to have heard the ticking!

To return to the parking lot, follow the trail back the way you came. For a little variety at the end, go straight on Peltier Road where the trail you came in on bears left. Continue 0.2 mile to a gate, turn left, and walk 0.2 mile along Chambers Rocks Road to the parking lot.

Other trails of interest: Old Peltier Road continues on the south side of Chambers Rock Road. A hike of about 0.5 mile on the old road leads past raspberry bushes to a visitor center in a restored eighteenth-century mill house.

24. Mystery Hole and Buck Trails

Type: Day hike
Difficulty: Easy
Distance: 1.5-mile loop
Hiking time: 1.5 hours
Elevation gain: 150 feet
Hikable: Year-round
Map: Nottingham County Park map
Rest rooms: Toilets, water 0.4 mile along park road
Fee: None

There are a few places in the northeastern United States that are geological oddities, and Nottingham Park in Chester County is one of them. The area is known as The Barrens, and is one of only three areas in the country where serpentine, a rare, light-green rock, is located. Surrounded by lush eastern forest habitat on all sides, this former serpentine, feldspar, and chrome quarry has soil that supports only limited prairie plants and succulents, and stunted trees. Several of the plants found here are in danger of extinction; one, the serpentine aster, lives nowhere else in the world.

This loop hike takes you through a portion of The Barrens and past the Mystery Hole, a fenced-off (for safety) but very visible old quarry, now filled with water. The mystery is how deep it is. Continue through The Barrens, then return through the dramatically different forest, coming back along the shore of pleasant McPherson Lake. The park has some very nice tent camping, which never seems to be crowded or overused, and many picnic areas. Numerous trails in the park make possible a whole host of loop hikes, of varying length and difficulty.

To get to Nottingham Park, take US 1 south from Philadelphia and get off at the Nottingham/PA 272 exit. Turn left and in 100 yards turn right onto Herr Drive and follow it to the stop sign. (Herr's potato chip factory is straight ahead.) Turn right onto Old Baltimore pike, go 0.2 mile, and turn right onto Park Road. The park entrance is 0.9 mile on the left. Once in the park, follow the park road 0.5 mile through the park to the lot at McPherson Lake.

Begin at the dirt service road to the left of the parking area. Go through the gate and in about 100 yards turn right onto an old dirt road, which is Mystery Hole Trail, blazed with blue markers. Pass a trail on your left and cross Black Run Creek on a wooden footbridge. Look for frogs here. You are on the fringes of The Barrens now. Notice the short trees, mostly pitch pine, cedar, and sassafras. Pitch pine can be distinguished from other pines in that it has three needles per cluster. The thorny green brier vine covers most of the undergrowth, and few birds are heard here. Climb briefly and soon see a trail (on another dirt road) to the right after about 0.2 mile. Take the right fork to a view of the Mystery Hole.

At the top of the road the well-fenced quarry is visible. The water that fills it is dark and deep. Return to the main trail by bearing left 50 feet and then right, nearing the top of the hill. Watch for a small water-filled quarry hole to the right of the trail, but use caution because there is no fence around this one.

As you look around, taller people can see The Barrens extending to the left, distinguished by the scraggly pitch pines that dominate the area. The air tends to be still and hot here. The area is managed by using controlled burns, which help keep the undergrowth down, reducing the overall fire hazard and helping the plants that grow here

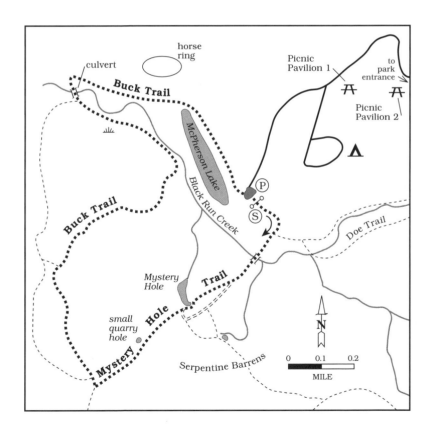

Where there are milkweed flowers there are sure to be butterflies.

to regenerate. This is the largest area of true prairie and savanna (dominated by grasses and scattered trees) in the state.

At the next trail junction at 0.4 mile, bear right on the Buck Trail, marked with red blazes. Very soon after is another trail junction; stay to the right. The change in the environmental zones is immediate and dramatic. All of a sudden you are in a cool, lush eastern forest, with a whole variety of green vegetation and tall trees. Head downhill gently on the old road that is Buck Trail. Listen for cicadas in the trees. Milkweed plants on the left host monarchs and other attractive butterflies and bees. Go downhill more steeply and pass an unmarked trail on the left at 0.6 mile. As the path levels out, return to Black Run Creek. A small wetlands is on the left.

As Buck Trail comes out into the open mowed field, it crosses the creek over a large culvert after 1.1 miles. The trail is indistinct, so simply follow the edge of the woods past the horse ring to where it becomes a clear path again by small but pretty McPherson Lake. Cattails grow on the edge of the lake, in which swimming is not allowed, but catch-and-release fishing for widemouth bass is. Little sunfish and blue gills can be easily spotted from the water's edge. Often a family of Canada geese take up residence at the lake. Look for other waterbirds—we saw a green heron wading here. The trail ends at the parking lot at the south end of the lake.

Other trails of interest: To get a good view of The Barrens, hike the Chrome Trail, beginning behind picnic pavilion 6, then turn left on the Doe Trail, which leads to a fire tower.

---

25. Pine Tree Trail

Type:	Day hike
Difficulty:	Easy
Distance:	1.5-mile loop
Hiking time:	1.5 hours
Elevation gain:	100 feet
Hikable:	Spring–fall
Map:	Lake Aldred trail map
Rest rooms:	Toilets, water at trailhead April–October
Fee:	None

Lake Aldred is a lake within the wide and mighty Susquehanna River, dammed by Pennsylvania Power and Light Company for hydroelectric power. A hike on the Pine Tree Trail begins at the Pinnacle, a dramatic overlook of the lake and its islands. From there it loops back into the woods, following old stone walls that once marked the boundaries of farmland. Black raspberries, wineberries, and blackberries line this pleasant woodland walk.

To reach the trailhead, take US 30 west from the Philadelphia area to PA 82 south. Follow PA 82 south, turning onto PA 372 south through the town of Buck, continuing south to Bethesda. Just past the village of Bethesda, turn right on River Road and go 1.8 miles. Make a left on Pinnacle Road, which is not plowed in the winter. Go to the end of the road, and turn right through a gate to the Pinnacle Overlook parking lot. (To reach the trailhead from Lancaster, take PA 272 south and make a right on PA 372 in Buck, and follow the rest of the directions from Philadelphia the remainder of the way.)

The trail begins at the overlook, which can be a dramatic view, especially in bad weather. Look upstream at Reed and Duncan Islands. To begin the loop, turn around and head back through the picnic tables to the edge of the woods, crossing but not following the orange-blazed Conestoga Trail that heads downhill. Follow the red-blazed

Pine Tree Trail as it enters the woods on a path that parallels the road you took in. A stone wall composed of schist, a flat flaky rock, is clearly visible on your right. The trail follows this wall until just before it emerges from the woods on Pinnacle Road at 0.25 mile.

Cross the road, going 25 feet diagonally to the right across to the closed yellow gate. Go past the gate. The trail is now a wide, mowed path on an old roadbed for the remainder of the loop. Head uphill, passing by a grassy road on the left. Watch for poison ivy here. There are plenty of interesting vines along the path, but make sure your children learn the difference between poison ivy and the harmless vines.

Pass a grassy road on the right but continue straight ahead. The trail curves right as you parallel a gravel driveway and house on the left. Plenty of berries thrive here. Black raspberries are the fewest but the sweetest and ripen first, in late June and early July. Plentiful, tangy wineberries ripen next in mid-July, and blackberries are ready in late July or August.

As the trail begins to head downhill, also notice wild roses (in bloom in June) and a variety of deciduous trees, including green ash, tulip poplar, red maple, and shagbark hickory, all of which make this a colorful trail in the fall. The trail continues to curve to the right and children may spot a variety of mushrooms in the damp soil.

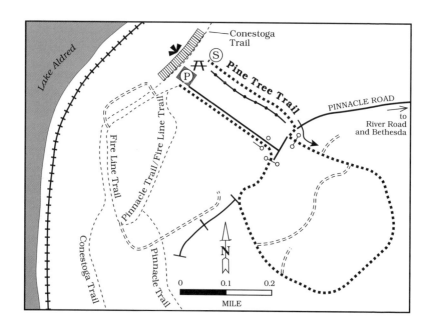

A view of Lake Aldred from the overlook, just before a summer thunderstorm hits

Soon begin a gentle climb, noticing young cherry trees along the trail. A deteriorating stone wall is on the left below the trail. Children may notice small stones of schist and enjoy looking for thin, almost transparent sheets of mica, which flake off the schist and look like tiny mirrors. Still curving right, continue on a gentle ascent through an area thick with grape, Virginia creeper, bittersweet, and other vines. Vines are not bad plants, but they can damage trees by their heavy weight and they steal sunlight from smaller seedlings. Disregard the red blazes from now on; there are some old trails also blazed red that confuse if followed.

Reach a junction where a trail bears right, but continue left. At the next junction, bear left again where another trail goes right. Still on an old road, come to a T junction at 1.1 miles and turn right, now following a powerline cut a short distance to a gate, which leads to Pinnacle Road again. Turn left and stay on the left side of the road as you walk along the wide, grassy roadside back to the overlook.

Southcentral Pennsylvania

Father and daughter are ready for a fun afternoon of exploring.

26. Tall Timbers and Thick Mountain Trails

Type: Day hike
Difficulty: Easy–moderate (some rocks)
Distance: 3.25 miles
Hiking time: 3 hours
Elevation gain: 200 feet
Hikable: Spring–fall
Map: Bald Eagle State Forest public use map
Rest rooms: Toilets, water at trailhead
Fee: None

A hike through the Tall Timbers Natural Area is just what it sounds like: a beautiful walk through a virgin hemlock forest along pretty Swift Run. The trail follows an almost imperceptible uphill grade past moss-covered rocks and decaying logs, where hikers can stroll up to about 1.3 miles before backtracking and crossing a bridge over the creek and returning higher up on the opposite side. Families can turn around at any point, and can go up and back on the Tall Timbers Trail to avoid a short climb on the opposite side of the creek.

To reach the natural area, take US 11/15 north from Harrisburg, exiting onto US 522 south, which leads to Beaver Springs. Turn right

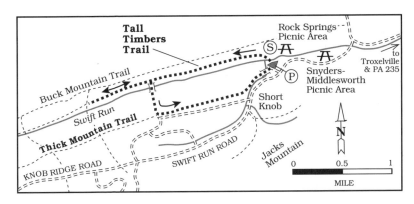

on PA 235 north and head into Troxelville. In Troxelville, turn left onto paved Timber Street, which soon turns into Swift Run Road. Bear left at the intersection just after the paved road turns to dirt and bear left again at the next intersection. Shortly after the second intersection, pass the first picnic pavilion on the right. Go another 0.2 mile to the second picnic area, turn right, by a large sign for Snyders-Middlesworth Picnic Area, and head downhill to the parking area.

The hike begins at the western edge of the parking lot, on the Tall Timbers Trail, which heads straight along the north side of Swift Run. Encounter the big trees almost immediately. Nice pools of clear water offer chances for creek exploration. Soon reach a rocky area where water overflows into the trail during spring runoff, but you are soon past this and back on the easy dirt path. Children may notice very sparkly rocks along the creek and on the path.

Swift Run rushes between moss covered rocks along the Tall Timbers Trail.

Continue on the very gentle grade along the creek, continually awed by the magnificent trees, which are 200 to 400 years old here. The trail curves right and you walk above the creek for a while. Reach a trail junction at 1.2 miles, a good turn-around point (young hikers may want to take a left and cross the bridge and a left again on the Thick Mountain Trail, which leads back to the parking area for a total of 2.7 miles.) To see more trees, continue straight on the Tall Timbers Trail, where you may occasionally have to duck under or crawl over a blown-down tree. Pass a natural bench—a large rock that juts out by a tree root and makes a perfect place for a rest break.

Move back closer to the creek again and after awhile the imperceptible climb becomes noticeable. Watch for a trail junction at 1.8 miles, with a connecting trail on the left which goes to the Thick Mountain Trail; this junction can be easy to miss. At the junction, turn around and head back to the bridge. If you miss this junction, you will soon notice that the Tall Timbers Trail straight ahead is not well maintained and many blow-downs block the path.

Back at the bridge, cross over Swift Run and head uphill briefly; at a T intersection bear left onto the Thick Mountain Trail at 2.7 miles. Soon the trail levels a bit and rolls up and down on the hillside above the creek. After a short distance, descend and cross a bridge over a creek, bearing left back to the parking area.

27. Alan Seeger Trail

Type: Day hike
Difficulty: Easy
Distance: 0.75-mile loop
Hiking time: 30 minutes
Elevation gain: None
Hikable: Spring–fall
Map: None available
Rest rooms: Pit toilet at picnic area; no water
Fee: None

The giants of the eastern hemlocks are hidden away throughout the state in little pockets off side roads. The Alan Seeger Natural Area is one of these sanctuaries for the ancient trees that once were common everywhere in the state. A very flat, easy, pleasant stroll in this area takes hikers through the old hemlocks, one of which is estimated to be 500 years old. Somehow these trees managed to escape the logging and fires that destroyed the rest of their contemporaries. The trail is lined with very aged rhododendrons too, which create an arch over portions of the trail—a beautiful sight in late June through July when they bloom. A bubbling brook crisscrosses the trail, making this a very relaxing outing, manageable for even the youngest family member. Be prepared to get shoes muddy, because there are wet areas on the trail most of the year.

To reach the Alan Seeger Natural Area, take US 22/322 north from Harrisburg to Reedsville. Get onto PA 655 south to Belleville, then take PA 305 north to a road junction by the Greenwood Furnace State Park sign. Turn right at this junction onto (dirt) Rag Hollow

Road, and follow this road up the mountain 9 miles to the Alan Seeger Picnic Area, where there is parking on both sides of the road.

At the junction of the three dirt roads in the picnic area, there is a large sign with a map on it for the area. The map is not entirely accurate due to some trail relocations, but the trail is easy to follow. Begin at the left of the trail map sign, and take the trail into the woods. Signs labeling the trees are located along the way. Though there are primarily hemlocks here, other species, such as white oak, white pine, chestnut oak, and red oak, are mixed in.

Children may notice that there is almost no undergrowth in the dense shade of these trees. Point out to them the difference in the forest floor when you pass by a more open area, where numerous white pine seedlings are flourishing. Alan Seeger, for whom this trail is named, was an American poet who was born in 1888. He loved the outdoors. He was killed in World War I while serving with the French Foreign Legion.

Soon intersect with the Mid-State Trail, Greenwood Spur, which coincides with the trail you are on for a while. Cross a small creek on a bridge into a thicket of rhododendrons, which form a tunnel you can walk through. Pass between two giant hemlocks which act as if they were standing guard to a gate hiding the largest trees. Begin to pass many large hemlocks, estimated to be 300 to 500 years old.

Rhododendrons grow into shaded tunnels of green among the hemlocks in the Alan Seeger Natural Area.

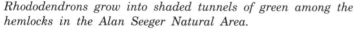

In a short distance pass a side trail on the left to a large hemlock. Then come upon a truly massive hemlock, the oldest in the state, having seen five centuries—a half millennium. (Note: the map sign shows a spur trail to this tree, but there is none now; the main trail goes right by it.) Children enjoy discussing what it was like here 500 years ago. This tree had its birth around the time that Columbus discovered America. Unfortunately, every living thing has its time and this tree's time is up—it is dying. Younger trees will replace it, and hopefully some of them will live to be as old as this granddaddy.

The rhododendrons are quite close now as you follow along a creek, crossing it on a bridge. Notice how clear the water is. Cross the creek again on a bridge and then go uphill, away from the creek. Next walk downhill where you soon reach Rag Hollow Road. Turn right and walk along the road back to the parking lot.

---

28. Lake, Mountain View, and Old Faithful Trails

Type: Day hike
Difficulty: Moderate (hills)
Distance: 2-mile loop
Hiking time: 2 hours
Elevation gain: 325 feet
Hikable: Year-round
Map: Stone Valley Recreation Area trails map ($2.75 from Penn State University)
Rest rooms: Toilets, water at visitor center
Fee: $2.50 ages 4 and up

There are plenty of trails to explore in the Stone Valley Recreation Area and plenty of interesting things to see and do at the environmental education center. The trails around the center are best for toddlers, and many other loops are possible. There are over 25 miles of trails in the area. At Shaver's Creek Environmental Education Center, you can investigate natural and cultural history topics in the exhibit room with puzzles and quiz boards, watch songbirds coming to a bird-feeding area, observe a honey bee hive from behind a glass window, enjoy resident turtles and frogs, and learn about the thirteen species of injured eagles, hawks, and owls in the raptor center that are part of the permanent live animal collection. These birds were so severely injured that they can never be released back into the wild. The loop described here begins at the environmental education center and crosses a wetland area on a boardwalk, heads up to a ridge where there are some mountain views when the leaves are off the trees, and heads back down along the edge of Lake Perez where there is recent beaver activity. The fee covers use of the trails, visiting the raptor center and exhibit room, and use of the picnic area, rest rooms, and drinking water.

To reach Shaver's Creek Environmental Education Center, take US 22 north from Mount Union, then PA 26 north from Huntingdon, past McAley's Fort. Shortly after passing the road to Whipple Dam State Park, turn left on SR 1029 (Charter Oak Road), go 1.7 miles, and turn left on the paved east entrance to the recreation area. Go 0.3 mile, bearing right at the Y intersection, and park along the looped parking area. From State College, take PA 26 south past Pine Grove

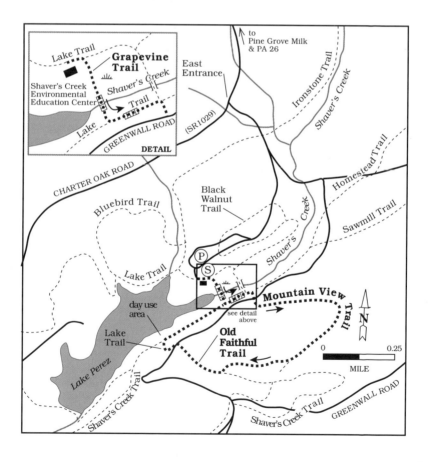

Mills and turn right on SR 1029 (Charter Oak Road) just before Whipple Dam State Park. Follow the rest of the directions above from that point.

A trail leads from the parking lot to the environmental education center by the herb garden, where signs direct you to the Lake Trail. Cross the staff parking driveway and head into the woods on the orange-blazed Lake Trail. Pass a side trail on the right almost immediately, but go straight and very soon turn right onto the red-blazed Grapevine Trail.

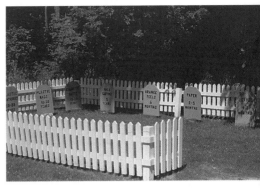

Did you know that plastic bags take 10-20 years to decompose? Find out how long other items take at the trash cemetery at Shaver's Creek Environmental Education Center.

Head downhill and pass a wet meadow habitat restoration project, where trees have been cut to create more space for wildflowers. Cattails line the trail on your left as you walk alongside the meadow and pass several tree identification markers, which are cut in the shape of the leaves and have on them interesting facts about the species. A catbird may call as you pass by; reach Shaver's Creek and walk across the wide wetland area on a boardwalk path, which is great fun, as it meanders a bit through the wetland area.

At the end of the boardwalk, turn left, back onto the Lake Trail. Look for signs of beaver activity in this area, such as downed trees and chewed trees. Walk a short distance through young hemlocks and cross another smaller wet area on a boardwalk. At the trail junction where the Lake Trail heads northwest to your left, go straight very briefly on the sky blue-blazed Sawmill Trail, then at the next junction turn right on the rose-blazed Mountain View Trail. (Hikers with very small children may want to turn left at the Lake Trail intersection and head back to the environmental education center for a loop hike of less than 0.5 mile.)

Cross Greenwall Road at 0.3 mile and head into the woods again, where the trail curves left into the hemlocks, past a water gauging station. Begin a climb, at first gradual, then more steep. Maple viburnum and other low shrubs do well here. Soon the grade lessens and you reach a level area on the side of a small ridge and walk along it a short distance before heading uphill again, curving right to reach the top of another small ridge. From here are some views of the surrounding mountains when the leaves are off the trees. A cool breeze greets you here as you pause to rest.

Follow along the ridgetop now and begin to notice deer fencing, put in place so the shrubs and saplings in the logged-over area behind it will have a chance of not being eaten. Soon come quite close to the deer fence and have good views of the new forest below.

At a Y junction after 1.25 miles, take the righthand, indigo-blazed Old Faithful Trail. From here descend and perhaps be scolded by blue jays as you amble downhill, passing a small portable white structure that was left behind from a research project. Whatever its purpose once was, it has been commandeered by some creature nesting in its top cabinet on a soft bed of moss.

Come to a junction with a ski trail and bear right again, keeping on the indigo-blazed Old Faithful Trail. In a short while, reach Greenwall Road again, turn left on it, and walk less than 0.1 mile to the driveway into the day-use area. Walk across the grass to the water's edge, where you meet again with the orange-blazed Lake Trail and take a right. Reach a junction with the red-blazed Grapevine Trail, where you began your loop, and take it back over the boardwalk to the environmental education center.

Other trails of interest: The orange-blazed Lake Trail, which follows the perimeter of the lake for 2.2 miles, is a fairly flat trail with plenty of opportunities to observe the lakeshore up close. The Lake Trail begins at the same place as the hike described above, and makes a complete loop back to the environmental education center.

29. Forest Heritage Trail

Type:	Day hike
Difficulty:	Moderate (rocks)
Distance:	1.6-mile loop
Hiking time:	1.5 hours
Elevation gain:	200 feet
Hikable:	Spring–fall
Map:	Kings Gap trail map
Rest rooms:	Toilets, water at Mansion Use Area
Fee:	None

Kings Gap has many interesting trails and family-oriented activities. Most trails are suitable for children, some easier than others. There is an interesting garden at the Mansion Use Area, site of the former owner's fine home, now the park office and the training center.

The Forest Heritage Trail makes a loop below the mansion area through a chestnut oak forest where remains of the once-busy charcoal-making industry are still visible. (Note: For information about the center's environmental education activities, call (717) 486-5031.)

To reach Kings Gap, take Interstate 81 south from Harrisburg to exit 11 and go south on PA 233 a short distance to the intersection with PA 174. Take PA 174 east 2.3 miles and make a right on Montsera Road, staying on the main road as two other roads curve off it. At the sign go right, then immediately left on Kings Gap Road. Continue 4 miles on the road to the Mansion Use Area.

Begin at the visitors parking lot, taking the Rock Scree Trail to reach the Forest Heritage Trail. The trail descends and crosses just below the front of the mansion patio. Come to a junction with the Scenic Vista Trail on the right, but continue left downhill and cross Kings Gap Road, bearing left on a wide old road.

Be on the lookout for American chestnuts; some small trees still remain scattered here and there. After 0.3 mile, reach a trail junction where the Rock Scree Trail goes straight ahead, and take the left fork of the Forest Heritage Trail loop. You will return to this spot on the way back. Follow the lime-green, dot-shaped blazes through low-bush

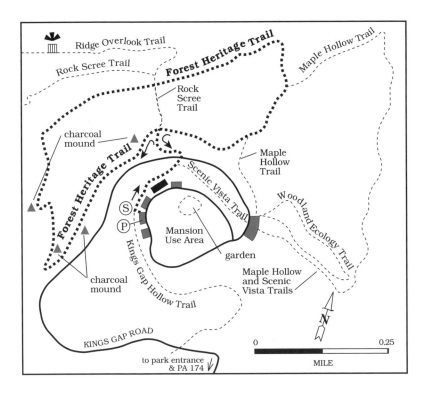

Chestnut oak acorns are important food for squirrels and chipmunks in Kings Gap.

blueberries under a chestnut oak canopy. The forest here has been logged heavily so the trees are young. The mossy trail descends gently, and soon reaches a flattish area that is the site of an old charcoal-making mound. In the 1700s and 1800s, charcoal was what fueled the many nearby iron furnaces before the discovery of coal. In the late 1700s, one furnace used up charcoal from 1 acre of forest in just 1 day, so vast amounts of trees were needed to make charcoal.

To make charcoal, a collier selected a site, then cut and stacked wood in a cone shape by standing logs on edge surrounding a central chimney. The pile was covered with dirt and lit. The fires were tended 24 hours a day for 10 to 12 days as the wood turned to charcoal. Once it was done, the fire was extinguished and the charcoal loaded into wagons to take to the furnaces. Once coal was discovered, charcoal making ceased by the end of the 1800s. At this mound and others, the ground still bears the fire scar and charcoal pieces are mixed in with the dirt. Very little grows here except moss and some blueberry bushes.

Continue on, uphill for a while, pausing occasionally to look up at turkey vultures that like to ride the thermals at Kings Gap. Pass another mound, and then another. At the third mound, bear right and begin a gradual descent. The trail switchbacks once and you see yet another mound on the left. Continue downhill.

Cross the Rock Scree Trail after 1 mile and begin to climb uphill on an old road now. Listen for cicadas in the top branches of the oaks. Chestnut oak acorns, small and oblong, litter the forest floor. They are an important food for squirrels and other forest creatures.

At the next junction, at 1.2 miles, the Maple Hollow Trail goes left, but you turn right and walk up a gentle hill to another junction with the Maple Hollow Trail; continue to the right to reach the junction where the loop trail began, at 1.4 miles. Bear left on the Rock Scree Trail back across Kings Gap Road and by the mansion to the parking area. Before leaving, stop and look at the terrific garden located on the east side of the mansion.

Other trails of interest: Three major areas here have their own sets of trails; each area has other trails, in addition to those listed below:

- The Mansion Use Area has a self-guided interpretive trail, the 1.3-mile Woodland Ecology Trail, which has signs to help visitors identify plants typical of a chestnut-oak forest.
- The Pond Use Area has the paved 0.3-mile White Oaks interpretive trail, which loops through a deciduous forest, with signs in braille and script.
- The Pine Plantation Area has a paved 0.3-mile Whispering Pines Trail, whose braille and script signs help hikers experience the ecology of a coniferous forest.

30. Pole Steeple Trail

Type: Day hike
Difficulty: Challenging (short, steep climb)
Distance: 1.2 miles round trip
Hiking time: 1.5 hours
Elevation gain: 500 feet
Hikable: Spring–fall
Map: Pine Grove Furnace State Park map
Rest rooms: Toilets, water at Laurel Lake, Fuller Lake, and campground
Fee: None

The entire valley in which Pine Grove Furnace State Park is located can be seen from the top of Pole Steeple, a quartzite rock outcropping on the edge of Piney Mountain. Though the trail is very steep at the top, it is a short walk with room at the top for a rest and to take in the view. On the way up, pass the remains of charcoal-burning hearths, which most likely supplied charcoal for Pine Grove Furnace and Laurel Forge during the eighteenth and nineteenth centuries. This hike requires some hand-over-hand climbing and has a steep dropoff on the edges of the rocks at the top, so only experienced or older children should attempt it. Also, since you will need your hands, carry everything you need in your day or fanny pack. Take binoculars and a camera and enjoy a bird's-eye view of the heart of Pennsylvania's Appalachian Range. Pine Grove Furnace State Park has two lifeguarded beaches in summer and an interesting historical walking tour surrounding the old furnace. An AYH hostel is located in the park in the Ironmaster's Mansion.

To reach Pine Grove Furnace State Park, take Interstate 81 south from Harrisburg to exit 11, exiting onto PA 233 south to Pine Grove Furnace State Park, where you come to an intersection across from the park office. There is a visitor center 0.25 mile on PA 233 south, on the right. Turn left onto Pine Grove Furnace/Hunters Run Road. Follow this road 2.4 miles past Laurel Lake to an intersection with Old Railroad Road, and make a hairpin turn to the right on this road. Go 0.6 mile further and park in the gravel lot on the right by the lake.

The trail begins across Old Railroad Road from the parking lot; walk past a cabin on a wide, well-used trail that immediately heads uphill. Listen for scampering gray squirrels as you walk steadily up the trail. Sassafras seedlings are getting a start along the trail. Most of the trees here are maple and chestnut oak.

Soon come to a landing where you can catch your breath before the trail curves right and continues uphill, but much more gradually. Look along the trail for the signs of old charcoal hearths, which are circles of flat ground with darkened soil, with no trees or rocks on them, 30 to 40 feet in diameter. Piles of wood were burned to produce charcoal, which was used to power the iron furnaces and forges before coal became widely used. The trail crosses three of these sites, and several others are not far off the trail. Poke around in one of them to see if you can find any bits of charcoal. Once coal was discovered, charcoal was not used, because it was time consuming and dangerous, and required huge numbers of trees.

Crows may call as you walk along; note that both high- and low-bush blueberries grow here. Both types of bush look alike except for height, though the high-bush tends to have bigger berries. Size is not everything, though; the tiny low-bush berries are sweet and tasty.

The trail soon steepens dramatically and heads almost straight up to the top. This has created some erosion problems. Take your time climbing; even if you go very slowly, you reach the top soon enough. Notice a pile of boulders ahead as you approach the top. Follow the

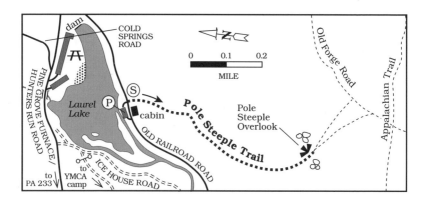

A view of Laurel Lake from the Pole Steeple Trail

blazes up the middle of the rocks, where the fractured rocks create step-like ledges to stand on. This area is a fault zone, where the rock split along these cracks millions of years ago. Look for shiny areas on the rocks where the rocks slid against each other, polishing the surface.

In 0.6 mile you are at the top and have a seat on either the right or left outcroppings. Do not let children climb to the very edges of the rock outcropping, which drop off steeply. A couple of thoughtless people have defaced a rock on the left; this may be a good opportunity to discuss ways to avoid ruining nature so it remains unblemished for everyone to enjoy it.

The view is excellent and particularly nice on a clear day in fall, when the colors are at their peak. You can see Laurel Lake below, and a YMCA camp. Across from you is South Mountain, whose high point along the opposite ridge is 1,582 feet. Little Rocky Ridge is to the left of South Mountain, and a high point on Piney Mountain, elevation 1,515 feet, is on the far left. Behind you a side trail leads 0.3 mile to the Appalachian Trail.

Return the way you came up, taking your time, because down climbing is harder than climbing up. Sometimes it is helpful to turn around backwards as you climb down, as if descending a ladder.

Other trails of interest: Two trails suitable for children are located near Fuller Lake beach in the western part of the state park, reached by heading west from Pole Steeple to PA 233 south, and turning onto Quarry Road just past the visitor center.

The Koppenhaver Trail is a 1-mile loop accessed at the far end of the Fuller ballfield. It crosses Tom's Run and passes through hemlocks and pines.

The Swamp Trail is about 0.25 mile long and loops around a small, forested swamp. Access it from the Appalachian Trail—pick it up at the dressing stockade at Fuller Lake and follow it north to reach the Swamp Trail on the right.

31. Rocky Knob Trail

Type: Day hike
Difficulty: Challenging (distance, terrain)
Distance: 4.6-mile loop
Hiking time: 4.5 hours
Elevation gain: 350 feet
Hikable: Spring–fall
Map: Rocky Knob Trail Map
Rest rooms: Toilets, water at Caledonia State Park
Fee: None

Rocky Knob is an interpretive trail on the ridge of South Mountain, just east of the Appalachian Trail, which it crosses. Much of the trail is located on an old road that was a failed attempt to connect Ridge and Birch Run Roads, which parallel each other. The trail includes several interesting features, such as large ant mounds colonized by the Allegheny mound-building ants. There are views of Rocky Knob (best in spring and fall), and an optional spur trail that is quite challenging goes to the summit of Rocky Knob, where there is also a good view. Blueberry and huckleberry bushes grow along the old road—their berries make nice munching in late July and August. An interpretive brochure is available from the district office. (Note: To get a copy of the brochure for the trail, write to Michaux State Forest District Forester, 10099 Lincoln Way East, Fayetteville, PA 17222.) Camping and a swimming pool are located at Caledonia State Park.

To reach Rocky Knob Trail, take US 30 from either east or west to Caledonia State Park and head north on PA 233. After several miles, turn left at the first paved intersection onto Arendtsville–Shippensburg Road. Go about 2.5 miles up to the ridge and turn left onto (dirt) Ridge Road. When I was here, there was no sign marking the trailhead, so clock your mileage from here and go just over 2 miles to a gated old road on the left, which is the trail. If you come to where the Appalachian Trail crosses Ridge Road, you have just passed the Rocky Knob trailhead. Park by the gate (but not blocking it) alongside Ridge Road.

Rocky Knob Trail begins on the old road, past the gate, and is marked with turquoise keystone-shaped blazes. Walk through rows of mountain laurel (pretty in early summer) and reach an intersection with the Appalachian Trail. This area is near the midpoint of the Appalachian Trail. If you were to walk south about 1,050 miles, you would end up in Georgia; north 1,050 miles would take you to Maine.

Continuing straight ahead, you begin to notice the ant mounds, which can get quite large, some as large as 4 feet high and 20 feet around. It is wise not to disturb the ants by poking their mound, because they can be aggressive and their bites sting. They are fun to watch from a distance. Along this trail you see active mounds and ones that are inactive, grown over with moss. The ants prefer small openings in the forest.

The Allegheny mound-building ants should post a sign by their large mounds that reads, 'Do not disturb!'

Pass under some overhanging chestnut oaks, which continue to grow despite being bent over by another tree. Reach a trail junction at 0.4 mile, to which you will return, and take the left fork by interpretive marker 1. Continue on the forested ridge and notice that the trees here are short due to poor soil, repeated fires, and overbrowsing by deer. Still, most of the trees here are older than they look, some forty years old. Head uphill gradually and step over a tree whose trunk is growing laterally across the trail. Soon the trail flattens as it traverses a hill at about 1,900 feet elevation. The trail gets somewhat rocky and you begin to walk downhill, on the edge of the ridge, with occasional views of the valley and Piney Ridge across from you.

As you descend, you may notice the American chestnut trees by interpretive marker 7, some of which have not yet succumbed to the blight that wiped them out—but they will. At 1.5 miles, interpretive marker 9, is a view of Long Pine Dam and Rocky Knob, and in the spring or fall you can see Wolf Hill and Mitten Hill on the right. Children may have noticed milky streaks in the rocks along this trail—this is quartzite, the same stuff of which Rocky Knob is made. Soon turn away from the edge of the ridge and walk uphill briefly to flat-topped Sier Hill. If it is hot, notice the wet rocks that look like they are sweating. They are not—it is actually moisture from the air condensing on the relatively cool rocks.

Beyond Sier Hill, descend steeply for a while on the side of the hill. Soon the trail becomes less steep. Notice how quiet it is here. The flute-like song of the wood thrush may be the only noise you hear.

Reach a saddle (a low point between two hills) and notice that the trees are taller due to better growing conditions. Soon reach a junction at 2.5 miles, by interpretive marker 11, with the spur trail to the summit of Rocky Knob. There are loose rocks on this very rugged side trail, which is recommended only for the experienced. Take the spur trail to the summit and back if you want, for a 0.5-mile side trip; if not, continue to the right on the trail downhill to interpretive marker 13, where the trail meets with the old road again.

The path is wider here and passes some patches of hemlock and

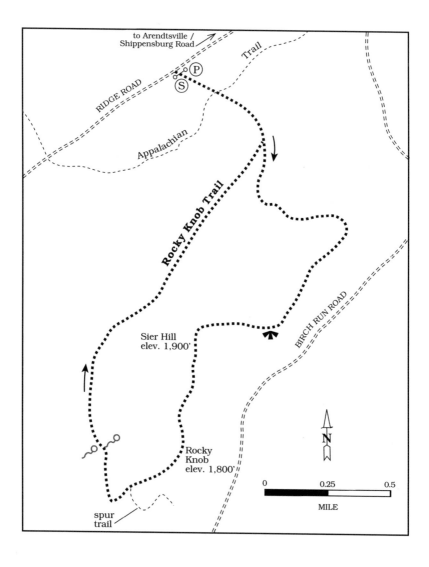

pine. Soon pass two small springs at interpretive marker 14. Look for a resident frog here. The trail continues uphill at a steady incline for nearly 1 mile to the junction with the loop trail at 4.2 miles. To keep kids' minds off the climb, stop frequently to pick blueberries or huckleberries in late summer. Blueberry fruit is bluer in color; huckleberries are shiny and almost black. Both are delicious. At the junction of trails, go left to continue on the old road, recrossing the Appalachian Trail and, shortly after, ending at the gate.

Other trails of interest: The Beaver Trail is a 1.25-mile trail just north of Caledonia State Park that follows the water's edge around the peninsula protruding into the Long Pine Run Reservoir. Access is from PA 233 north of Caledonia—turn left onto Milesburn Road, then right onto Birch Run Road. The trail is on the right.

32. Tunnel and Iron Horse Trails

Type:	Day hike
Difficulty:	Moderate (rocky tread)
Distance:	1-mile loop
Hiking time:	45 minutes
Elevation gain:	360 feet
Hikable:	Spring–fall
Map:	Iron Horse Trail Map
Rest rooms:	Toilets, water at picnic area
Fee:	None

Conococheague Mountain has not only a difficult name but a contrary geology as well. In the late 1800s, ambitious railroad companies tried to link railroad lines between New Germantown and Franklin County, Pennsylvania, by tunneling through this mountain. The tunneling was started from both ends, but the geological features of the mountain caused the tunnel to crumble in on itself. This, combined with money troubles, caused the project to be given up. The Tunnel Trail loop in Big Spring State Park takes hikers to one side of the tunnel that never was, where hikers can feel the cold blast of air coming from right under the mountain.

To reach the Tunnel Trail, take US 22/322 north from Harrisburg, exiting onto PA 34 south toward Newport. In New Bloomfield, take PA 274 south. Continue on PA 274 past Blain and go 10 miles further.

A hiker enjoys the cool breeze near the mouth of the failed tunnel in Big Spring State Park.

Make a left on (dirt) Hemlock Road, and turn left immediately into the parking lot.

The trail begins behind the bulletin board, which gives details about the tunnel effort. Cross Hemlock Road and head uphill, paralleling the road for a time. The trail is somewhat rocky and very mossy. Many young hemlocks grow along the path here.

Head down a flight of steps and bear right, following the now-rocky path uphill. It flattens again and passes rows of pretty mountain laurel, the state flower, which blooms in the spring. Look for young American chestnut trees, which still grow for a while before succumbing to the blight that destroyed their ancestors in the early 1900s. The saplings never reach maturity, which makes the species in some sense extinct. Their blade-like leaves resemble those of chestnut oak, but their edges are toothed.

Head downhill briefly, then scramble up a pile of rocks, joining with the old railroad grade that would have carried trains through the mountain. Make a gentle climb on the railroad grade and at 0.3 mile come to the short spur trail that leads to the tunnel. Even from the spur trail, the cool air from the tunnel entrance can be felt. At the entrance, there is a fence to keep people out of the tunnel itself, which is dangerous. Children can close their eyes and listen, and

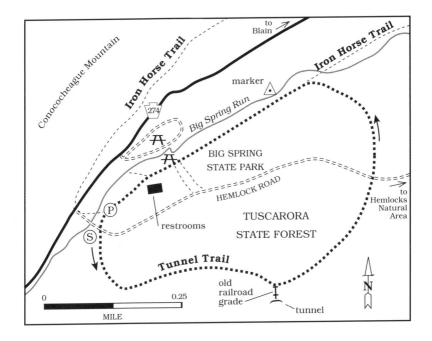

should be able to hear the dripping of water from the tunnel roof. It is cool because the tunnel is an artificial cave. The temperature of a cave is between 55°F and 60°F year-round, and that is true of this cave. So, in the summer, the air feels like air conditioning; in the winter it may feel more like heat.

Back at the junction, turn right on the main loop trail and head downhill off the railroad grade. The path becomes rocky again and you cross Hemlock Road at 0.5 mile and head downhill, switchbacking once into a very young forest. Notice the whitish rocks—feel their soft, almost powdery feel. They are a type of quartzite. Quartz and quartzite are common in this area of Pennsylvania. Pass by some young birches whose twigs, you will discover, taste like root beer. Go into more open forest soon, through a bouldery area, then, at a junction of trails near Big Spring Run at 0.75 mile, turn left.

You are now on the Iron Horse Trail, a 10-mile loop that focuses on the railroad history of the area. As the trail parallels Big Spring Run, pass a blackberry patch and come to a marker that shows where the railroad tracks ended. Walking up a gentle hill, follow left along the pavilion at the picnic area, and pass two side trails on the left as you go straight. Come to a set of rest rooms on the left and bear left at the trail junction to return to the parking lot.

33. Hemlock, Laurel, and Rim Trails

Type: Day hike
Difficulty: Moderate (rocky, uneven trail)
Distance: 1-mile loop
Hiking time: 1.5 hours
Elevation gain: 200 feet
Hikable: Late spring–fall
Map: Hemlocks Natural Area map
Rest rooms: Toilets, water at picnic area in Big Spring State Park, at the beginning of Hemlock Road
Fee: None

The original beautiful hemlock forests of Pennsylvania were mostly devastated by logging about 100 years ago except for a few special areas that escaped, such as this narrow ravine along sparkling Patterson Run in Perry County. Then hemlock was valued for its bark, which contained tannin useful for tanning leather. We value the trees here for their beauty, where the virgin hemlock–white pine forest is preserved as a national natural landmark. The trail described here follows alongside Patterson Run through the 300- to 400-year-old trees, crossing the creek several times. Return along the ridge for a good view of the ravine. (For a copy of an interesting brochure describing Hemlocks Natural Area, write Forest District Headquarters, Tuscarora State Forest, RR 1, Box 42 A, Blain, PA 17006.)

To reach the Hemlocks Natural Area, take PA 274 south from Duncannon (north of Harrisburg) to 10 miles past Blain, and turn left onto (dirt) Hemlock Road in Big Spring State Park. Stay on the dirt road 4 miles further to a small gravel parking lot on the left side of the road, where there is a plaque.

Begin at the plaque and head downhill, soon crossing the creek on a bridge and coming to a trail junction. You will return to this point on the way back. Go left onto the Hemlock Trail and immediately cross the creek again on a bridge. The trail is rocky and the rocks are mossy and can be slippery, so take your time. Soon after the creek crossing a trail comes in from the left, connecting to Hemlock Road; stay to the right.

See huge hemlocks almost right away. More than 50 percent of the hemlocks in this area are over 24 inches in diameter, measured 4.5 feet from the ground. The largest hemlock measured was 51 inches in diameter and 109 feet tall. The tallest measured was 123 feet with a diameter of 38 inches. Any way you measure it, that is big. How many children does it take to encircle one of these beauties?

Continue downhill, towards the creek and feel its coolness. In the deeper pools, brook trout hide. As you pass several blown-down trees, children can try their patience by counting tree growth rings, which indicate a tree's age.

The ravine smells lovely with all the evergreens. Reach a junction at 0.6 mile and bear right on the Laurel Trail. Almost immediately cross a bridge, bear left a few feet, then watch carefully for the indistinct beginning of the trail uphill on the right. The trail becomes more distinct in just a few feet, then climbs to a junction with the Rim Trail, on which you take a right.

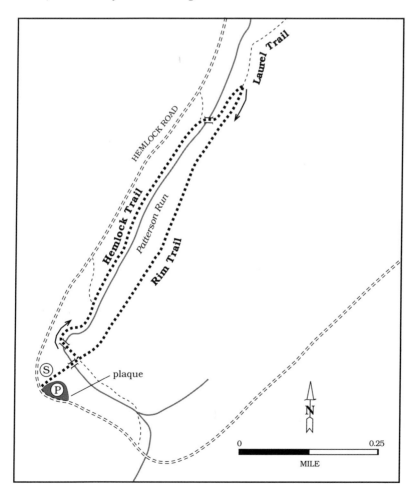

Hikers gaze up at the towering hemlocks in Hemlocks Natural Area.

On the Rim Trail ascend steeply for a short distance, then the grade eases and contours along the side of the ridge. From here you have a good view of the tall trees and Patterson Run below.

Soon you approach the creek and notice that all along the trail there are many young hemlocks, which will someday replace the aged ones when they die. These young ones, like children, ensure a bright future. Reach the junction by the bridge where the loop began, and go straight ahead to head back uphill to the parking area.

34. Doubling Gap Nature Trail

Type: Day hike
Difficulty: Easy
Distance: 1.2-mile loop
Hiking time: 1 hour
Elevation gain: 25 feet
Hikable: Spring–fall
Map: Colonel Denning State Park map
Rest rooms: Toilets, water at campground; water at trailhead
Fee: None

This self-guiding nature trail in Colonel Denning State Park begins at the Doubling Gap Lake dam and follows the edges of pleasant,

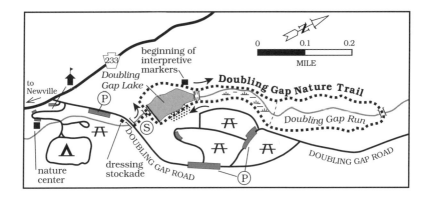

babbling Doubling Gap Run. Numerous stations along the way explain the interrelationship among forest dwellers, both plants and animals. The trail and park are located in Doubling Gap, so named because of the s turn Blue Mountain makes when it doubles back on itself in this area. Fishing is permitted along Doubling Gap Lake, as is swimming when there is a lifeguard in the summer. There is a campground in the park.

To reach the trail, take Interstate 81 south from Harrisburg to exit 11, taking PA 233 north, past Newville, continuing into the park about 9 miles further. At the park office on PA 233, bear right onto Doubling Gap Road, and go about 0.1 mile to the parking lot (lot 1) on the right, by the dressing stockade, across the road from the dam.

The hike begins at the bulletin board by the spillway for the dam, across the road from the parking lot. Walk up the steps and bear left, crossing the bridge over the spillway. Turn right immediately on the handicapped-accessible ramp and walk along the path on the west shore of the small lake. This is a popular area for trout fishing.

Walk through a mixed forest of hickory, spruce, oak, poplar, beech, and white pine. Reach a junction of trails and turn left into an area with larger trees, and soon bear left again. The creek is on the right and soon you pass an orienteering marker and reach the first interpretive marker of the nature trail. There are numerous side trails to the creek's edge and there are several nice places along here to explore the creek, looking for crawfish, minnows, or frogs. Lucky hikers might observe a box turtle along the trail.

Cross a tributary on a small bridge and proceed uphill through hemlocks, white pines, and tall deciduous trees that tower above them— for now. Continue easily uphill past the hemlocks, after which go downhill. Cross another small creek on a bridge and at a trail junction at 0.4 mile, go left. (The trail on the right is a shortcut to the other side of the creek and back to the beginning of the trail.)

From the small ridge you are on you can see the floodplain below. Pass interpretive marker 2 and continue on the now-flat trail past some blackberry bushes and thistles in an open area on the left. Many years ago there was a homestead here, but the evidence of it is mostly gone. Pass interpretive marker 3 and go downhill, curving back toward the creek. At interpretive marker 4, you are beside the creek and cross it on a bridge at 0.6 mile. The fifth interpretive marker explains the various layers of the forest: canopy, shade-tolerant trees, shrub layer, and herb layer. Can children identify which plants grow in what layer? For example, the New York fern that grows by the trail is in the herb layer. Find other examples for them to guess.

After 0.9 mile, reach the shortcut junction again and bear left, through a moist area. Walk through hemlocks at the base of a hill and bear right, crossing a small tributary on a bridge. Pass interpretive marker 6 near an area in which many different kinds of fungi can be found on the trees and ground. By some beeches, meet a junction with some side trails, but go straight by the final interpretive marker alongside the creek.

Just before the bridge over Doubling Gap Creek, bear left and follow the eastern shore of the lake to the beach area, then to the dam, where you began.

35. Lakeside Trail

Type:	Day hike
Difficulty:	Easy
Distance:	1.3-mile loop
Hiking time:	1 hour
Elevation gain:	20 feet
Hikable:	Year-round
Map:	Cowans Gap State Park map
Rest rooms:	Toilets, water at trailhead
Fee:	None

Tucked in the spiny Tuscarora Mountains of central Pennsylvania, Cowans Gap is a great place for families. The pleasant Lakeside Trail surrounds Cowans Gap Lake and is easy enough for strollers. A colony of beavers can make the hike interesting; everyone enjoys seeing what the beavers are up to. Several trails in the park are suitable for children. An environmental education center has displays and photographs of interest to children and adults. The park also has good fishing, rowboat rentals, a lifeguarded beach, and a campground.

To reach Cowans Gap, take US 30 west from Chambersburg to the summit of Tuscarora Mountain and turn right at the summit on Aughwick Road. Go 5 miles to the park entrance, and 1.3 miles further north to the beach area parking lot (lot 3) on the left.

The Lakeside Trail begins by the rest rooms on a paved path that goes past the concession stand. Go to the right to walk on a gravel road a short distance, then on a dirt path. Soon you are in the shade of the forest, a welcome respite on a

Boys hoping for a good catch from Cowan's Gap Lake.

hot summer day. Pass two water fountains and reach a junction with the Tuscarora Trail, which follows the Lakeside Trail across the dam ahead. Go to the left at the junction (the trail to the right soon ends at Allen Valley Road). Watch for poison ivy as you approach the dam, then cross it.

After 0.4 mile, a bridge spans the spillway and the Tuscarora Trail bears right, where it eventually connects with the Appalachian Trail. Bear left here and get a view of the beach across the lake. This shoreline is a popular place to fish in summer and winter. Pass under the welcome shade of some spruces, and begin to notice signs of beaver activity on the shoreline. Felled trees lie halfway in the water, their bark chewed off by the busy beavers. The whiter or yellower the wood, the fresher the cut. Red squirrels live here also, chattering to each other and scampering up and down the trees.

Cowans Gap has an interesting story behind it. It was named for Major Samuel Cowan, who was a British officer during the Revolutionary War. His future father-in-law disapproved of him because of his alliance with the British, and he and his girlfriend eloped to Chambersburg. They eventually decided to move to Kentucky, but their wagon broke down en route and they traded it to an Indian chief in exchange for this property. The gap, viewed from the Knobsville Road

Trail, is a wind gap, meaning the water no longer goes through the gap—only the wind.

Cross two small creeks and see more beaver-felled trees and some girdled trees. Cross another small creek and pass the handicapped-accessible fishing pier, reaching the narrow end of the lake. Cross three more small creeks on bridges, the third one over a beaver-dredged canal. Beavers are more agile in water than on land, so they build canals to help them transport branches back to the lodge more easily by swimming with the floating branches. Look across to the small island and see if you can spot the beaver's lodge at the end of it. Freshly chewed sticks are a clue to its location. In this area, the beavers do not need a dam, because the humans already did that part for them. Eventually, when their food supply in this area runs out, the beavers will move on.

Cross Little Aughwick Creek on a large bridge at 0.9 mile and walk on the park road briefly, then bear left onto a gravel path. Pass a picnic pavilion on the right, the posts of which the woodpeckers have been vigorously attacking. Farther on, on the right, is the interpretive center, which has some interesting displays on birds common to the area. After a visit to the interpretive center, return to the trail and continue on to the beach area where you began.

Other trails of interest: Knobsville Road Trail—a 1.1-mile trail on an old road—leads uphill to a pretty overlook of Cowans Gap and the lake. Access is from the west end of the park road, past the beaver lodge.

The 1-mile Plessinger Trail along Little Aughwick Creek is recommended. Access is by bridge near the beaver-lodge end of the lake.

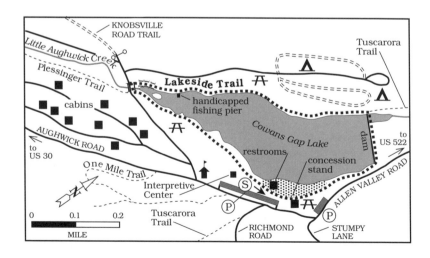

The Twin Spring Self-Guiding Nature Trail is closed due to logging activity in the area.

---

36. Rhododendron, Raven Rock, and Abbott Run Trails

Type: Day hike
Difficulty: Easy–moderate (climbing)
Distance: 0.7 mile one way
Hiking time: 45 minutes one way
Elevation gain: 60 feet
Hikable: Spring–fall
Map: Trough Creek State Park map
Rest rooms: Toilets, water by nature center near park office and at campground
Fee: None

This short loop of the Rhododendron, Raven Rock, and Abbott Run Trails packs about as many interesting features into it as possible: a suspension bridge, a lovely waterfall, an unusual balancing rock, a cooling stroll along a mountain brook, and intriguing rock ledges with cave-like forms carved in their sides. The trail is located in Trough Creek State Park, which has camping, fishing, picnicking, and a historical iron furnace.

To reach Trough Creek State Park, take US 522 south from Mount Union, and then take PA 994 west past Newburg and make a right on Old Forge/Hill Farm Road. Go 2 miles to the T intersection. Go left on Trough Creek Drive, and follow the road about 1 mile to the well-signed trailhead (for Balanced Rock), and park on the right in the lot beside the road.

To begin, cross Trough Creek Drive and head downhill to the Rhododendron Trail, staying on the high trail to the left. Reach the well-fenced suspension bridge on your right and have a great time crossing it over Trough Creek. At the end of the bridge, turn right and follow the creek on a wide path, past the many rhododendrons for which the trail was named. You have good views of the rushing creek below. Watch for an area where there are steep dropoffs with no railing.

At 0.2 mile reach pretty Rainbow Falls, which cascades down

terraced, moss-covered rocks. From here cross a bridge over Abbott Run and go up a set of stone steps to some ledges, which are sculpted with cave-like hollows in the sides where rocks dropped out. At a Y intersection here, turn right and go up more steps to another Y intersection; go right to reach Balanced Rock. Once there were cliffs above this area, and this boulder dropped off of them. The cliffs are worn away now, but this rock remained remarkably balanced. Someday it will fall into the water below. How long do children think it will stay balanced?

Back at the trail junction just below Balanced Rock, head to the right, uphill into the woods on the Raven Rock Trail, above the ledges, through young hemlocks and white pines. Pass a bridge on the left over Abbott Run, then descend alongside Abbott Run. At the next bridge, cross Abbott Run and at the trail junction with the Ledges Trail, turn left, taking the low Abbott Run Trail at 0.4 mile.

Follow the Abbott Run Trail, passing another bridge on your left; the trail crosses the creek on another bridge, and you walk along the other side of the ledges you passed on your way up. After 0.5 mile you are back at the junction above Rainbow Falls. Bear right to return to the trailhead, following the path that you started on.

Other trails of interest: A 1.6-mile, easy portion of the Terrace Mountain Trail is accessible at the end of Trough Creek Drive by the Ice Mine. It follows along a narrow inlet of Raystown Lake for about 0.8 mile before heading up Terrace Mountain, which is steep.

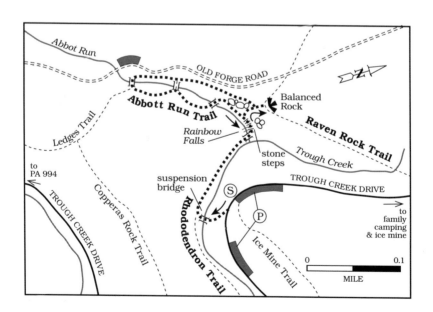

37. Homestead Trail

Type: Day hike
Difficulty: Moderate (hills)
Distance: 1.8 miles round trip
Hiking time: 3 hours
Elevation gain: 300 feet
Hikable: Spring–fall
Map: Blue Knob State Park map
Rest rooms: Toilets, water at Willow Spring Picnic Area
Fee: None

Situated near Altoona, Johnstown, and Bedford is this 5,614-acre park, which contains the second-highest peak in the state, Blue Knob. Excellent views can be seen on the way to the trailhead at the Willow Spring Picnic Area. This pleasant walk on old roads is a walk through time. Old fields in a rolling valley still have some reminders of the former inhabitants who built homes in this area many years ago. The Homestead Trail is mostly downhill until the very last section. This tends to be a quiet trail, so there is an opportunity to observe wildlife if you hike quietly. The state park has a pool and camping.

To reach Blue Knob State Park, take US 219 north from Johnstown and turn right (east) on PA 869, taking it all the way to the village of Pavia. At the stop sign in Pavia, turn a hairpin left onto Knob Road, SR 4035. Continue north and once you reach the park, turn right, by the ranger station, onto Whysong Road, and take it up to the Willow Springs picnic area, where there is a loop road with parking.

The trail begins where the picnic area road loop comes together, at the south edge of the road. Begin on the Saw Mill Trail very briefly and pass by a gate, heading downhill, almost immediately coming to a trail junction; turn right onto an old road, the orange-blazed Homestead Trail. The trail drops steeply at first, through a forested area that has recently suffered from some damage by insects. Reach a junction with another old road that connects back to the Saw Mill Trail, but bear

How many legs does a millipede have?

right to stay on the Homestead Trail. Bright green fox grass swooshes softly at your feet.

Continue descending, and at 0.3 mile come to a clearing where one old homestead once stood. I spooked three deer and a very chubby groundhog here. Children may enjoy deciding where they would put their home along this trail if they could choose. Notice the small trees which will someday fill in this meadow and turn it back into a forest.

Cross a seasonal creek and pass grapevines as you go up a gentle hill on the mossy, grassy path. Do not be surprised to hear the cries of a hawk echoing through the valley. Blue Knob Peak is above just to the northeast and the valley below drops off dramatically and steeply, making a great place for hawks, black vultures, ravens, and other great birds that enjoy riding the thermal currents created by the rugged topography. Low-bush blueberries line the hillside on the left as you descend past more grapevines and come to a junction with another old road, where you curve right.

Cross another seasonal creek and continue on the old road, which is neatly lined with trees. One can imagine what the road was like when houses lined its edges. Come to another old road junction on

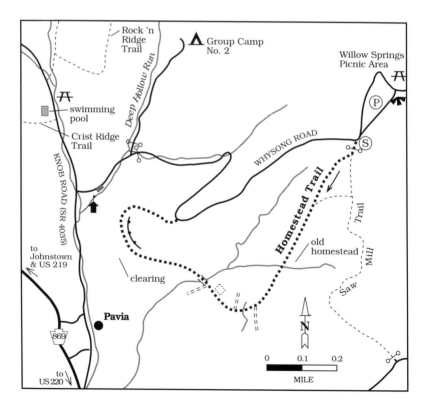

the right and go straight. The creek trickles below. Several homesteads were located along this creek. Look carefully for a mossy old foundation just below the trail. Soon after spotting the old foundation, at another junction with an old road, turn right and cross the creek on a wooden bridge at 0.8 mile. Many wildflowers bloom here, as do apple trees, which were surely planted by early pioneers. An old rose remains in the thickets, probably also planted by some pioneer.

Head uphill now and soon come to a clearing, bearing right on the old road, and notice the remains of an old stone wall and fenceposts. The trail flattens somewhat, then begins a gradual climb. Crows scold from above and hikers might spook a ruffed grouse or a turkey. The path steepens and curves right, passing many young maples with their smooth, silvery bark. Watch for poison ivy on the trees, keeping away from even the hairy roots. As the trail grade lessens, soon find you have reached Whysong Road and the end of the trail at 1.3 miles. Walk 0.5 mile to the right, along the sparsely traveled road, back to the parking area.

Other trails of interest: Rock 'n Ridge Trail is a a 2.8-mile loop trail (about 2 hours) that starts at the pavilion in the picnic area above the swimming pool and follows a brook to a ridge and back.

The Crist Ridge Trail takes off from the third curve on Knob Road and heads downhill 0.9 mile to the swimming pool area. There is a chance for wildlife viewing.

38. Bog Path

Type:	Day hike
Difficulty:	Moderate (uneven path)
Distance:	2-mile loop
Hiking time:	2 hours
Elevation gain:	100 feet
Hikable:	Spring–fall
Map:	J. P. Saylor and Lost Turkey Trail Map 2, Gallitzin State Forest
Rest rooms:	Toilets at Babcock picnic area; no water
Fee:	None

Few people have ever been in a bog, where the sphagnum moss is so thick it will support a person's weight—for a while. The Bog Path, adjacent to the Clear Shade Wild Area, takes hikers on a tour of just such a bog. An interpretive trail, the Bog Path encircles an area that was devastated by lumbering in the early 1900s and then ravaged by forest fires, exposing the topsoil to erosion. The poorly drained area became saturated with water, and thus the boggy character. The path goes through second-growth forest and open meadows around the bog, passing many bog-friendly plants such as low-bush blueberry and thick sphagnum moss. The trail crosses the bog and hikers can view the area from an observation deck.

To reach the area, take US 219 from the north or south to Johnstown, exiting onto PA 56 east (Geistown/Windber exit). Follow PA 56 east past the Babcock Picnic Area and the Gallitzin State Forest Ranger Station (where you can pick up an interesting interpretive brochure, which includes an inventory of trees and shrubs). Shortly after the ranger station is a road to the left; continue straight ahead. At the second road, which is on the right past the picnic area, turn right onto the dirt road with a sign for Clear Shade Wild Area. Park on the right in the parking lot immediately off the road.

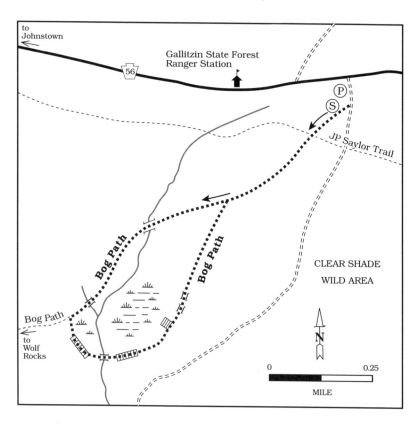

The Bog Path begins at the corner of the parking lot by the trail map sign. It is blazed red and yellow at first. Enter the forest and descend easily past some hemlocks, soon crossing the J. P. Saylor Trail, which makes two large loops in this area. Continue downhill and the trail becomes somewhat rocky. At the Y junction at 0.3 mile, bear right to begin the loop; you will return to this point.

Notice low-bush blueberries, which bear small fruits in August. Soon the trail heads through a more open area, where the trees are young and short and the area still fairly sunny. It is a bit wet as you head downhill through a grassy area (the trail is somewhat indistinct here, but well blazed), crossing a creek on a bridge.

Soon find yourself surrounded by some very pretty spruces and watch the blazes for a left turn. In shadier forest now, the trail is mildly rolling, then the forest opens up again. Pass maples and aspen and cross a grassy meadow—tell children to listen to the dry, rustling sound of the grass as it swishes apart in front of their feet.

Pass two young intertwining beeches on the right and cross a small creek on a bridge. After 0.9 mile, come to a junction, the right path of which leads about 1 mile west to Wolf Rocks. This trail is rugged and the rocks would be interesting were it not for the spray-painted graffiti that plasters them. Instead, bear left at the junction, following the Bog Path with just the red blazes now, and see the bog on the left. Feel the softness and springiness of the thick moss, which can absorb vast quantities of water. That is one of the qualities that makes sphagnum moss marketable—it is still sold as a gardening aid for potted plants. Do not wander off the trail; the moss masks wet areas that may be deeper than they look.

Cross a boardwalk over a wet area and continue to a grassy patch. Notice the brown color of the creek water on the left. Tannic acid from the hemlocks and other organic matter turns the water this color. Cross the creek on a bridge and walk across another boardwalk that goes directly over the wet bog area, where you can hear the bubbling water underneath.

Rustle through another grassy area, then cross an open meadow where the trail is a bit indistinct but well blazed. See an observation deck on the left at 1.25 miles and go up for a look. Notice the hemlock stumps in the bog area—once there were many hemlocks here, as well as other trees. Hemlocks are rather rot-resistant, so they remain, many with fire scars.

Cross two small bridges and look for big juicy blueberries nearby. Reach an area of semi-open woods and enter it, then head uphill into the shadier woods. Reach the junction where the two ends of the trail come together, and bear right back to the parking lot.

Southwest Pennsylvania

Bear Run offers a feeling of solitude and wonder.

39. Damsite Trail

Type: Day hike
Difficulty: Moderate
Distance: 2.5 miles round trip
Hiking time: 2 hours
Elevation gain: 100 feet
Hikable: Spring–fall
Map: Yellow Creek State Park map
Rest rooms: Toilets, water at beach area
Fee: None

This trail, which is mostly on an old road, follows the west shoreline of Yellow Creek Lake, formed in 1969 when the dam was completed. The hike leads through pretty woods on the ridge above the lake, then drops down to the old road and stays on it until its end, from which there is a view of the dam and its spillway. An excellent blackberry patch at the end of this trail makes it worthwhile hiking for young berry pickers—there is more than enough here for a pie or some jam if you reach it when the berries ripen in late July through August. The park has a visitor center with exhibits by the farm pond, which is located on the southeast shore of the lake by the beach. Stop here first, before going to the trailhead. Children under twelve can fish in the farm pond. The beach is lifeguarded for swimmers during the summer.

To reach the trailhead, take US 422 west from Ebensburg, passing the tiny town of Nolo. Two miles past Nolo, turn left on PA 259, which enters the park. Pass the park office on the right and continue 2.3 miles further on PA 259, past the beach area. Follow PA 259 as it makes a righthand turn after about 1 mile, to Hoffman Road. Turn right on Hoffman Road and go almost to its end at Yellow Creek Lake—there is a parking area on the right side of the road and the trailhead is on the left side of the road just before the edge of the woods.

(Young hikers might prefer to take the old road both ways, rather than the trail on the way in, for an easier walk of 2.3 miles. To reach the old road from the parking area, head downhill to the right on Hoffman Road toward the lakeshore, and turn left onto the woods road. When you reach the junction with the trail in 0.3 miles, resume following the main trail description below.)

The trail begins across the road from the parking area and bears right on a mowed path through cherry and apple trees. Walk steadily uphill through a sunny meadow with many wildflowers. Small trees dot the meadow, which will eventually become a forest.

Soon the trail enters the woods; an old pine plantation is on your right. Continue gradually uphill. Children may notice pretty orange butterfly weed along the path. Come to a junction and bear left off the old road onto a more narrow path on the rolling hillside above the lake. Hitchhiking seeds might stick to young hikers' socks here. Ground cedar carpets the path as it descends, gently at first, then more steeply, to cross a small stream. Next cross over an old building foundation. Children may notice daddy longlegs crossing the path. These gentle insects are not true spiders and will not bite people. They tickle when they walk on you.

Cross several small seasonal creeks and finally come to a junction with an old road at just over 0.3 mile, and turn left. Notice this junction, as you will return to it on the way back.

The route flattens now, and you can get glimpses of the lake through the trees on the right. Pretty, red-flowered bee balm and other flowers line the path in July. Pass large oak and hickory trees and begin a gentle climb. The road curves left, by some grapevines the thickness of some tree trunks. As the trail levels again, pass over two small creeks, which drain into the lake. Pass a grassy old road on the left at 0.8 mile, but continue ahead, downhill now, through an area of wet

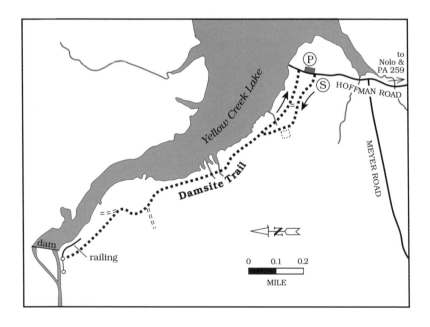

trail, due to several springs. One-tenth mile further, a muddy old road on the right heads downhill, but stay on the path straight ahead, which becomes more grassy and level, then goes downhill past some steel posts. Children may find millipedes along the trail, which scrunch into a tight curl when picked up. They do not have a million legs, but they do have a lot.

Ripe blackberries are a hiker's reward along the Damsite Trail.

The path becomes sunnier as the trees thin out, and soon you see a fence on your right. The trail ends by a gate at the end of the fence at 1.2 miles. From here you can see the dam and spillway below. Do not go around the fence to the ledges, because there is no guardrail and it drops off steeply. The blackberries are on the left of the trail across from the fence.

When you have eaten your fill of berries, backtrack to the junction at 2.1 miles where you first entered onto this old road. On the return, go straight and continue on the old road rather than taking the higher trail you took on the way in. Cross over a stream and walk up a gentle hill, passing an old road on your right. Come close to the lakeshore several times. Pass some aspen trees and, after a little while, reach an old paved road, which is the very end of Hoffman Road.

For a side trip to the lakeshore, take this road left 100 feet; at the lake, observant hikers might spy wading birds among the yellow-flowering splatterdock plants. Look for freshwater mussel shells along the shore, which were probably opened by raccoons.

To return to the trailhead, go up the hill on Hoffman Road, reaching the parking area in 0.1 mile.

Other trails of interest: The Laurel Run Trail, a 0.5-mile loop, is pretty in spring when wildflowers are out. Park at the park office. The trail leaves from the side of PA 259 along Laurel Run just north of the office.

40. Picnic Area, Spruce Flats, and Wolf Rocks Trails

Type: Day hike
Difficulty: Easy
Distance: 2.3-mile loop
Hiking time: 2 hours
Elevation gain: 25 feet
Hikable: Spring–fall
Map: Laurel Highlands Snowmobile Trail System Map
Rest rooms: Toilets at trailhead; no water
Fee: None

Spruce Flats is an incredibly lush area on the wide, flat top of Laurel Summit in the Laurel Highlands area. At over 2,700 feet, this is one of the higher parts of Pennsylvania, but the terrain is easy to handle. When the fog rolls in here, as it often does, you would think you were in New England if you did not know better. This loop trail is also an excellent beginner cross-country ski route. A picnic area is located at the trailhead.

To reach Spruce Flats, take US 30 east from Pittsburgh past Ligonier and Laughlintown. Soon after the village of Laurel Mountain, turn right on Laurel Summit Road, which is paved but turns into dirt later. Follow Laurel Summit Road 5.7 miles to where it makes a righthand turn and 0.1 mile further to the Laurel Summit picnic area. Park in the rear parking lot circle.

The hike starts on the Picnic Area Trail, which is not signed, but begins straight ahead on the northeast side of the parking area. The trail curves right from the parking lot, then reaches a dirt road in about 0.1 mile, where you turn left. Walk on the road briefly, then make a right onto the Picnic Area Trail as it continues into the woods. Cross a grassy old road and continue through this mixed deciduous forest. Alongside the trail, the impressive interrupted fern thrives. Deer frequent the area and their tracks are often seen in the mud. Young white pines seem to like it here as well, their new growth showing up on their tips in a bright green color. Moss grows just about everywhere—on rocks, decaying logs, the edge of the trail—there are several different varieties, too, including thick sphagnum, which is dried commercially into peat moss.

At a junction with a gravel road at 0.7 mile, turn left on the road and soon cross a pipeline cut. There are many stumps in this area, which was logged heavily at one time. Fires razed the area afterward, and the forest has taken a while to regenerate. Some of the oldest trees around line the edges of the road, though they are all second growth.

Reach a junction with the Black Bear Trail on the right, but continue on the road, which is easy walking and may allow you to see deer, back bear, or wild turkeys if you are quiet. Pass a picnic table in a clearing on the right, and see a gate up ahead, which you pass by. The Silvermine Trail goes right here. Notice the color of the water of the creek you go over just beyond the gate. This "black water" is so called because of a buildup of decaying organic matter, particularly hemlock needles, which contain tannic acid. Many of the creeks on this flat summit area run black, until a big storm with lots of water flushes them out and they run clearer. Then the buildup begins again.

Soon turn left off the road onto the Spruce Flats Trail, on a grassy old road at 1.4 miles. Notice the fenced-in deer exclosures, most likely there to protect plants inside it. Come to a muddy area and walk on the edges around it, because the mud is deeper than it looks. Hikers may surprise a ruffed grouse, the Pennsylvania state bird, which has good habitat here with lots of cover.

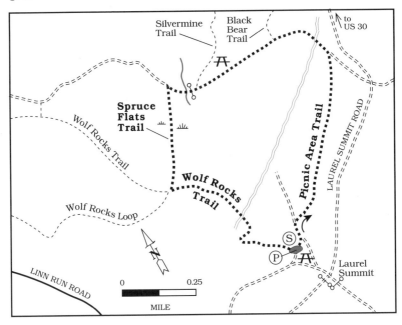

Princess pine and other moisture loving plants blanket the ground around lush Spruce Flats.

Head down a gentle hill and turn left at the junction with the Wolf Rocks Trail at 1.75 miles. (Those who want a longer walk may want to go right on the Wolf Rocks Trail for a 3-mile side trip, round trip, out to an interesting rock formation on the edge of the ridge.) For the main hike, go left on the Wolf Rocks Trail, cross a black water seep, and walk up a gentle hill through rhododendrons and some large white pines. Indian cucumber, with its six leaves radiating from the middle, is found here. When it goes to seed it sends up an antenna with three more leaves in a whirl on top. Cross the pipeline cut again and soon thereafter end your hike as the trail comes out at the northwest edge of the picnic area.

41. Hemlock Trail

Type:	Day hike
Difficulty:	Easy–moderate
Distance:	1.2-mile loop
Hiking time:	1 hour
Elevation gain:	100 feet
Hikable:	Spring–fall
Map:	Laurel Hill State Park map
Rest rooms:	Toilets, water across street at picnic grove 4
Fee:	None

This moderately rolling trail along Laurel Hill Creek in Laurel Highlands is particularly nice, as it reaches a stand of virgin hemlock in just 0.5 mile. This self-guided interpretive trail is having its interpretive guide updated, so ask at the park office to see if it is available yet. Several routes are possible here—a 1-mile round-trip hike to the

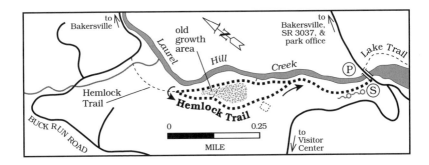

big trees on the lower side of the loop is easiest. The stand of virgin hemlock seen on this hike is the only stand of old-growth trees remaining in Laurel Hill State Park. Children enjoy seeing how many arms it takes to encircle one of these stately giants. The rest of the park features dammed Laurel Hill Lake, with a swimming beach, a family campground, and other trails that head up to the Allegheny plateau.

To reach the trailhead, take Interstate 76 east from Pittsburgh to the PA 31/Donegal exit (exit 9) and take PA 31 east to Bakersville. Make a right on SR 3037 and go 1.6 miles. Turn right on the park road by the stone entrance gates. Go 0.4 mile to the park office and then 0.5 mile further to a gravel parking lot on the right just before the bridge over Laurel Hill Creek. Park here.

The Hemlock Trail begins on the other side of the bridge and heads into the forest alongside the creek. Pass several small springs that run across the trail into the creek. Reach a junction after 0.2 mile, where you will return. Bear right; the trail follows the edge of the creek. Cross two log bridges across seasonal creeklets. The trail goes through mostly young deciduous trees here. The large-leafed striped maple can be found mixed in among the underbrush. Look for a short side trail to a small sandy area on the creek's bank after about 0.2 mile. This is a nice area for water play, perhaps to look for crawdads and worms.

Head uphill briefly and soon enter the virgin hemlock area. Grand old hemlocks sway in the breeze here, as they have for centuries. Notice how little undergrowth there is in the deep shade. Pass a side trail on the left. These trees were lucky to escape the lumbermen. Their bark was valued for tannic acid, which was used to tan leather.

As you go up some steps, the path rolls up and down and leaves the old hemlocks behind. At the next trail junction, turn left onto the loop at nearly 0.5 mile. Pass numerous seeps that drain into Laurel Hill Creek, which receives runoff from its 80,000-square-acre watershed.

Descend and come to a Y junction where the left fork leads back to the old-growth area. Take the right fork and begin a climb. Notice the tall trees below you now. Walk into a young grove of hemlocks—or so it seems. Notice the ground is covered with oak leaves. Oaks tower above them. Hemlocks like shade, however, and someday will grow taller than the oaks and overshadow them. Fungus and pine sap (related to Indian pipes) grow well in the damp shade. Pass the remains of an old log lean-to and descend downhill on terraced steps to rejoin with the lower loop trail at nearly 1 mile. Turn right and follow it back to the trailhead.

Other trails of interest: Those wanting to stay on the lower side of Hemlock Trail can follow it past the old growth to its opposite end at Buck Run Road, for a hike of 1.2 miles each way.

The Pump House Trail is a wide, easy trail on an old road that leads 0.6 mile to Jones Mill Run Dam and the pond behind it. Access this from the marked trailhead along the park road in the center of the park, about 1.2 miles south of the Hemlock Trail parking lot, on the west side of the road well before reaching the visitor center.

42. Shelter Rocks Trail

Type:	Day hike
Difficulty:	Moderate (rocky)
Distance:	0.1–1 mile round trip
Hiking time:	1 hour round trip
Elevation gain:	100 feet
Hikable:	Spring–fall
Map:	Forbes State Forest public use map
Rest rooms:	No toilets or water
Fee:	None

Mount Davis is the highest point in Pennsylvania—3,213 feet. Kids and adults appreciate getting a look around from the 50-foot observation tower on this flattish summit that offers views of the surrounding mountains. From the summit you can take a short hike to Shelter Rocks, an interesting jumble of large boulders that kids enjoy scrambling around. Try this hike in the fall for the best views.

To reach the trailhead, take US 40 south from Uniontown to PA 523 north. Go 1.4 miles to Listonburg. Make a right turn onto SR 2004

A hiker takes a close look at Shelter Rocks.

and take it 10.8 miles to South Wolf Rock Road. Turn right and drive to the summit parking lot, which is on the left.

Walk past the gate on a hard-surfaced road bearing left, which takes you 0.1 mile to the observation tower. The tower steps are well fenced so there is no chance of falling, and a map at the top shows the surrounding topography. Mount Davis was formed about 200 million years ago during an upheaval called the Appalachian Revolution. That was a long time ago, even in mountain time, so it is no wonder its flanks are rounded with age.

At the bottom of the tower, go left around the circular paved road till you reach the Shelter Rocks Trail. Walk through short scrubby trees that do not reach great height due to the harsh weather and winds on this summit. Low-bush blueberries line the trail, thriving on the shallow, rocky soils here. Soon reach a burned area, which you saw from the summit. The skeletons of the trees here still bear the scars of a fire. At the edge of the burn area, notice that along with blueberries, sassafras seedlings are taking advantage of the sunlight and regenerating the forest here.

Back in the woods again, begin a gentle ascent on the somewhat

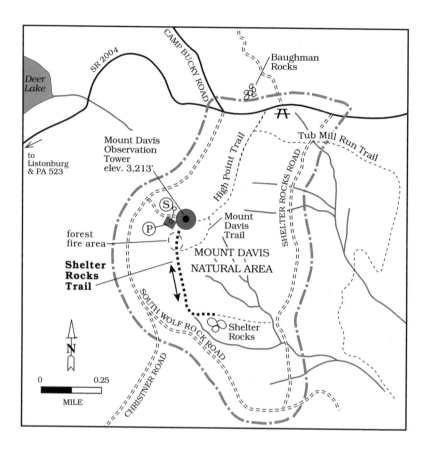

rocky Shelter Rocks Trail. Moss covers many of the rocks here, a testament to the moisture. The trail is a bit indistinct for about 50 feet. Continue downhill, through mountain laurels and interrupted ferns. The trail curves left and flattens as you notice pitch pine scattered through the otherwise deciduous forest. After 0.5 mile, reach a brushy side trail (no sign) and see the Shelter Rocks on your right. There is no view here, but the rocks are interesting. They are covered with black lichen, which turns moist green on top when wet and pales to gray when dry. The area under the lower rock probably explains why the rocks were so named, as the overhanging boulder would indeed provide shelter during a storm. Explore all the nooks and crannies here, then backtrack to complete your hike.

Other trails of interest: It is possible to hike up the summit of Mount Davis. The High Point Trail leads from the picnic area just east of South Wolf Rock Road on SR 2004. To make a long loop, take

High Point Trail from the picnic area up to the summit, then take the Shelter Rocks Trail to grassy Shelter Rocks Road, turn left, then make a left on the Tub Mill Run Trail back to the beginning of the High Point Trail, a distance of about 2.3 miles.

---

43. Bear Run Nature Reserve Trails

Type: Day hike or overnight
Difficulty: Easy–moderate (rocks)
Distance: 2.1-mile loop
Hiking time: 1 hour
Elevation gain: 100 feet
Hikable: Spring–fall
Map: Bear Run Nature Reserve Trail Guide map
Rest rooms: Toilets, water at Ohiopyle State Park
Fee: None

In the midst of the often crowded Laurel Ridge Area is this wonderfully uncrowded reserve with 20 miles of very well maintained and marked trails that meander through well-watered hills and valleys. Here, mountain laurel and rhododendron thrive along with turkey, deer, and other wild creatures. Many loop hikes are possible here and camping is allowed on the property at designated sites. There is a campsite near the loop described here and in other areas throughout the reserve. (Note: Maps are available at the trailhead, showing many other possible hikes and campsites.) This 5,000-acre area is run by the Western Pennsylvania Conservancy. Though hunting is not allowed, fall hikers are encouraged to wear blaze orange because hunters sometimes have been seen in the edges of the reserve's boundary. This place is bound to become a favorite family destination.

To reach Bear Run, take US 40 south from Uniontown and turn north on PA 381 toward Ohiopyle. Stay on PA 381 and pass through Ohiopyle, continuing 3.5 miles further north and turning right into the well-signed parking lot for Bear Run Nature Reserve. Park at the upper lot.

Begin at the far end of the upper lot, entering a pine plantation on the Wagon Trail, following it only about 50 feet to the Arbutus Trail, where you make a right. The trail is a soft carpet of pine needles as you make an easy downhill through the plantation. Virginia creeper

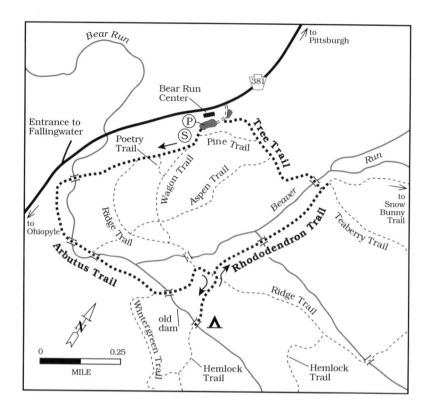

and poison ivy both grow here—this is a good chance to teach youngsters the difference between them.

The trail curves left and reaches a junction with the Poetry Trail, where you bear right. A depression that sometimes holds water for a seasonal pond is on the left. At the junction with the Ridge Trail, go straight and cross a seep. The trail is rockier now. Hickory trees tower above, leaving their green husked nuts on the trail as evidence. Walk on a boardwalk and begin to hear Bear Run on your right. Feel for warm and cool air pockets here. Cross Bear Run on a bridge at 0.3 mile in the first of several crossings. Cross it again shortly on another bridge and duck through a tunnel of rhododendrons, their white and pinkish blossoms blooming in July. Go straight at a junction with the Aspen Trail and cross Bear Run again on a bridge at 0.7 mile.

At 0.9 mile, reach the Wintergreen Trail and here leave the Arbutus Trail, going left on Wintergreen. Follow alongside the creek briefly, then cross another bridge over Bear Run, noting the old spillway that is cracking due to water pressure. Now on the opposite side of the creek you can see an old dam.

Next turn away from the creek and head uphill on the rocky path and descend to a junction with the Ridge Trail after 1.1 miles. Turn right onto the Ridge Trail, an old road. In about 0.1 mile turn left onto the Rhododendron Trail. If you are wanting to camp overnight, go less than 0.1 mile farther uphill on Ridge Trail and make a right at the next trail junction, following it about 0.2 mile to a designated campsite by Bear Run.

Back on the Rhododendron Trail, descend through ferns and listen to all the birds found here. Inter-

Midsummer is the best time to see the rhododendrons in bloom.

rupted ferns line the path, sometimes reaching 3 feet tall. Head uphill briefly, cross a stream on a bridge, then descend gradually to a junction with the Tree Trail at 1.6 miles. Go straight onto the Tree Trail, on an old road now, and cross a bridge over Beaver Run. The trail curves left and then right. Pass the Aspen Trail on the left at 1.8 miles and continue downhill on the Tree Trail through the plantation; soon after, the Pine Trail comes in from the left. Watch for wild turkeys here— I saw numerous feathers on the trail. At the bottom of the hill, the trail ends by the lower parking lot—walk uphill to the upper lot.

Other trails of interest: Hikers seeking a wide, level, easy trail can try the 1.1-mile Snow Bunny Trail, which can be reached just east of the intersection of the Rhododendron and Tree Trails. From the intersection, follow the Rhododendron Trail for 0.2 mile, and then bear left on the Snow Bunny Trail for a pleasant woods walk.

The 2.3-mile Ridge Trail is on an old road that begins in the lowlands near the parking area and heads south from the Arbutus Trail; it passes through various stages of forest succession on its way to the highlands of the reserve.

The Laurel Run Trail crosses PA 381 about 1.5 miles north of the Bear Run Center. This 2.3-mile trail follows scenic Laurel Run.

44. Ferncliff Trail

Type: Day hike
Difficulty: Easy–moderate (narrow path, cliffs)
Distance: 1.7-mile loop
Hiking time: 1 hour
Elevation gain: 100 feet
Hikable: Spring–fall
Map: Ohiopyle State Park map
Rest rooms: Toilets, water in parking area just before bridge in Ohiopyle
Fee: None

A walk in a hemlock-dominated forest is usually quiet, but here in Ohiopyle State Park, the roar of the mighty rapids on the Youghiogheny River, which makes a horseshoe curve around the Ferncliff peninsula, is ever present. This hike through Ferncliff Natural Area, a national natural landmark, is beautiful and lush. There are views of a powerful waterfall and places to stop and wade in the water when the trail reaches the east bank of the "Yough," which has some of the most challenging white-water rapids in the East. Early to mid-July is a nice time to hike the trail, when the rhododendrons are out and it is hot enough to enjoy cooling breezes from the river.

To reach the trailhead, take PA 51 south from Pittsburgh, exiting onto US 40 east at Uniontown. In Farmington turn left on PA 381 north into the park and continue on PA 381 north to the village of Ohiopyle. Cross the bridge over the Youghiogheny River and immediately turn left into a gravel parking area.

The trail begins at the right edge of the parking area. Bear right into the woods and come to a stone monument where the loop trail begins. Turn right here onto the Ferncliff Trail (not to be confused with the Fernwood Trail, which cuts through the interior of this natural area).

Soon head into the hemlocks. In summer, the smell of warm needles is very pleasing. Numerous side trails branch to the right off the main trail, offering glimpses of the river. On this side of the peninsula the trail is high above the river. Urge patience, however, as you come around to see the waterfalls and the river close up near the end of the hike.

The trail goes uphill for a while. Hikers might startle chipmunks as they scurry about their business in the forest. Pass through an area of deciduous forest, with young trees above, and soon come to a trail junction with the Fernwood Trail at 0.6 mile; bear right, still on the Ferncliff Trail. New York fern and Indian cucumber line the path here. Indian cucumber is a delicate-looking plant with six leaves emanating from the center, so named because its tiny root tastes like cucumber.

Begin to descend now. The sound of the rapids gets louder. Soon come to a junction with the Oakwoods Trail on the left, and continue straight ahead on Ferncliff. The trail comes out to an overlook of the river, which is fairly calm here, but still very fast moving. There is no guardrail here, so warn children to stay away from the edge. The Buffalo Nut Trail veers off to the left, but head downhill through a tunnel of rhododendrons. If you have very little ones, hold hands here, because the trail narrows and has steep dropoffs in a few places. Continue downhill and hear, then smell, the water from the falls. See a glimpse of it on the right, then at 1.1 miles take the side trail down stone steps for a nice overlook of the falls.

Down the trail, continue to descend and come out to some sandstone rocks where there is another view of the thunderous falls. The falls were formed by water wearing away joints in the Pottsville

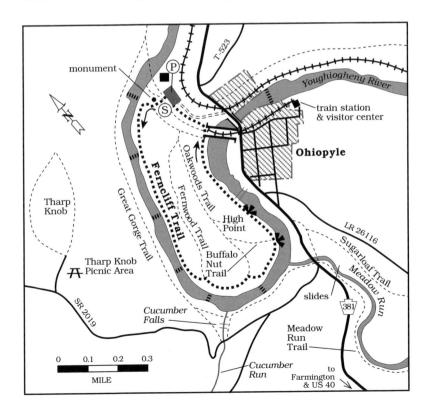

One of the incredibly powerful waterfalls on the Youghiogheny River, as viewed from the Ferncliff Trail.

Sandstone, which finally broke apart and fractured pieces dropped away. As a waterfall wears down, it becomes a rapid, which is what the Youghiogheny is famous for among white-water rafters, canoeists, and kayakers.

Follow along the edge of the river. Swimming and wading are not permitted here. Pass through more rhododendrons on a rocky and rooty tread. Look at the rocks and see if children can spot fossils from the ancient Lepidodendron tree, which look like tire treads. The Lepidodendron grew here approximately 300 million years ago when this area was a vast tropical coastal swamp and the middle of the United States was under an inland sea. This tree, also known as the scale tree, grew up to 60 feet tall, and had long, smooth-edged leaves, which you might also see fossilized. This is a good place to try a fossil rubbing.

Reach a sign warning of the dangers from the rapids and falls, and a lifeline stretched across the river. As you continue, the path backs off a little bit from the water's edge and you pass first a trail junction on the left and then you go under a railroad bridge. Shortly after the bridge, reach the parking lot.

Other trails of interest: The 1.8-mile loop around the Old

Mitchell Place, accessed at the Old Mitchell Place parking lot, takes you through the woods and meadow. Follow SR 2019 northwest from PA 381 for several miles to the parking area on the right.

The Meadow Run Trail is 3.3 miles with two loop options—loop 1 goes over a knob and loop 2 has natural water slides located at its beginning. The trailhead is on PA 381 just south of the village of Ohiopyle.

Tharp Knob Trail leaves from the Tharp Knob picnic area, located over a mile northwest of PA 381 on SR 2019. This loop trail of about 0.7 mile goes to an overlook and back.

45. Main Loop, French Camp, and Inner Loop Trails

Type:	Day hike
Difficulty:	Easy
Distance:	1.9-mile loop
Hiking time:	1.5 hours
Elevation gain:	100 feet
Hikable:	Spring–fall
Map:	Fort Necessity Hiking Map
Rest rooms:	Toilets, water at visitor center
Fee:	$2 ages 17 and up

Fort Necessity is far less famous than Valley Forge, but this small stockade in a picturesque meadow and woodland area is historically significant as site of one of the conflicts that led to the beginning of the French and Indian War. Hikes here are all fairly easy. This loop goes by the reconstructed stockade, which replicates the one built by George Washington, and heads up through a meadow filled with wildflowers to a vista and back downhill through a deciduous forest. The park is a wildlife sanctuary. The park has interpretive signs throughout, a visitor center, a picnic area, and an old tavern. Slide shows and exhibits are available at the visitor center. Seasonally guided tours and soldier talks start here also.

To reach the park, take US 40 east from Uniontown past tiny Chalk Hill. Just past Braddock's Grave Memorial on the left, enter the park on the right. At the road fork, stay to the right to park near the visitor center.

The hike begins at the visitor center. Take the paved pathway behind the center, into a meadow, and cross Meadow Run on a wooden bridge. The paved path bears right to the site of the stockade, which looks exactly like the one built here by Washington during a conflict between the English and the French for control of the Ohio River Valley in 1754. Washington was only twenty-two years old at the time. Enter the stockade and listen to the audio program, which dramatizes the events of this short-lived conflict. Washington's men had a successful raid on the French prior to coming here to hunker down and defend themselves against retaliation. When the French came it was not long before the English surrendered due to their losses, the only time in Washington's career that he had to surrender his troops.

Leaving the stockade, head into the meadow in front of it on a bark-chipped path, go straight ahead at a trail junction with the Outer Loop trail on the right, then bear right a short distance before the trail curves left and becomes a mowed grass path. Go uphill, cross a dirt access road at about 0.5 mile, and soon come out into an open meadow, teeming with bees, butterflies, and wildflowers. A variety of honeysuckle with translucent red berries grows thickly here, as do many varieties of flowers, including the orange butterfly weed. Rabbits and groundhogs duck for cover as you follow the Inner Loop Trail. At a junction where a side trail joins with the Outer Loop Trail, go

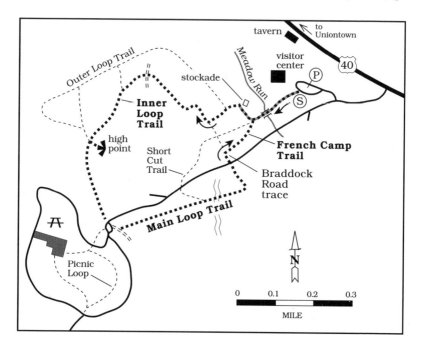

straight, heading steadily uphill. Huge purple thistles are a favorite of the honeybees here.

Reach another junction and bear left. At 0.7 mile see a side trail on your left, which you can take to reach the high point of the park, with a nice view of the entire park under the pleasant shade of a maple tree. There is usually a good breeze here and it is a good spot for a lunch.

Continuing on ahead, pass some nice blackberry patches and reach the top of the hill by the Picnic Loop Trail and the park road. Cross the pavement, head left onto the dirt road, and see the trail on the left. Take this trail—the Main Loop Trail—down through the woods, full of maples and tulip poplar, passing a junction with the Short Cut Trail on the left at 1.2 miles. Cross a pipeline cut and descend a gentle hill to the edge of a pine plantation. Cross the park road and continue downhill. You are now on the old Braddock Road trace. This road was built by Washington as he advanced toward the Great Meadows. The next year the road was improved by General Braddock as he marched out of Fort Cumberland, Maryland, and extended to the Monongahela River near present-day Pittsburgh. Turn right at the next junction and take the paved path back to the parking lot where you began.

46. Lazear Trail

Type:	Day hike
Difficulty:	Moderate (steep hill)
Distance:	2.4-mile loop
Hiking time:	2 hours
Elevation gain:	400 feet
Hikable:	Spring–fall
Map:	Ryerson Station State Park map
Rest rooms:	Toilets, water at trailhead
Fee:	None

There is something especially satisfying about hiking up to a good view. The Lazear Trail offers a chance to do just that. The trail climbs up on a shaded old road to an excellent overlook of Ryerson Station State Park and its R. J. Duke Lake and Dam. Height is not the trail's only attraction. On the way up you can pause at the Wolf Tree, a grand 300-year-old white oak. There are several other large trees of

Hikers who reach the overlook are rewarded with a view of the whole park.

similar stature on the rest of the hike, which is a pleasant shaded downhill walk to Munnell Hollow, returning along the edge of the lake where quiet hikers might surprise a wading great blue heron. The state park has a campground, a swimming pool, rowboat rental, and a children's playground near the trailhead. (Note: The state park has just begun a naturalist program; for information on guided hikes and programs, call (412) 428-4254.)

To reach Ryerson Station State Park, take Interstate 79 south from Pittsburgh to PA 21 west. Where PA 18 and PA 21 split just past Rogersville, take PA 21 west 15 miles and turn left on SR 3022, then right on Fordway Road, where signs lead to the beach. Park in the furthest, lowest parking area.

The trail begins to the right of the parking area, at a bulletin board at the edge of the woods. It begins to climb immediately. The trail is named after the family who used to own this land before it was acquired as a state park in 1958. The state park itself is named after Fort Ryerson, which was located nearby and used as a refuge from Indian raids in the late 1700s.

As you climb, watch for deer trails, faint but sure paths that usually contour the side of a hill—it is easier walking that way than straight up. Soon come to a junction with the Fox Feather Self-guided Trail. Turn right and continue uphill on Lazear Trail. Scattered spruces help shade the climb.

After 0.2 mile, arrive at the Wolf Tree on the right, just in time for a break. A bench here allows hikers to rest, reading the interpretive sign and contemplating how the area must have looked when this was one of the few trees around. This old oak is called the Wolf Tree because its dense shade allows no significant undergrowth, so it towers above all else like a lone wolf. However, there are some white oak seedlings on the hillside to your left. Which of these will be here in 300 years?

Continue the climb, careful to avoid poison ivy vines on some of the tree trunks. The trail flattens briefly and you pass the Orchard Trail on the left and head uphill again. Soon come to a sunny open area where fox grapes have just about taken over. This is a favorite grouse habitat because of the good cover the vines provide; trees, however, do not fare so well here, as the weight of the choking vines smothers them.

The climb is a bit gentler now, and you can listen for the blue jays' raucous calls. At 0.8 mile, reach the overlook, which is, at 1,389 feet, the highest point in the park. From here you can see the lake, dam, road, and the town of Wind Ridge perched on the opposite ridge. This is a nice breezy spot for a well-deserved rest, snack, or lunch. For a short hike, turn around here and backtrack.

The rest of the trail continues downhill following the old road. Wild rose and sassafras line the trail. It switchbacks once and continues past another old oak, which is in the black oak family. White oaks have rounded lobes and elongated oval-shaped acorns; those in the black oak family have pointed lobes and short, fatter acorns. Can children tell the difference?

Pass numerous other interesting trees on the way down, some contemporaries of the Wolf Tree. Hikers may surprise a groundhog, as I did, munching on tender grass. Reach the first junction with the Tiffany Ridge Trail on the left at 1.2 miles, and soon parallel Munnell Hollow Creek, which flows into the lake. Pass the second junction with Tiffany Ridge Trail. You might notice bee balm with its raggedy-looking petals that bloom in July—both bees and butterflies favor its flowers. At the next junction, at 1.7 miles, the Fox Feather Self-guided Trail goes left and you go straight. You are now on the tail end of Fox Feather's self-guided loop. Pass the Iron Bridge Trail on the right and go straight, soon reaching the lakeshore.

Keep watch for great blue herons, which nest downstream from the dam and are frequently seen wading here. Beavers swim around the area in the early evenings. The trail follows the grassy edge of the lake, where there are nice spots for fishing. Pass a short connecting trail to Fox Feather Self-guided Trail that comes in from the left. Continue along the lakeshore. Come out at the picnic area by the playground, and head back to the parking lot on the gravel path.

Other trails of interest: Three Mitten Trail leaves from SR 3022 near the park office. The somewhat hilly loop follows Polly Hollow creek on its east side, then loops back through the forest, with a total distance of about 1.1 miles.

The Pine Box Trail, which begins at the east edge of the park's border, passes by an old cemetery with graves from the 1800s. The trail is just over 1 mile long, but the cemetery is reached in about 0.2 mile from the trailhead, located on SR 3022.

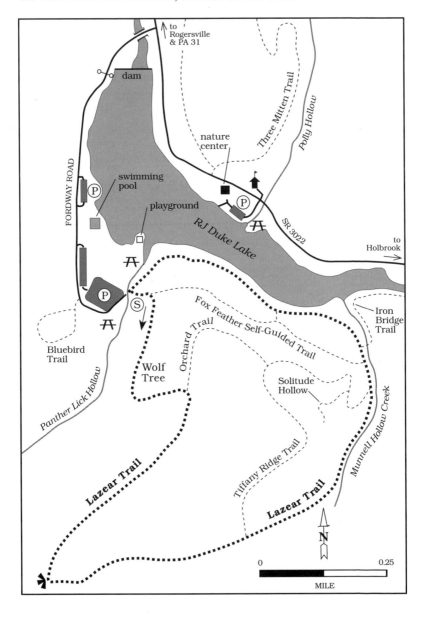

47. Jennings Trail, Old Wagon Road, and Meadow Trail

Type: Day hike
Difficulty: Easy–moderate (hills)
Distance: 2-mile loop
Hiking time: 1.5 hours
Elevation gain: 200 feet
Hikable: Spring–fall
Maps: Wildflower Reserve map; Raccoon Creek State Park map
Rest rooms: Toilets, water at nature center
Fee: None

When April showers are over and you want to see May flowers, this is a great place to be. From late April through mid-May, many of the 500 species of wildflowers found in this reserve in Raccoon Creek State Park can be found blooming. But if you cannot go in spring, you will still find plenty of wildflowers along trails that lead through a variety of habitats—from oak–hickory forest to floodplain forest to a cool stroll along Raccoon Creek. All this, 25 miles from Pittsburgh. The hike described here follows the perimeter of the reserve. Many shorter loops are possible. Before your hike, stop at the nature center and look at the photographs of some of the flowers you might look for. (Note: For information about interpretive activities call (412) 899-3611 or (412) 899-2200.)

To reach the Wildflower Reserve, take US 30 west from Pittsburgh past the town of Imperial. Go 7 more miles, past the town of Clinton, then make a right into the Wildflower Reserve, 0.2 mile before reaching the main park road on the left. Park at the parking lot to the right, before the end of the driveway, which leads to a private residence.

Begin on the Jennings Trail, which heads uphill from the east (right) side of the parking lot. The trail ascends on an old road to a small cabin in a clearing. Pass by the cabin and bear left across the field to where the trail re-enters the woods. Pass the narrow Deer Trail on your left and follow the path downhill, rather steeply, switchbacking twice before leveling off somewhat.

Pass an unnamed side trail on the left and cross a seasonal creek. At 0.3 mile come to a junction with Big Maple Trail on the left, but

This stuffed black bear in the nature center serves as reminder that there are still plenty of live black bears in Pennsylvania.

go straight. The trail parallels US 30 for a while. The dampness of this area makes it good mosquito habitat, so come prepared with bug stuff if you are hiking in summer. Soon cross a small creek on a wooden bridge. Notice the ground cedar, which is sometimes mistaken for seedlings. This is as big as it gets!

The trail veers away from the highway and draws closer to Raccoon Creek. Notice 3- to 4-foot-high maple viburnum. In fall, it is one of the few plants whose leaves turn purple. Its purple berries, also found in fall, are not edible. Reach a set of wooden steps which lead steeply down to the floodplain area. It can be muddy and wet here in the spring. The trail bears left, and nettles and jewelweed line the trail. Look for numerous old oaks scattered throughout this young forest. At one time this would have been an open area, marsh, or field, with a few scattered trees that are now the forest sentinels.

Reach a junction and turn right onto the Old Wagon Road at nearly 0.8 mile. At a junction of trails reached in another 0.1 mile, go straight on the Meadow Trail. As you come to the meadow, you are greeted with a burst of flowers—black-eyed susan, goldenrod, Queen Anne's lace, coneflower, yarrow, and a host of other flowers thrive here in the sun. In the summer the plants get quite tall. A loop bears left around the perimeter of the meadow, but is occasionally too overgrown between mowings. Pass a junction with the other end of the Hickory Trail on your right and all too soon you are through the meadow. Kids may enjoy looking for unusual trees. I noticed one that was completely hollow in the middle, being supported only by its ends. Look for trees that curve in different ways. Think about what caused them to bend.

Come to a junction with the Jennings Trail at 1.1 miles and take

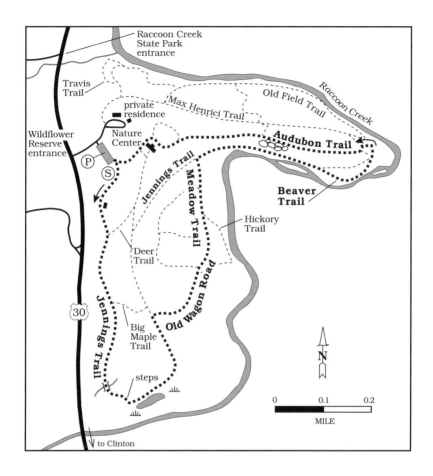

a right onto it. Following Raccoon Creek, notice the artistically sculpted limestone cliffs on the left. Along the creek you can see evidence of past beaver activity. Chiseled old stumps still bear the distinctive teeth marks. Next, at a junction with the Beaver Trail, go right. Along this trail you might not see beavers, but there are several close-up views of Raccoon Creek.

Curving left, rejoin the Jennings Trail and continue alongside the limestone cliffs. Soon reach a junction that leads to the Audubon Trail. Continue straight ahead past a few old oaks and young trees. Cross a seasonal creek on a bridge and at the next junction at 1.5 miles, go left uphill fairly steeply and soon join the Audubon Trail. The trail switchbacks, then reaches the top of a ridge, from which you can see the creek far below on your left. Pass an obscure junction with a connecting trail to the Old Field Trail. Pass a large red oak. A rope handrail begins on the right. Past a row of white pines the path comes out to a clearing behind the nature center, where the trail ends. Take the connecting path back to the parking lot to complete your hike.

Other trails of interest: The Mineral Springs Trail loop is a short, self-guided trail accessed off a park road just south of the park office on PA 18. It features a waterfall and the Frankfort Mineral Spring near the beginning of the loop. The area was a nationally known health spa during the 1800s and once attracted thousands of visitors who believed in its healing powers.

---

48. Loop, Indian Pipe, and Warbler Trails

Type:	Day hike
Difficulty:	Easy–moderate (rocky)
Distance:	1.5-mile loop
Hiking time:	1.5 hours
Elevation gain:	150 feet
Hikable:	Spring–fall
Map:	Todd Sanctuary map
Rest rooms:	Toilets by cabin, no water
Fee:	None

Just an hour north of downtown Pittsburgh is a 172-acre preserve managed by the Audubon Society of Western Pennsylvania. Children enjoy the cool walk through the hemlock forest described here, or may choose any of the other 5 miles of trails that go through a ravine, by a meadow, by a pond, or by an old quarry. Though this land was donated to the society in 1942, it seems to be a well-kept secret. The sanctuary is sometimes closed during deer season because the areas surrounding it are popular with hunters. The cabin at the trailhead serves as the visitor center and the site of interpretive programs, which are offered regularly. (Note: For information on the interpretive activities, call (412) 963-6100.)

To reach Todd Sanctuary from Pittsburgh, take PA 28 north to exit 17 and turn right on PA 356. In less than 1 mile, turn right onto Monroe Road, which is not signed but is at the corner where a restaurant and real estate office are located, as well as signs to Buffalo

Golf Course. Go 1.3 miles to a fork in the road and bear right onto Kepple Road. Follow it 1.7 miles to the sanctuary driveway on the right. This driveway is easy to miss; it is just before the crossing over Knixon's Run, and if you cross over Hesselgesser's Run, you have gone too far.

All trails begin at the left corner of the parking lot. Enter the woods here and turn right on an old road. Head downhill about 0.1 mile and turn left on a path over a mossy bridge leading to the cabin visitor center.

Take a right in front of the cabin visitor center onto the Loop

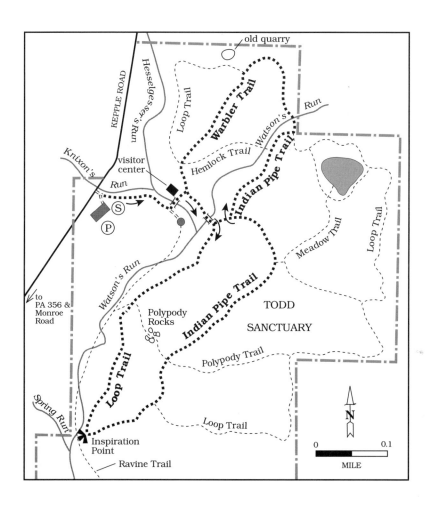

Trail along a hedgerow of honeysuckle and soon head into the woods under hemlock trees. The trees here are young but healthy. Take a minute to smell their sweet, piney scent.

Cross a bridge over Watson's Run, then make a right at the trail junction and head uphill through the hemlocks. The trail is a bit rocky here and the rocks may be slippery, so wear your boots. Pass a short trail on the right that leads to the Ravine Trail, and pass the Polypody Trail on the left at 0.3 mile. Go straight, pass another side trail, and bear left uphill. The trail follows the rolling contours of the ridge you are on. After 0.6 mile, reach Inspiration Point, which probably used to have a great view of the ravine below but is now obscured by the hemlocks that have grown up around it, so there is not much to see. Watch small children here, because there is no guardrail along the edge of the dropoff.

Follow the trail as it makes a hairpin turn back along the ridge. At a trail junction, leave the Loop Trail, which was closed off when I hiked the trail, and go straight onto the Indian Pipe Trail. Look for Indian pipes, naturally, along the trail. They are tiny pipe-shaped flowers without chlorophyll. Hikers might notice the nests of tent caterpillars, which have infested some of the trees in this area.

At a junction with the other end of the Polypody Trail, continue straight ahead, perhaps noting the 3-foot-tall maple viburnum shrubs. Now head downhill and pass a junction with the Meadow Trail at 0.9

Rustic Todd Sanctuary is a well-kept secret in southwestern Pennsylvania.

mile, which leads to a pond. Bear left through the hemlocks and make a right at the next trail junction, still on the Indian Pipe Trail. Many ferns grow here, which probably also means that there are plenty of deer, which eat most underbrush except ferns. Pass a junction with the Hemlock Trail on your left and soon come to the end of the Indian Pipe Trail at a т intersection at 1.1 miles. Make a left onto the Loop Trail and hop across Watson's Run, which is shallow here.

Proceed up a gentle hill. Children might want to look for evidence of young tree seedlings taking root, such as hickories and oak. At the next trail junction, go straight onto the Warbler Trail at 1.3 miles, which leads gently downhill past a dense grove of hemlocks. Notice how few things can take root in this shade. Finally, reach a trail junction with the Hemlock Trail, go straight, then immediately turn left onto the Loop Trail again, which brings you out to the cabin visitor center.

Other trails of interest: The Ravine Trail follows Watson's Run in a small ravine surrounded by hemlocks. This 0.6-mile trail often crosses the creek as it continues to the edge of the sanctuary boundary, where hikers must turn around and retrace their route. Reach the trail by going to the end of the old road from the parking area.

49. Spring Hollow Trail

Type: Day hike
Difficulty: Easy
Distance: 0.5-mile loop
Hiking time: 45 minutes
Elevation gain: 50 feet
Hikable: Year-round
Map: Beechwood Farms Nature Reserve map
(Audubon Society of Western Pennsylvania)
Rest rooms: Toilets, water at nature center
Fee: None

City-bound folks do not have to go far to get a taste of nature at Beechwood Farms, 10 miles northeast of downtown Pittsburgh. This area is managed and supported by the Audubon Society of Western Pennsylvania, which does not charge a trail fee, but offers special programs and benefits to members, such as access to its lending library, discounts at its store, year-round activities, and children's environmental birthday party programs. Most of the hikes in the reserve are appropriate for children. The Spring Hollow Trail is a great place to start exploring the area. This loop trail goes through a meadow to a small pond, into the woods, and up to a small ridge where everyone enjoys the treetop view from a unique high observation deck, and back through meadows where wildflowers and songbirds abound. All trails are well signed and it is almost impossible to get lost. (Note: Trails are open dawn till dusk daily. The store and center are open Tuesday to Saturday 9:00 A.M. to 5:00 P.M., Sunday 1:00 to 5:00 P.M. For information on programs call (412) 963-6100.)

From Pittsburgh, take PA 28 north, exiting onto PA 8 north (Butler exit). At the first stop light, turn right onto Sharps Hill/Kittanning Road. This road becomes Dorseyville Road. Go 4.3 miles, passing two stop signs. Beechwood Farms Nature Reserve is on the left.

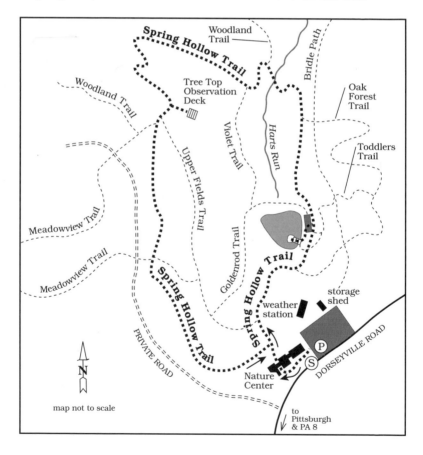

The Spring Hollow Trail, which begins behind the nature center, is reached by walking through the center's breezeway to the trailhead. Go straight on the bark-chipped trail through a meadow full of thistles, milkweed, and blackberry bushes. Cross a boardwalk and note the signposts with numbers that correspond to a discovery guide for sale in the store. The Oak Forest Trail comes in from the right. See the pond and pass a huge old silver maple, probably 100 years old. The Toddler's Trail crosses Spring Hollow Trail in the vicinity of the pond. After 0.1 mile, take the side trail on your left to see the pond. A walkway leads into the water for a close-up view of the cattails and young willow trees. Frogs "garumph" amongst the water plants.

A hiker enjoys the treetop view.

Back on the trail, pass numerous young sugar maples mixed in with some very old oak trees. Head downhill and then straight at a junction with the other end of the Oak Forest Trail. Children can get a close-up view of a huge old stump trailside whose insides are disintegrating.

Soon spot shallow Hart's Run, then cross over it at 0.2 mile. Watch for witch hazel, which has some odd habits. It blooms in the fall rather than spring, and its seed pods explode around Halloween. No wonder it got that name.

At a junction with the Woodland Trail, turn left and proceed uphill now. Pass the Violet Trail, which is on the left, and cross a seasonal creek. Numerous dead snags provide homes for nesting birds and food for woodpeckers. Look for a short informal path on the left where little ones can poke their heads into a very large hollow log. Continue uphill as the path passes between an oak and chestnut oak. Note the different shapes of leaves for these related species. At the top of the hill at 0.3 mile, take a side trail on the left to the fantastic Tree Top Observation Deck, which lets you see what it is like to look down on the forest.

Soon reach an open meadow and a junction with Upper Fields Trail on the left and Meadowview Trail on the right—go straight. There are many wildflowers here, including Queen Anne's lace, yarrow, crown vetch, goldenrod, honeysuckle, milkweed, dog daisies, morning glories, field daisies, buttercups, teasels, and blackberries. Pass another junction with the Meadowview Trail and go straight, downhill past some elm trees. Return to the back of the nature center where you began.

Other trails of interest: The Toddler's Trail is a 0.1-mile trail accessible from the pond area; it leads young hikers on a slightly hilly path through a maple forest, through a field, and by the pond.

The Goldenrod Trail is named for the flowers that grace the trail in autumn. This 0.1-mile trail is also accessible at the pond and passes through land that is in transition from field to forest.

The Oak Forest Trail branches off the Spring Hollow Trail just before the pond. This 0.5-mile trail meanders through a mature oak forest in an area that was once the site of a home.

---

50. Blazing Star, Prairie Loop, and Massasauga Trails

Type:	Day hike
Difficulty:	Easy
Distance:	1-mile loop
Hiking time:	1 hour
Elevation gain:	50 feet
Hikable:	Spring–fall
Map:	Jennings Environmental Education Center map
Rest rooms:	Toilets, water at trailhead
Fee:	None

Once a vast prairie extended from the Rocky Mountains to the Appalachians, but few people in Pennsylvania have ever seen a prairie in their home state. Yet a few relict prairies still remain, one of them in the midst of Jennings Environmental Education Center, north of Moraine State Park. This prairie is home to the spectacular blazing star flower, which is uncommon in the state. These rose-purple flowers that bloom in late July to early August are the reason the reserve was established. The reserve is also home to the endangered but shy Massasauga rattlesnake, but hikers are unlikely to see one of these. Remind children it is illegal to pick flowers here, or to disturb the Massasauga rattlesnake. Rather, if you see it, give it wide berth and walk away quietly. A nature center with interpretive programs is located across the highway from the trailhead. (Note: For information

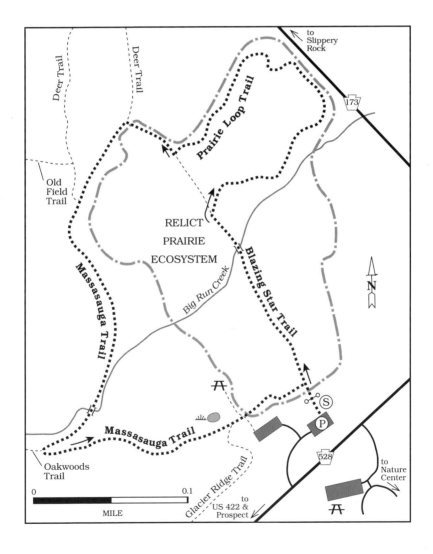

The Blazing Star flower

on programs call (412) 794-6011.) There are many loop hikes here of varying length to explore.

To reach the reserve, take Interstate 79 north from Pittsburgh, exiting onto US 422 east. Follow US 422 east to PA 528 north near Prospect. Once on PA 528, go 7.5 miles and turn left into the parking lot. The nature center is located about 0.1 mile farther along PA 528, on the right.

The Blazing Star Trail begins at the stone gate memorializing Dr. Otto Emery Jennings, a famous botanist and naturalist who first discovered the prairie area here. Pass through the gate and come almost immediately to a junction with the Massasauga Trail. You will come back this way, but for now go straight on the Blazing Star Trail. The blazing star is visible shortly. It has the unusual characteristic of blooming from the top down. By late July the prairie is alive with its purple color. Many other colorful wildflowers bloom here as well— children may enjoy counting how many different flowers they can find, or how many different colors.

At 0.2 mile, cross a plant-choked tributary of Big Run Creek on a bridge, and just after reach a junction with the Prairie Loop Trail. Take this loop to the right, which follows around the northeastern perimeter of the prairie. This prairie was believed to be established here around 2000 B.C. on the site of a prehistoric glacial lake basin. The soil here is made up of fine silt, sand, and clay deposited by glaciers. It is believed that the poor growth conditions present at the

prairie site prevented the establishment of forest growth and permitted the plants here to remain. This is the only public and protected relict prairie in the state of Pennsylvania.

At the end of the Prairie Loop Trail, reach a junction at 0.4 mile and turn right, back onto the Blazing Star Trail. Come to another junction, this time with the Deer Trail, and turn left onto the Massasauga Trail, into the forest. Notice the dramatic temperature difference now that you are under the trees. After 0.5 mile, come to a junction where the other end of the Deer Trail turns off to the right; continue straight ahead, still on the Massasauga Trail.

Many different colors of fungus grow here under the moist forest shade. Children may be interested in looking for different-colored mushrooms. I saw white, brown, red, green, and orange mushrooms here.

The small tributary to Big Run Creek comes in on your left and hikers may hear the loud buzzing of cicadas up in the treetops. Cross this creek on a wooden bridge at 0.6 mile and shortly afterward bear left at a junction with the Oakwoods Trail. Still on the Massasauga Trail, go uphill a short distance and pass a side trail with a miniature swampy pond on the left. Right after, go straight at junction with the Glacier Ridge Trail at 0.9 mile. See a picnic pavilion on the left and go straight, back to the junction where you began. Turn right and walk back to the parking lot.

---

51. Hell's Hollow Trail

Type:	Day hike
Difficulty:	Easy
Distance:	1 mile one way
Hiking time:	45 minutes–1 hour one way
Elevation gain:	100 feet
Hikable:	Spring–fall
Map:	McConnells Mill State Park map
Rest rooms:	Toilets, water at McConnells Mill Historic Site
Fee:	None

Despite the devilish-sounding name, Hell's Hollow Trail is a pleasant short hike through a cool, moist forest ending at a cascading waterfall by an old kiln. The path is flat and gentle, except for the final descent to the falls. Wear hiking boots here, despite the short distance, because the smooth rocks are usually wet and can be very slippery. The area is full of beautiful wildflowers in the spring—around Mother's Day is a good time to catch the spring flowers at their peak. The stream is home to native brown trout, one of the few streams left in the state that has naturally reproducing brown trout.

To reach the trailhead, take Interstate 79 north from Pittsburgh to US 422 west. Take US 422 west, then make a left on PA 388 south. Immediately past the intersection with PA 65, turn left onto Shaffer Road. At the stop sign, go straight and at 1.4 miles from PA 388, turn right into the parking lot.

Begin the hike at the edge of the parking lot, heading into the woods past the picnic table to a bridge that crosses Hell Run. Bear right on the wide, flat trail. For this short distance you are on the North Country National Scenic Trail, a long trail that will traverse seven states when completed. At 0.2 mile, the North Country Trail (in the park called Slippery Rock Gorge Trail) bears left and you turn right, crossing Hell Run again on a bridge.

The creek is on your left now as you pass by some stinging nettles. If you get stung, try wiping some juice from the jewelweed plant,

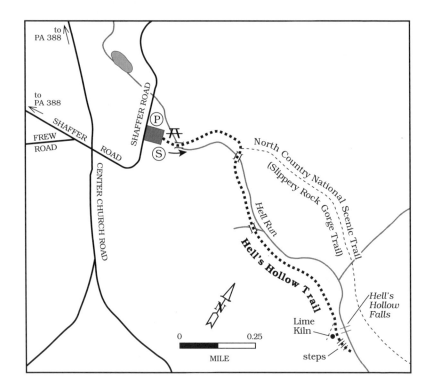

A view of cascading Hell's Hollow Falls from the end of the trail

which grows in the same area as nettles, onto the sting, which it helps soothe. The forest here is composed of red and sugar maples (pretty in the fall), shagbark hickory, and other young hardwoods.

Descend a gentle hill and cross a tributary of Hell Run on a bridge. Go uphill very briefly and then downhill. On the left the creek begins to undercut its limestone banks. Soon reach a nice pool on the left, which is home to native brown trout. (Swimming is not permitted in the park.) The creek drops quickly now. Reach a junction at 0.9 mile, where the right fork goes a short distance to a railing that encircles the top of the open lime kiln. Take the left fork and descend steeply now. On the right, three-quarters of the way down, reach the bottom of the lime kiln, which hikers can duck into to see the view from inside.

Wooden steps lead the rest of the way to Hell's Hollow Falls. The falls are gentle cascades over mossy ledges. Look for frogs and other creatures here. It is also a good place to look for fossils. To get back to the trailhead, backtrack.

Other trails of interest: The Kildoo Trail is a 2-mile trail with a paved self-guided section that makes a loop around a portion of Slippery Rock Gorge. The trailhead is at Covered Bridge in the center of the park, which can be reached by following Interstate 79 north from Pittsburgh to US 422 as described above, then turning south on McConnells Mill Road as it heads into the state park.

177

Northwest Pennsylvania

Wood lilies reward hikers along the Shenango Trail.

52. Shenango and Towpath Trails

Type:	Day hike
Difficulty:	Easy
Distance:	1.5-mile loop
Hiking time:	1.5 hours
Elevation gain:	100 feet
Hikable:	Spring, fall
Map:	Shenango Trail map
Rest rooms:	Toilets, water at Army Corps of Engineers campground a few miles west on Rutledge Road
Fee:	None

Follow the route of the historic Erie Extension Canal for this short loop trail that takes you along a portion of the Shenango Trail through fields and woodlands and returns along the old towpath by the banks of the placid Shenango River. Located on the east side of the Shenango Reservoir, this trail features a bounty of wildflowers in the spring, and a suspension bridge with plenty of swing that youngsters will want to cross and recross. In summer this trail is best avoided, because it is overgrown in places with poison ivy and has many mosquitoes. (Note: To obtain the map for this hike, send $1 to Shenango Conservancy and Outing Club, 94 East Shenango Street, Sharpsville, PA 16150.)

To reach the trail, take PA 60 north from New Castle, and at West Middlesex continue north on PA 18 to the village of Clark. Turn right at the light in Clark onto PA 258 east. Go 5.7 miles and turn left onto (dirt) North Bend Road. Go 0.9 mile further and park in the gravel lot on the right, just before North Bend Road intersects Rutledge Road.

The trail begins across the road from the parking area, under a wooden arch. This is the beginning of the Shenango Trail, which follows the Shenango River northwest for 8 miles, ending near Kidds Mill Covered Bridge. As the hike begins, walk through fields thick with vegetation and see staghorn sumac, wild cherry, and wild roses along the path. Look for bluebirds along the pathway in this area, as there are nesting boxes set up for them here. A side trail cuts back on your right—this area is the site of an 1850s iron furnace called Big Bend Furnace. Its owners used the canal to transport their goods. Nothing remains of the furnace now except for small mounds of slag fill, which can be found with a little exploring. Big Bend, a town located near here at about the same time, grew up and had short-lived success as a canal boom town.

Be alert for cottontail rabbits hopping down the trail ahead. Young aspen trees with trembling leaves and greenish-tinted bark line the trail here. Cross under a road bridge and continue ahead. Look for cardinals and other songbirds here where there is plenty of food and shelter.

Pass some pines and come to a short suspension bridge at 0.2 mile. The bridge has railings but no side fencing, so remind children to hold onto the rails to avoid slipping. On your left pass the Towpath Trail—you will return this way. Continue straight ahead, past spruces

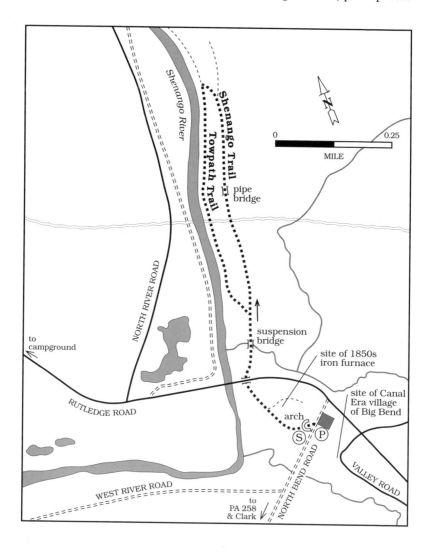

and pines encroaching on the meadow. Children may recognize the call of the rufus-sided towhee, whose song sounds like "drink your tea, drink your tea. . . ."

Next enter the young forest. Children can look for the few old oaks that were here during the days of the canal, when this was an open meadow. Passing a gas pipeline and an unofficial side trail on the left, cross a seasonal creek on a pipe bridge. Pass the other end of the unofficial side trail, and reach a trail junction where a path continues ahead through the field. Turn left, heading downhill, to stay on the Shenango Trail. Look for deer tracks in the moist dirt. The narrow end of their heart-shaped prints points in the direction in which they were walking.

At a signed trail junction with the Towpath Trail, make a hairpin left turn onto the Towpath Trail at about 0.7 mile. The Shenango River is on the right now, quite close. Look for animal burrows on the creek bank and near the trail. Pass by a marshy area, then recross the gas pipeline. Before and after the gas line is the most well-preserved section of towpath. Canal boats were towed by horses and mules in the river channel on the right, which in canal days was dammed and nearly at the level of the towpath. There was not a separate canal channel on the left, as there was along most of the canal route, although it looks that way.

Children enjoy looking for evidence of past beaver activity along the banks of the river. Several trees were felled by the chisel-sharp teeth of these amazing creatures who make their homes in the bank of the river. Along the river, they do not need to build dams and lodges because the water level is already high enough that they can float their logs around with no trouble. Sometimes a bank den still has sticks piled on top of it. Maybe it looks more like home that way.

Rejoin the Shenango Trail on your left at 1.3 miles and, on the way back, look for insect galls in the weeds and wildflowers along

This arch marks the beginning of the Shenango Trail.

the trail. Slice one of these open to see what bug lives inside. Retrace the route across the suspension bridge back to the trailhead.

Other trails of interest: The Seth Myers Trail in the Mahaney Recreation Area nearby is a self-guided trail of about 0.6 mile with a most whimsical interpretive guide, available from the Army Corps of Engineers Office.

53. Beaver Dam and Tamarack Trails

Type:	Day hike
Difficulty:	Easy
Distance:	1.5-mile loop
Hiking time:	1 hour
Elevation gain:	20 feet
Hikable:	Spring–fall
Map:	Pymatuning State Park map
Rest rooms:	Toilets, water at park office and Jameson Camp (just west of trailhead)
Fee:	None

This short, easy hike in Pymatuning State Park offers a close-up view of a beaver dam as the trail follows the edge of a bay in Pymatuning Lake, crosses the bay at the beaver dam, where recent beaver activity might be observed, and loops back into the woods where white-tailed deer are frequently seen bounding off through the trees. The loop described here combines the nicest features of both the Beaver Dam and Tamarack Trails. It is best to do this hike early or late in the day for the best chance of observing ducks, beavers, deer, and other wildlife. If you go in midsummer, however, take along some insect repellent. The mosquitoes in this moist area are hungry.

To reach Pymatuning State Park from Erie or Pittsburgh, take Interstate 79 to Meadville and take the US 6/322 west exit. In Conneaut Lake continue on US 322 west to Jamestown. Just past Jamestown, enter the park and turn right at signs for the park office, onto West Lake Road. Follow West Lake Road, pass the first trailhead for the Tamarack Trail, and at 1.9 miles from the park office, park along the right side of the road across from the second trailhead, on the left.

The Tamarack Trail begins at the large trail map. Head into the woods on a wide path. In about 100 yards, come to a junction. Bear

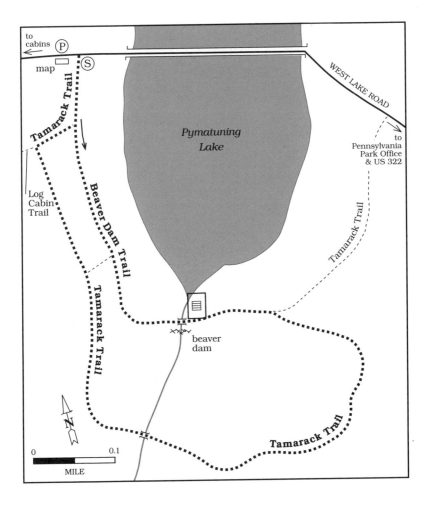

left on the Beaver Dam Trail. Black raspberries line the wide, bark-chipped trail. A bay of Pymatuning Lake comes into view shortly on the left. Soon a trail that cuts over to the Tamarack Trail joins on the right. Continue straight ahead and come upon the beaver dam, which spans the narrow end of the bay. This is a good place to surprise a mallard duck with her ducklings. A wooden bridge follows along right on the edge of the beaver dam after about 0.4 mile.

Beaver dams are remarkably strong and can remain intact years after the beavers have moved on. In areas where beaver dams have flooded roads or railroad beds, some troublesome dams have had to be removed with backhoes, or even dynamite. It is no wonder, then, that many modern man-made dams resemble beaver dams in shape and placement. Wildlife biologists theorize that beavers are stimulated to build and repair dams by the sound of rushing water. An active dam is vigilantly maintained by addition of fresh sticks and mud.

As you cross the bridge, the Beaver Dam Trail bears left and follows the edge of the water to an observation deck. Look around for recent beaver activity. A large tree in the bushes to the left had been recently girdled by a beaver when I hiked this trail. Perhaps the beaver will return and fell the whole tree by the time you hike this trail.

The trail next curves right, away from the water, while an unofficial side trail continues left along the water's edge. Stay right and, at the trail junction at 0.5 mile, meet with the Tamarack Trail and take its right fork. Look for white-tailed deer browsing in this area, and see if your children can spot any of the numerous deer trails that criss-cross the trail. Deer trails are fainter, but still recognizable as paths. Why do you suppose deer would want to use trails, too?

Watch for poison ivy as you walk through the quiet woods. Sadly, all the tamarack trees for which this trail is named are dead. Head down a gentle hill and cross over a creek on a wooden bridge at 1 mile. Look for animal tracks in the moist soil here. Besides deer tracks, you might see raccoon prints, which look like tiny human handprints. A wetland is on your right and you soon cross a seasonal creek, and then pass a short connecting trail that leads to Beaver Dam Trail. Still in deep shade, reach a junction at nearly 1.4 miles and make a right where the Log Cabin Trail goes off to the left, then in about 50 yards at the junction with the Beaver Dam Trail, take a left and head back to the trailhead.

Beaver dams like the one this bridge is built against are amazingly strong.

54. Gull Point Trail

Type: Day hike
Difficulty: Easy
Distance: 2-mile loop
Hiking time: 2 hours
Elevation gain: None
Hikable: Spring–fall
Map: Presque Isle State Park map
Rest rooms: Toilets, water at Budny Beach
Fee: None

Presque Isle is a peninsula that curves northeast along the city of Erie's waterfront and lays claim to several special features. It is a favorite stopover point for thousands of migratory birds in the spring and fall, and is considered one of the ten best birding locations in the state. Over 300 species have been identified here. Peak migrations are usually May 10 through 25, and in September. A walk on sandy Gull Point Trail takes hikers to several locations along Thompson Bay in the wildlife sanctuary, where many birds may be observed year-round, including the impressive great blue heron. An observation deck permits folks a view of the seasonal nesting area. The National Geographic Society says that Presque Isle has the second best sunsets in the world, which adds to its appeal. Eleven lifeguarded beaches are available for swimming and sunning during the summer months. Note that there are no dogs allowed on this trail, because it runs through a wildlife sanctuary.

To reach Presque Isle State Park, take Interstate 79 north from Meadville to PA 5 west. In a short distance take PA 832 north and go 1 mile before entering the park. To reach the trailhead, take the main park road—which starts as Peninsula Drive and changes to Marina Drive, West Fisher Road, and Thompson Drive—counterclockwise around the edge of the peninsula 7 miles until you reach the Budny Beach parking lot. Park in the first lot on the right.

The trail begins at the upper righthand corner of the parking lot by a large interpretive sign that has some interesting facts about the area. Children may be fascinated to know that the peninsula ended right at Budny Beach a little over 100 years ago. Wind and waves have created this sand spit that continues to grow daily, at the rate of 1 mile every 200 years. Children can look for where the cottonwood trees are smallest—these areas are the most recently formed parts of the sand spit. They may also enjoy discussing the fate of the *Thelma*,

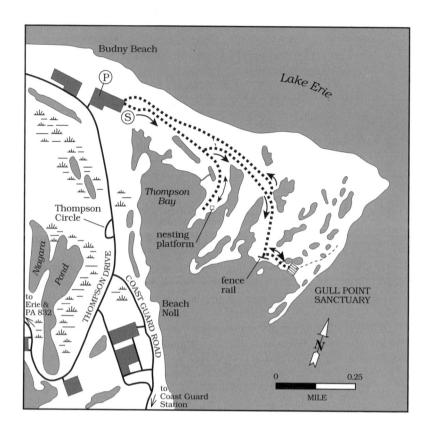

a ship that ran aground in 1956 near here. Enter the trail at the edge of the sign, onto a sandy path lined with fragrant wild roses and young paper birches.

Soon reach a trail junction and take the side trail on the right to the tip of a small peninsula in Thompson Bay. Hear frogs singing in an unseen small pond on the right. Grass that is taller than you are lines the path on both sides. (This grass, which resembles pampas grass, is called "phragmites," or common reed. It is an invasive plant that appears everywhere.) Quickly come to the point, where a nesting platform may hold an osprey nest made of sticks. Go to the water's edge and get out the binoculars, scanning the shoreline for wading birds. A beaver lodge was active in the west side of the bay when I hiked here; look for evidence of recent cuttings along the lakeshore and for the lodge far out in the water. Did your children know that beavers build their lodges in the water to protect themselves from enemies? The entrances to the lodge are underwater and the beavers swim in and out year-round, even if the water is iced over.

Backtracking to the trail junction, take the right fork ahead through some high bushes. Pass a junction for a trail that cuts back to the parking lot on the left. (This is a possible turnaround point, for a shorter hike of 0.7 mile.) Listen for the sound of big ships in the Port of Erie blowing their horns. Children may be interested to know that before there were interstate highways, Erie was an important port because big ships could reach here from the Atlantic Ocean via the Saint Lawrence Seaway and the Erie Canal to bring goods to western Pennsylvania, Ohio, and beyond.

Passing whispery young willows, soon reach another trail junction at 1 mile and bear right. Pass a pond ringed with phragmites. The trail becomes very sandy from here on, and as you near the edge of the peninsula, you have a view of heavily industrialized Erie. Reach a fence rail with a view of the bay and note signs that warn you to stay off the shoreline between April 1 and November 30, the prime nesting time for birds. (Walking on the trail and observation deck is permitted.) Continue ahead bearing left, careful to stay on the trail until you reach the observation deck at 1.25 miles. From here you can look to the edges of the sand spit, watching for a variety of birds gathered here. Year-round you may see gulls and Canada geese; at other times the arctic tern and other migratory fowl may be observed.

A trail heads north from here to the shore, but backtrack on the trail to the last intersection by the phragmites-lined pond at 1.5 miles. This time, take the northern path to the right, which follows the edge of the beach. See dunes on the left and hear the waves from the shore. Children may enjoy playing detective and looking for bird tracks in the sand. Reaching the other end of the short connecting trail on your left, bear right and begin to see views of Lake Erie. Though the water looks tempting, swimming is not allowed here; wait until you return and head for Budny Beach. The trail ends by the interpretive sign.

A view of the shorebird nesting area from the observation deck along Gull Point Trail

Other trails of interest: The 5.8-mile paved Multi-Purpose Trail begins at the park entrance and is very popular with bikers and in-line skaters. This trail ends at Perry monument.

55. Wetland Trail

Type: Day hike
Difficulty: Easy
Distance: 1-mile loop
Hiking time: 1 hour
Elevation gain: 100 feet
Hikable: Spring–fall
Maps: Wildcat Hollow map; Oil Creek State Park map
Rest rooms: Toilets along trail; toilets, water at park office
Fee: None

There are probably no wildcats left in Wildcat Hollow, but there are plenty of other creatures in this second-growth forest. This area would have been unrecognizable 130 years ago when oil was first discovered in the area. The original forest was leveled to make room for oil derricks and the town of Petroleum Center, which grew up almost overnight and earned a reputation for being one of the wickedest towns east of the Mississippi. Thankfully, everything is quiet now and the area is once again a forest. This trail loops around the base of Dance Hall Hill, following the edges of a cattail marsh surrounding Wildcat Run where some of the remains of the heyday of the oil boom remain. This trail is wet in the spring and best hiked later in the summer after mud season is done, or in the fall when things are drier. Still, expect to get feet wet somewhere along the trail.

To reach Oil Creek State Park from Oil City on US 62, take PA 8 north, turning right onto PA 227 east in Rouseville. At the village of Plumer, turn left onto SR 1004, which winds through a residential area, passing smaller roads first on the left, then the right, entering the park in about 1 mile, and continuing on the road 1.7 miles further to the park office in Petroleum Center. Stop at the visitor center and go through the display area, where there are several child-oriented displays. Then drive past the office, cross the steel bridge over Oil Creek, and turn left onto SR 1007. Cross the railroad tracks and park in the lot on the left.

The trail begins across the road from the parking lot. Pass by the wooden posts and walk on an old road grade to reach rest rooms and a picnic pavilion. Right past the pavilion, where the two ends of the Wetland Trail loop meet, bear right onto the Wetland Trail; you will return to this junction on the way back. The Wetland Trail follows an old road grade alongside Wildcat Run. Notice the many wild grapes draped on the trees, which provide food for many species of birds. Red raspberries, which ripen in mid-July, line the path, as do tall interrupted ferns.

The road grade continues ahead, but turn left into the cattail wetland at 0.3 mile. Children enjoy feeling the soft cattails, which grow right next to the trail. Wooden boardwalks keep your feet mostly dry. Watch your step along the trail, as old oil pipes still crisscross the ground, and some of them intersect the path.

The trail curves left, then right, as you walk amongst young hardwood trees. Before long begin to climb and reach a wet area where forget-me-nots thrive. Look to see if you notice the shiny remains of oil that are still on the surface of some of the wet areas. When the oil boom was in its prime, oil overflowed into all the creeks in this area. Reach a junction with the Oil History Trail and go left at just over 0.4 mile to remain on the Wetland Trail. Continue to climb, looking for the shagbark hickory, with its characteristic shaggy-looking bark that hangs in loose gray strips. Mushrooms thrive in such environments. If you look closely at some of the mushrooms, you might notice that tiny bites have been taken out of them by some of the current woodland residents. Do not ever try this yourself, however.

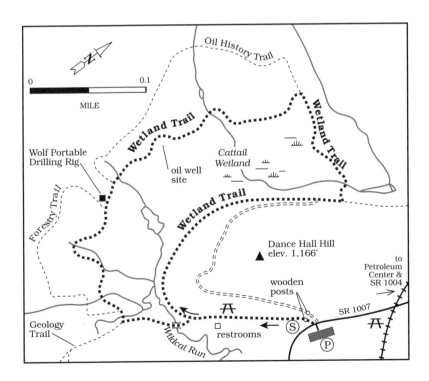

This old oil drilling rig was considered 'portable' in the 1800's.

Soon reach a junction with an old oil well on the left. Remains like these are common throughout western Pennsylvania. Next reach a junction with the other end of the Oil History Trail on the right after 0.6 mile. Continue straight ahead on the Wetland Trail and almost immediately come upon a structure with huge pulley wheels. This machine, called the Wolf Portable Drilling Rig, was once topped with a 20- to 30-foot tower. An engine powered the rig, which was used for drilling oil wells or for pulling up piping once a well was finished. Children may be surprised to hear that this rig was considered portable—it certainly does not look that way by today's standards. The Forestry Trail heads off to the right from here; stay to the left on the Wetland Trail.

The trail heads downhill now and crosses a creek. Mayapples are plentiful here in the spring. Cross another small creek and pass a junction with the other end of the Forestry Trail on your right. Cross yet another small creek and then reach the Geology Trail at nearly 0.8 mile. Bear left on the Wetland Trail and cross Wildcat Run on a wooden bridge. Continue ahead and soon reach the beginning of the Wetland Trail loop, where you took the path now on your left. Stay to the right and follow the old road back to the parking area.

Other trails of interest: Three other trails in Wildcat Hollow, each having its own theme, branch off the Wetland Trail. The 0.25-mile Oil History Trail contains remnants of the once-prosperous oil industry. The 0.25-mile Forestry Trail winds through a second-growth forest. The more rugged 1-mile Geology Trail passes several rock piles and climbs about 300 feet to a rock outcrop, then returns through a rock underpass.

The Delzell Trail is a 1-mile-long self-guiding historical trail that begins at the park office in Petroleum City, where an interpretive pamphlet is available.

56. Longfellow, Joyce Kilmer, and Rhododendron Trails

Type:	Day hike
Difficulty:	Moderate (some steepness)
Distance:	2-mile loop
Hiking time:	2 hours
Elevation gain:	500 feet
Hikable:	Spring–fall
Map:	Cook Forest State Park map
Rest rooms:	Toilets, water at trailhead
Fee:	None

If walking through a forest of ancient trees has ever felt like a spiritual experience, there is a chance to relive that feeling while walking through the Forest Cathedral in Cook Forest State Park. This area is home to one of the largest virgin white pine and hemlock stands in Pennsylvania. This land was purchased in the 1920s by a citizen group and the state legislature for $650,000, a sizable amount of money then. This walk takes you up through the heart of the Forest Cathedral, downhill through the rhododendrons, and across a suspension bridge, returning along picturesque Toms Run. The hike described here is only one of many possible—there is a network of short trails throughout the Forest Cathedral and in other locations in the forest, most of which are short and very scenic. The park has an interesting visitor center in an old log cabin and a playground at the trailhead.

To reach Cook Forest State Park from the east, take Interstate 80 west from DuBois and get off at exit 13 at Brookville and head north on PA 36. Go 17 miles to Cooksburg. Near the bottom of the hill in Cooksburg, bear right onto Vowinckel Road and go about 1 mile to the Log Cabin Inn visitor center on the right.

After touring the natural history and logging artifacts in the visitor center, head up the Longfellow Trail, which leaves from the right side

Everyone loves a suspension bridge!

of the building and goes by the peace tree, a symbol of goodwill and peace between Native Americans and United States citizens. Bear to the right past the memorial fountain, which tells the history of the park's purchase. Cross a small creek on a wooden bridge and begin a gentle climb uphill on a wide path. Soon begin to see very large trees, some of which are up to 350 years old and 200 feet tall. Pass the B Trail on the right and bear left. A small spring runs across the trail and in a bit you pass the D Trail on your right.

Come to a sign explaining what happened in 1956 when a tornado ripped through and felled many old trees. Continue climbing, more steadily now, and pass an intersection with the G Trail, but continue on ahead through the silent giants. About 0.1 mile past that junction, turn left on the Indian Trail for 50 yards, then at 0.4 mile take a right on the Joyce Kilmer Trail, which leads into the very heart of the Forest Cathedral. Notice how quiet it is here, how lush and green. The trail levels out, then descends gently to a junction. At 0.5 mile, turn right on the Rhododendron Trail, named for the bushes that bloom in mid-July.

Continue downhill through great old trees. These trees were here when William Penn was purchasing Pennsylvania lands from the Native Americans. Imagine being in Pennsylvania when the state was covered with trees like these. Would you like some of these trees in your backyard? Children may enjoy laying down on the ground and looking up to get a better view of the treetops, which even then are hard to see. Soon begin to hear and see Toms Run on your right, below you. Not long after the creek comes into view, at about 1 mile take a short unnamed side trail that veers right and leads to the suspension bridge, which is visible from the trail. Kids love this bridge because of its bounce, and parents feel safe knowing it is well fortified with handrails and wire fencing to prevent accidents. A drinking fountain is located at the far end of this bridge. Go right on the Birch Trail, which leads to a small parking area on the right in 0.2 mile. Paved Vowinckel Road is on the left. At the small parking area, 1.5 miles from the trailhead, head to the right, downhill, on the Longfellow Trail (the Birch Trail continues ahead parallel to the road), and cross a bridge over a tributary to Toms Run. Follow the trail on the west side of Toms Run, where there is a wide, shallow pool, nice for wading. Very shortly reach the second bridge in this area, where you do not cross (this is the continuation of the Longfellow Trail), but stay on the west side of the creek on an unofficial but very well-used cross-country ski trail.

Take this trail along the creek about 0.4 mile to a parking area by picnic shelter number 1, just past 1.8 miles. Cross Toms Run on a bridge and follow the footpath left another 0.2 mile to the trailhead parking lot.

Other trails of interest: Shorter versions of the loop described above can be made by branching off on the D Trail and following it to the southern portion of the Longfellow Trail, crossing the bridge over Toms Run and following the cross-country ski trail north back to the Log Cabin Inn parking area.

The 2-mile Liggett Trail, with its few hills, is good for families with small children. The trail parallels Toms Run, beginning at Breezemont Drive just south of the Log Cabin Inn parking area, and comes out on Toms Run Road.

The Seneca Trail is a 1.2-mile trail that leaves the highway at Cooksburg at the northern end of the Clarion River Bridge and leads to the fire tower and Seneca Point. A mineral spring is located on this trail along the Clarion River.

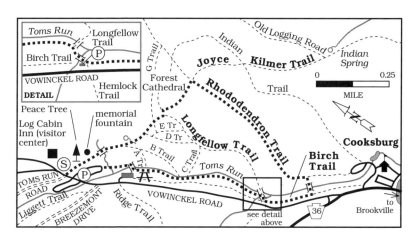

57. Songbird Sojourn Interpretive Trail

Type: Day hike
Difficulty: Easy
Distance: 1.7-mile loop
Hiking time: 1.75 hours
Elevation gain: 100 feet
Hikable: Spring–fall
Map: Buzzard Swamp hiking map
Rest rooms: Toilets, water in Marienville
Fee: None

Do not be put off by the name—there is plenty of life around Buzzard Swamp. The area is managed for wildlife and recreation, and a portion of the swamp is closed to people so waterfowl can propagate freely and undisturbed. The Songbird Sojourn Interpretive Trail is a very pleasant self-guided trail that lies northwest of the wildlife propagation area and the swamp, so the opportunities for viewing wildlife and hearing songbirds are good. Note that the area is best avoided during hunting season. The loop meanders through the forest, crossing several small streams. An interpretive brochure is available at the trailhead or from the Marienville ranger station, on Route 66 several miles north of Marienville.

To reach the trailhead, from Interstate 80 near Clarion, follow PA 66 27 miles north to Marienville. At the center of town, turn onto South Forest Street (by the Pennzoil station) and go 1.3 miles until you get to the Buzzard Swamp entrance sign. Turn left onto (gravel) Forest Road 157 and go 2.4 miles to the parking area on the left.

The Songbird Sojourn Interpretive Trail begins at the east end of the parking lot by the metal gates. Pass the gates and enter the trail near the sign at the edge of the woods on a wide, mowed path. Enter the forest underneath young beech trees surrounded by bracken ferns. The trail is blazed with blue and gray diamonds. The blue blazes belong to another trail that coincides with this one; the gray diamond blazes are what you follow for the entire length of the trail. Notice the many cherry trees in this area. The trees here have recently suffered from an attack by caterpillars that eat all their leaves. The cherry trees grow new leaves. All forests go through periods of pest infestation, which last for a few years, then end as the pests die out.

As the path narrows, children will want to keep their eyes and ears wide open to look for white-tailed deer, which have some trails and bedding areas near here. Reach the first of numerous Norway spruces, whose many short, spiky needles seem to droop from the long branches. At a trail junction, turn left to stay on the Songbird Sojourn Interpretive Trail, as the blue-blazed trail goes straight ahead. Following only gray blazes now, amble through many ferns into a young hardwood forest, mixed with Norway spruces and hemlocks. The trail is still flat here, though hikers need to watch their steps to avoid tripping on the many roots that cross the trail.

Pass by a small open area and take note of a red pine, with its long needles. A portion of the tree's bark has been scraped off and the injury appears to be "bleeding" sap, the lifeblood of the tree. Listen for the trill of chipmunks chattering in the trees. Hop over a small creek and watch for ground pine and princess pine, which blanket huge areas of the forest floor along the trail. Birds chirp and flit among the trees. Soon come to a small stand of pine, hemlocks, and spruce. Children may want to look for pine cones that have been eaten by squirrels and chipmunks. The core of the cone looks much like a corncob once it has been stripped.

Reach another trail junction by marker number 5 at 0.4 mile. Again, bear left, following gray and blue blazes for a while. There are many young yellow birches here. Cross a seep and head uphill. Cross another seep and come to a third trail junction at 0.6 mile. At this junction, the blue-blazed trail leaves for good, heading to the right, and you bear left, following only gray diamond blazes the rest of the way.

Look for dark green Christmas ferns in a shady forest floor. You are walking under many maple and oak trees now. Listen for woodpeckers as you pass marker number 7. The path climbs gently and

This attractive sandblasted sign marks the beginning of the trail.

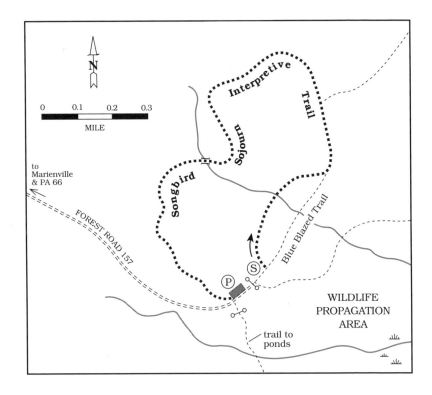

winds through the quiet forest. At the top of the hill, a small creek is flowing parallel to the trail on the right. The trail levels and on the right catch glimpse of a clearing, kept open for wildlife to browse. Passing through many yellow birch saplings, walk into the woods again and head downhill. At marker number 11, hikers may notice a large spring that begins just to the right of the trail.

The trail flattens out somewhat. Children may enjoy looking for mushrooms on the trees when the weather is damp. After marker number 13, at 1.3 miles cross a small creek on a wooden bridge, which is slippery when wet. The trail then curves left through delicate-looking New York ferns, a pale spring green color. Walk briefly through some more birch saplings and witch hazel, then head down a gentle hill. On the left, hikers can see the meadow through the trees where the sound of songbirds is ever present. Continuing downhill, come back out to the parking area where you began. Children may spot orange and black striped wooly bear caterpillars on the grasses at the edge of the parking area in the fall. Legend has it that the thicker the caterpillars' coat, the colder the winter to come.

58. River Trail

Type: Day hike
Difficulty: Easy
Distance: 1.6-mile loop
Hiking time: 1.5 hours
Elevation gain: 150 feet
Hikable: Spring–fall
Map: Clear Creek State Park trail map
Rest rooms: Toilets at trailhead; toilets, water at campground
Fee: None

This loop trail follows the wide Clarion River on the edge of Clear Creek State Park through evergreens and rhododendrons. The river can be viewed on two levels; on the lower part of the loop you walk directly along its banks and on the upper portion you hike through the mossy forest from which there are views of the river below. An optional spur at the top of the loop is available for hikers who wish to go a little further. The hike is described to follow the loop clockwise, but the trail can easily be hiked from either direction, or the riverside portion can be hiked out and back, for those who prefer to stick close to the water's edge. Note that hikers should use caution in this area during hunting season.

To reach Clear Creek State Park, take Interstate 80 west from the Dubois area, and get off at the Brookville exit, heading north on PA 36. In the small village of Sigel, make a right onto PA 949 and go 4 miles to a junction with the main park road by the park office on the left. Make a left and go 1.5 miles further, passing the museum (which has interesting exhibits about the history of the area) and

The Clarion River looks cool and peaceful on a summer day.

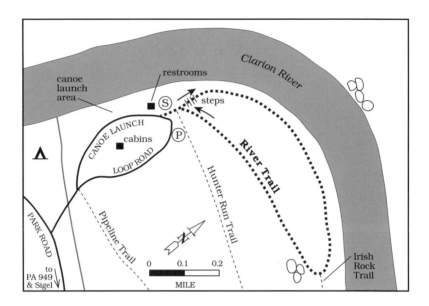

turn right on a small drive which has signs directing to the canoe launch area. Bear right at the γ intersection. Park on the right side of the drive, at the northern end of the loop driveway by a small building with rest rooms in it, or park further along the drive by the canoe launch and walk back toward the rest rooms to the trailhead.

The trail begins at the northern end of the loop driveway, by the rest rooms. The River Trail begins on an old dirt road. Pass the Hunter Run Trail on the right, and after about 50 yards, reach a γ intersection where the trail begins its loop. Take the lefthand fork and head down the terraced trail to the riverside. The Clarion River appears quiet here. Its current flows at about 4 miles per hour. The trail you take follows the edge of the river very closely, ducking under the eastern hemlock trees and rhododendrons, which bloom profusely in the summer and are quite beautiful. The narrow, flat trail affords good views of the river and the life in it. On a still day, hikers can see the tiny concentric circles formed by the water striders that skim lightly across the surface. Watch for some boulders across the river that jut out into the water. Fishing is permitted along the riverbanks.

Pass through an area where numerous trees blew down in the summer of 1995, when strong winds came through. The park roads and many trails were blocked following that storm. Watch for interesting boulders across the river. The trail curves right, going gently uphill and away from the very edge of the river. The rolling trail heads through some hardwood forest. Listen for the tapping of woodpeckers in some of the dead trees.

At nearly 0.9 mile, reach a junction with the Irish Rock Trail. (It is a spur that continues 1 mile further, heading moderately uphill along the Clarion River, passing Irish Rock, a landmark where rafters used to tie up their craft at night, and ends at the park boundary.) At the junction, head to the right, uphill, to stay on the River Trail. The trail switchbacks once and climbs up to some moss-covered boulders, frosted with rhododendrons on top. As the trail flattens again, thick moss covers the forest floor, some of it spongy sphagnum moss.

Soon the River Trail flattens. Catch glimpses of the Clarion River below. Descend easily. Thick wild grapevines hang from the trees and you pass a sign asking hikers not to damage the vines, as they are beneficial to the forest. Continue downhill as the path widens as you find yourself on an old road again. The trail flattens and you return to the junction where the loop began, and go straight to return to the parking lot.

Other trails of interest: Ox Shoe Trail is a .8-mile self-guided historical loop focusing on logging; the trail begins by the phone booth at the ranger station. A brochure is available at the interpretive center.

---

59. Buckaloons Seneca Interpretive Trail

Type:	Day hike
Difficulty:	Easy
Distance:	1-mile loop
Hiking time:	50 minutes
Elevation gain:	None
Hikable:	Spring–fall
Map:	Buckaloons Seneca Interpretive Trail map
Rest rooms:	Toilets, water at trailhead
Fee:	None

Families with toddlers appreciate this interpretive trail in the Buckaloons Recreation Area, on the site of a former Seneca Indian village. The trail follows the Allegheny River through the picnic area and along Brokenstraw Creek and Irvine Run on the outskirts of the campground through a restfully shady forest with many large trees. Rabbits, chipmunks, and songbirds abound and there are numerous places to leave the trail to explore the creeks. The recreation area has

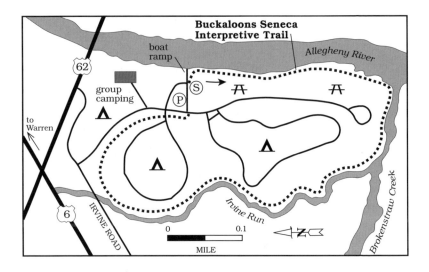

camping and picnicking. Check with the campground host in summer for copies of the interpretive brochure, which are posted at the trailhead during the rest of the year.

To reach Buckaloons Recreation Area, take US 6 west from Warren to the US 62 south exit. At the end of the exit ramp, make a right and almost immediately make the first right in about 100 yards, onto Irvine Road. Go 0.1 mile and turn left into the recreation area. Continue on the park road to the boat ramp by the Allegheny River.

Begin the hike across from the boat ramp. The Allegheny River is a major waterway that flows from New York to Pittsburgh, where it joins with the Monongahela and Ohio Rivers. It is no accident the Seneca Indians found this spot to be a good location for a village. Children may want to think about what things made this a good village site for the Senecas. Are there any reasons why it might not have been a good site?

The trail along the river is indistinct, basically following the edge of the grass and hedgerows alongside the picnic area. There are numbered markers along the trail that correspond to numbers in the interpretive brochure. Pass some very old white oaks, some with hollow areas underneath. There are some very large white ash trees here. Notice the many chipmunk holes near the trail. If kids are eager to get to the water, look for a side trail to the left that leads to a nice pebbly area where kids can get their feet wet in the river. This is a fun place to practice skipping rocks.

Notice the many sycamore trees, which thrive in moist areas. Their bark tends to shed, leaving a mottled camouflage-like appearance.

An angler tries his luck in the Allegheny River.

Children may find pieces of the shed bark in the ground. Soon come to the confluence of Brokenstraw Creek and the Allegheny River at 0.3 mile. Pause here to see if the Canada geese are around. Geese are not the only ones that like the river—many people enjoy fishing in this area. The trail curves right here, following alongside a split-rail fence that parallels Brokenstraw Creek a short distance. Then curve right some more and follow Irvine Run along the edge of the campground. Several small side trails lead to the campground, though you remain largely out of sight of it. Soon you are right up on the edge of Irvine Run, looking over the eroding bank into the small creek. When a storm comes, it carries away a little bit of the bank each time.

Pass an unofficial side trail on the right, then one on the left, and at both of these continue straight ahead, under low-hanging branches that form an arch over your head. Look for brilliantly colored tiger lilies near the trail on the left in midsummer. Stroll by some apple trees and white pines and descend slightly, past a grove of hemlocks. Soon afterward, the trail curves to the right, away from the creek, as you walk parallel to the campground road. Watch for cottontail rabbits and groundhogs. Cross the campground road, and soon reach the trail's end at the corner of the boat ramp parking lot.

60. Interpretive Trail

Type: Day hike
Difficulty: Easy
Distance: 1.1 miles (long loop); 0.25 mile (short loop)
Hiking time: 1 hour (long loop); 20 minutes (short loop)
Elevation gain: 100 feet
Hikable: Spring–fall
Map: Hearts Content Scenic Area Interpretive Trail map
Rest rooms: Toilets, water at trailhead
Fee: None

Just the name Hearts Content invokes a peaceful, quiet feeling. Indeed, a short walk among the giant hemlocks, beeches, and pines in this lush area of Allegheny National Forest is soothing. Some of the trees here are 400 years old, a remnant of virgin timber that was donated to the federal government in the mid 1920s by a logging company. Now part of a 120-acre scenic area, Hearts Content is designated a National Natural Landmark. This interpretive trail has

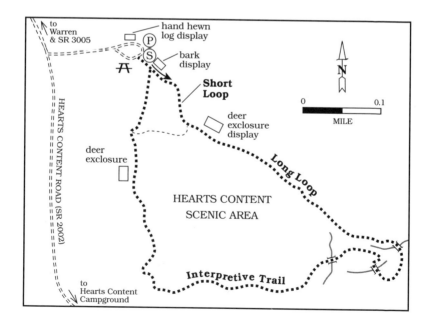

signs, interpretive displays, and fenced-off demonstration plots along the route that explain the composition of the aging forest and how it is changing as a result of influences from deer. There is a picnic area at the trailhead, a campground across the street, and other trails nearby leading into Hickory Creek Wilderness Area and to cross-country ski trails.

To reach Hearts Content Scenic Area, take US 6 east from the Erie area to Warren, and turn right at the Mohawk Avenue light, uphill, bearing right onto Pleasant Drive (SR 3005).

Some of the trees in Hearts Content were here before George Washington was born.

Stay on Pleasant Drive; though several roads branch off to the right and left, stay on the main road 11.9 miles until you reach a Y intersection. Bear left onto (dirt) Hearts Content Road (SR 2002). Follow the signs and go 3.7 miles on the dirt road until you reach the parking lot on the left for Hearts Content Scenic Area. Trailhead parking is here. Look for the hand-hewn log display and kiosk with interpretive brochures. Hearts Content Campground is 0.1 mile further down Hearts Content Road, on the right.

The Interpretive Trail begins at the upper lefthand corner of the parking lot. Almost immediately come to a junction where the two ends of the loop meet, and take the left fork by a hands-on display that allows children to touch different kinds of tree bark. Gnarly old beech trees are mixed in with the hemlocks and white pines, and a lush carpet of ferns grows underneath. The beeches here are dying from beech bark disease complex. An insect called beech scale bores into the bark to feed on the sap. The hole allows disease to enter the tree and kill it. Quite a few of the old beeches are already dead. Though it is sad they are dying, notice how the new openings in the forest now let in sufficient sunshine for saplings to grow.

Pass the junction at 0.1 mile where the short loop goes off to the right and circles back to the trailhead; take this turnoff for the shorter option. For the long loop, continue straight ahead and soon come to a fenced-in area, a deer exclosure with an interpretive display. An old picture here shows how the forest in this very spot used to look. Can children notice in what ways it is different now? There are so many deer in this area that they eat many species of trees and young plants, except ferns, which is why they grow in abundance. Challenge the children to see how many healthy hemlock and pine seedlings they can spot along the rest of the trail. These trees are the forest of tomorrow.

Proceed easily downhill by some ancient hemlocks and white pines. An easy way to tell which is which is to look at what type of cones surrounds the trunk. Hemlock cones are only about ½ inch long; white pine cones are much bigger. Notice some of the decaying trees that have become nursery trees, fertile soil for young hemlocks and mosses. Pass a plaque, then cross three small creeks on wooden bridges at 0.4 mile. Look for wood sorrel, which looks like four-leaf clover and whose leaves taste tangy. Also look for a huge old beech and white pine that have grown together, locked in an embrace. Seashell fossils can be found in the rocks that were imported to surface the trail.

Soon come to another deer exclosure. Fencing portions of the forest is one way to protect young trees from deer. Another way is to plant the seedlings inside 4-foot-high plastic tubes. When the saplings get tall enough to emerge from the top of the tubing, they are no longer as tender a treat for hungry deer. Look for these tubes along the side of Hearts Content Road.

Not far after passing the exclosure, meet the other end of the short loop at 1 mile. Continue ahead, past a stand of tall oaks that line the edge of the field, and cross the grass back to the parking area.

---

61. Penny Run Trail

Type:	Day hike
Difficulty:	Easy
Distance:	1.5-mile loop
Hiking time:	1.5 hours
Elevation gain:	150 feet
Hikable:	Summer, fall, winter (muddy in spring)
Map:	Chapman State Park map
Rest rooms:	Toilets, water in picnic groves
Fee:	None

Chapman Dam is a pleasant getaway year-round. This pretty, wooded path heads up a draw and down the other side, crossing many creeks and seeps on nine picturesque wooden bridges. Red maples,

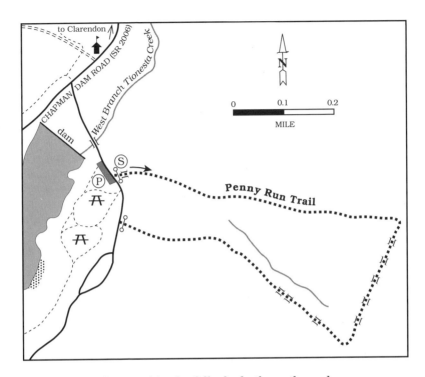

which turn brilliant red in the fall, shade the path, as do many young hemlocks with their feather-soft needles. Chapman State Park itself has many attractions for families. It offers several other trails in addition to this one, and has a lifeguarded swimming beach in the summer, an ice-skating area and sledding hill with a warming hut in the winter, and a family campground.

To reach Chapman State Park, take US 6 east from Warren to Clarendon and make a right at the only light in town onto SR 2006, Chapman Dam Road. Take the road 4.8 miles to the park and turn left just past the park office. Go about 0.2 mile further to the dirt parking lot on the right. The trailhead is across the road from the parking lot.

The trail begins at the wooden gate and immediately crosses a bridge. The path is wide as it heads into the woods, soon bearing right to begin a gradual ascent through the maple trees. Hikers may notice the land dropping away below. Grasses and ferns cover the ground. In the spring, many tiny seeps cross over and under the path, draining into the creek below. This makes for unpleasantly muddy hiking.

Soon reach a grove of hemlocks. Hikers may notice how mossy and lush this area is from all the moisture. Continue on the blue-blazed

A young hiker samples the raspberries in Chapman Dam State Park.

path through Christmas and New York ferns. In a while the trail finishes its ascent and bears right at almost 0.6 mile, meandering through the hemlocks. Cross the second bridge and then cross four more bridges. In the winter the snow weighs down the tree branches so they droop to almost touch the bridge railing, making this look like a real winter wonderland.

The trail curves right again, now heading easily downhill at 0.8 mile. Cross another bridge and notice a stream on the right, paralleling the trail. Cross two more bridges and come to a more open area of the forest. As the trail winds down, come to a gate at 1.4 miles, which you pass around, and make a right on the paved park road, following it another 0.1 mile to the parking lot where you began.

Other trails of interest: An interesting hike begins at the Gamelands Trail and follows the Lowland Trail to Tionesta Creek, where there is a suspension bridge. Access is from the other end of the lake. The gated dirt road there is the beginning of the Gamelands Trail. Follow the trail to the Lowlands Trail and turn left to the creek. Beaver can sometimes be observed in this area. Raspberry bushes line the Lowlands Trail in the summer months. To return, backtrack for a round trip of about 0.8 mile.

62. Morrison Trail

Type: Day hike or overnight
Difficulty: Moderate–challenging (distance, elevation change)
Distance: 5.3-mile loop
Hiking time: 4 hours
Elevation gain: 500 feet
Hikable: Spring–fall
Map: Morrison Trail Map
Rest rooms: Toilets at trailhead; water at marina on way in from Warren
Fee: None

This pretty loop trail in the lush Allegheny National Forest is an excellent place to try out a family backpacking adventure. The trail can be hiked in a day, but camping is permitted along the trail. The Morrison Trail follows Morrison Run through mountain laurel, ferns, young oaks, and hickory trees to a junction with another branch of Morrison Run, then heads uphill along that branch through some interesting bouldery areas. There are some nice places to camp in the area near the confluence of the two branches of the creek, as well as several sites along the west branch of the creek. In spring, the creek is considered good for brook trout fishing, and there is a chance to view wildlife along the trail, especially white-tailed deer, ruffed grouse, wild turkey, and perhaps even a black bear. In fall remember to wear blaze orange, or hike only on Sunday, because the trails in this forest are heavily used for hunting.

To reach the trail, take US 6 east from Warren to PA 59 east, which has signs directing to Kinzua Dam. Pass the dam and marina and continue up the hill to the ridgetop on PA 59 east, passing the Rimrock Overlook Road on the right. Go 0.5 mile past the Rimrock Overlook turnoff (SR 454) and turn right into the well-signed parking area for the Morrison Trail. Maps are available at the trailhead. (Note: The Bradford Ranger District office, a good source of Allegheny National Forest information, is at the junction of PA 59 and 321 4.4 miles east of the trailhead. Maps are also available from Allegheny National Forest Headquarters at 222 Liberty Street in Warren.)

The trail leaves from behind a sign with the trail map on it. Cross three small creeks and notice the heavy growth of ferns on the forest floor, evidence that there are many deer in residence here. (Ferns are one thing that the deer do not like to eat.) Soon come to a trail junction

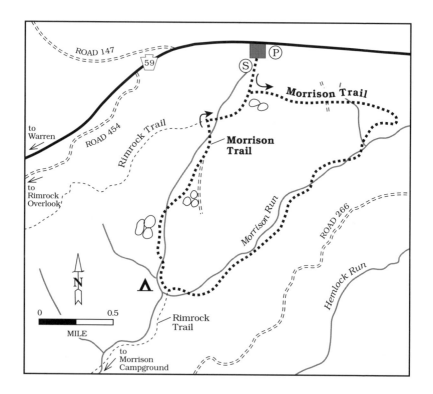

by a large boulder. You will return to this point on the way back. Bear left by the boulder and climb through thickets of mountain laurel, which bloom in early summer. The climb is short and soon the trail flattens out. Look for chipmunks scattering as you hike. Also look for tracks out of the tunnels made by wood borers in the fallen trees.

Head down a gentle hill, through more ferns. Children may hear a squeak tree—one that is rubbing against another tree, making an eerie creak when the breeze blows. Watch also for artists conch, a fungus whose smooth, white underside is sometimes used to draw or paint upon. Continue downhill, crossing an old road, and notice low-bush blueberries. Cross a creek as you find yourself on the side of a hill, headed down toward Morrison Run. Children may enjoy looking for daddy longlegs, harmless insects with very long legs that tickle when they walk on you. The trail switchbacks and soon afterward at 1.6 miles you hop across a tributary to Morrison Run. There are no bridges on creek crossings here, so take your time on the mossy rocks, which can be slippery when wet.

Now walk along the banks of Morrison Run. Soon come to an ambiguous junction with an informal trail that leads left to a field of ferns. Watch the blazes and bear right across Morrison Run. Walk on an old road for a time, which tends to be muddy most of the year. Notice a campsite on the left, cross two small creeks, then cross Morrison Run again. Walk on an old road now. A smaller creek is on your left parallel to the trail, and Morrison Run is on your right. Notice the ironwood trees here, also known as "musclewood." Can children tell why it is called that by looking at the rippled bark?

Cross Morrison Run once again. Look for trees that have burls in them—large growths on the trunks or branches. The flat trail reaches a junction with the west branch of Morrison Run at 3.4 miles. There are numerous campsites in this area; look for a spot at least 200 feet away from the water. There is a nice, fairly flat, open area across the creek to the left, uphill. There are no outhouses here, and water must be filtered or boiled. This junction is also a good place for a picnic or to play in the water.

For those desiring a longer day hike or overnight trip, the Rimrock Trail loop joins the Morrison Trail here, and continues downhill 2 miles to Morrison Campsite, on the banks of Kinzua Creek, which has outhouses, well water, and designated campsites with picnic tables. The campsite is accessible by boat as well as trail. (The Rimrock Trail loop by itself—from the same trailhead as the Morrison Trail—is 5.5 miles; it joins with the Morrison Trail loop near the end of the main hike.) The entire two-trail loop, adding the Rimrock Trail Loop onto the Morrison Trail, is 10.8 miles.

To continue on the Morrison Trail hike, turn right without crossing Morrison Run, and head up a gentle hill through a stand of hemlocks. Soon cross this branch of Morrison Run, noticing a tributary on the left. Cross the creek and notice a side trail that goes right. Continue uphill past some interesting boulders that are fun to climb on. Watch for woodpecker trees in the area. Notice the trees that are splayed against the side of the boulders, holding on for dear life with their amazingly long roots. Cross Morrison Run and notice milky quartz pebbles from the conglomerate rocks in the area.

Head up a steep hill

Ferns cover the forest floor along the Morrison Trail.

past some more boulders and come to a junction with an old road. Bear left here as the trail flattens out somewhat. Continue up a more gentle hill and watch for witch hazel shrubs along the way. Bear right around an old blow-down and cross a small seep, heading into mountain laurel thickets again. In spring look for three-petaled trillium flowers, with their three wide leaves. This is one of the prettiest springtime flowers that grows here, preferring shady areas.

Cross Morrison Run again and shortly thereafter come to a trail junction at just over 4.6 miles. The blue-blazed Rimrock Trail Loop comes in on the left (for hikers who took the combined loop described above, this is where you rejoin the main hike). Go right and cross Morrison Run yet again, continuing uphill. Note the old apple trees in an old meadow on the left. Soon come to the trail junction where you began, and bear left, back to the parking area.

Other trails of interest: The Rimrock Overlook, which you pass on the drive to the Morrison trailhead, has a great view. Take the Rimrock Overlook road up to the parking area and head downhill 0.25 mile on the trail to the numerous overlooks, which offer nice views of the Allegheny Reservoir and the surrounding ridges. This is a good vantage to view the sunset from, as it faces west.

63. Tionesta Interpretive Trail

Type: Day hike
Difficulty: Easy
Distance: 1.5 miles (long loop); 0.5 mile (short loop)
Hiking time: 1.5 hours (long loop); 30 minutes (short loop)
Elevation gain: 100 feet
Hikable: Spring–fall
Map: Tionesta Scenic Area Interpretive Trail map
Rest rooms: Toilets, water at National Forest Service Office in Sheffield
Fee: None

Tionesta National Scenic Area is one of the few areas in the Allegheny National Forest that has remained largely untouched by the logging industry. This section of virgin forest is a remnant of the original forest that once covered 6 million acres on the Allegheny plateau in Pennsylvania and New York. The interpretive trail here

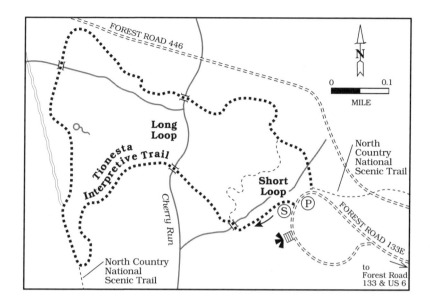

meanders through old-growth stands of stately hemlocks and beeches, some of which are 200 to 400 years old. Though the interpretive signs have fallen into disrepair, the trail is in good shape, skipping over four small creeklets and offering plenty of interesting natural features along its way. A portion of the trail coincides with the North Country National Scenic Trail. A long and short loop are possible. Camping is not permitted in the scenic area but there are undeveloped legal roadside camps along Forest Road 133 near East Branch Tionesta Creek, which is popular with anglers.

To reach the Tionesta National Scenic Area, take US 6 east from Warren. Pass the Allegheny National Forest office just outside of Sheffield, where you might want to stop to pick up an interpretive brochure. Continue south for 6 miles further along US 6. Just before reaching the town of Ludlow, turn right on South Hillside Road, go 200 yards to the ⊤ intersection, and make a left onto Water Street. Drive another 200 yards and turn right onto Scenic Drive, which is also called Forest Road 133. (Note that Forest Road 133 is plowed during the winter, but is passable only by four-wheel-drive vehicles when it is snowy.) Cross the railroad tracks and follow the road up the hill, where it turns into a dirt road. Stay on Forest Road 133 for 6 miles, following signs to Tionesta National Scenic Area, taking care to stay on the main road. After 6 miles turn right onto Forest Road 133E, which ends in a loop at the trailhead. Park along the end of the loop.

The woods are lovely, dark, and deep...

Before beginning the hike, walk 100 yards south from the trailhead to take in the views from the observation deck that is perched overlooking a portion of the forest devastated when a 1985 tornado cut a swath through the valley, leveling 800 acres. In other areas, loggers cleared a lot of the tangled wood following the tornado, but here the forest was left untouched. Many old snags can still be seen standing like silent sentinels over the regenerating shrubs and saplings that now blanket the area. Children enjoy sampling the blackberries that grow near the deck in summer.

The trail begins at the western end of the parking loop and returns at the north end of the parking area. Following the white diamond-shaped blazes, the trail enters the forest along the edge of the tornado-devastated area. Huge black cherry trees felled during the storm display their massive roots. As the trail heads toward the first bridge, it passes several 100-foot-high hemlocks. See if the children can find the tiny ¾-inch pine cones from which huge giants like these will sprout. How did something so big come from so small a seed?

Cross over a small wooden bridge after 0.1 mile. Urge caution when crossing the bridges, because the mossy planks are slippery when wet. The short loop turns right (north) just past the bridge, paralleling a tributary of Cherry Run for most of its length as it winds through the hemlock forest. For the long loop, continue straight ahead and pass numerous fallen trees that are disintegrating into the soil. Children can feel how soft and moist the rotten wood is. Soon cross another bridge over Cherry Run. Toads like to bask along the creek's moist banks. The trail then heads uphill into a stand of beeches. In the fall, squirrels like to bury the hemlock cones and beech nuts in the soft soil around the bases of these trees. By springtime they frequently forget where they left their stashes!

The trail climbs slightly. Some of the beeches have been infected with beech bark disease complex. Kids may not realize that trees, like people, can get sick. Watch your step here, as there are many exposed roots. A large hollow log on the left side of the trail makes a good place for a break, or to climb on and explore. The next 0.3 mile is boggy. Look for animal tracks in the muddy patches, where animals come to drink. Try to identify the two-toed heart-shaped tracks of white-tailed deer, which use the trail for browsing. If there is a breeze, children may want to close their eyes and listen for the creaking of tree branches rubbing together. High up on the left side of the trail, two trees lean on each other, making an eerie Halloween sound.

At 0.5 mile the trail leaves the dense undergrowth and enters a grassy gas-pipeline right-of-way, where it joins with the North Country National Scenic Trail. From here, the long loop and the North Country are one and the same, and the trail is blazed with blue and white diamonds. This open, park-like knoll is a nice place for a snack.

Turn right and follow the pipeline about 0.1 mile along the right-of-way, passing a fine old black cherry tree on the way. Soon the trail reenters the forest. Old beech trees here look like elephant trunks, as one of my companions noted. Youngsters might enjoy counting the growth rings on a downed tree that was cut to clear the path.

Soon the trail climbs gently uphill again, keeping just above a wide spring off to the right of the trail. Chipmunks and red squirrels scamper about here. In 5 more minutes reach a huge hemlock snag. Woodpeckers like to feed off the bugs still living in the thick, reddish brown bark. The trail ducks downhill and crosses the third bridge at 0.9 mile. Through the trees, dirt Forest Road 446 is visible. The trail comes close to the road, then parallels it at a distance back to the trailhead. The trail stays high here, and younger hardwood trees reach for the sun in this less dense part of the forest. Look for burls on the beech and maple trees—large basketball-sized growths on the trunks.

The trail again dips down to reach the fourth and final bridge at 1.2 miles, where 300-year-old hemlocks dominate. Children enjoy seeing how many arms it takes to encircle one of these mighty giants. If you close your eyes and sniff, the forest here smells like Christmas. As the hemlocks thin out near the high point of the trail, look for beeches and maples whose bark has been eaten by porcupines. The bark of several trees right next to the trail were munched on during one recent winter. See if your charges can spot the teeth marks left behind by these prickly creatures.

The other end of the short loop comes in from the right (south) to join the long loop again at 1.4 miles. Go 0.1 mile further, where the trail ends up at the north end of the parking loop.

64. Minister Creek Trail

Type: Day hike or overnight
Difficulty: Challenging
Distance: 6.7-mile loop
Hiking time: 7 hours (or shorter hiking days with 1 or 2 overnights)
Elevation gain: 500 feet
Hikable: Late spring–early fall (in the absence of snow)
Map: Minister Creek hiking trail map
Rest rooms: Toilets, water at campground
Fee: None

Though this is one of the longest hikes described in this book, it has many features that make it an ideal place for older children who have some miles under their belt, or for those who might need a scenic and relatively uncrowded area to take children on their first backpacking trip. The hike starts and ends at Minister Creek Campground and climbs up to a plateau with an excellent view of the valley, especially in the fall. It descends through boulder chasms and into the Minster Creek valley, following old railroad grades part of the way. There are two designated camping areas along the creek, and many other possible tent sites throughout the hike. The trail crosses several branches of Minister Creek where some folks like to catch native brook trout. The trail ends back at the campground. A short up-and-back trip to the overlook is possible, too. Use caution at the overlook, which does not have a guardrail and drops off steeply at the edges.

To reach Minister Creek from the Warren area, take US 6 east to Sheffield, bearing right on PA 666 west. Go 2.4 miles and turn right, still on PA 666 west, through Henry's Mill and Lynch. Past Lynch, stay on PA 666 as the road narrows and becomes rough and full of potholes. Pass by the few houses in Truemans and, at the 15th mile on PA 666, turn left into the signed parking lot area across the highway from the Minister Creek Campground.

The Minister Creek Trail begins on the campground side of PA 666, heading uphill on an old road to the left of the campground driveway. The trail is currently marked with white diamond-shaped blazes. At 0.1 mile reach another old road and bear right, bypassing another trail that heads uphill on the left. Continue on the old road for a few tenths of a mile, gradually climbing. Soon the sunny road

ends and you head uphill into the forest on a more narrow path.
The trail splits at 0.6 mile; the righthand path takes the shortest
route to Deer Lick Camp, an undeveloped camping area alongside
Minister Creek. I recommend going left here and following the loop
in a clockwise direction. The trail heads uphill, switchbacking twice
past huge boulders with intriguing shapes that host an assortment
of moisture-loving plants and young trees. Children can be distracted
from the uphill climb by having them look for interesting sights in
the boulders, such as trees that started growing on the sides and tops
of the boulders but had to stretch their roots 10 or 20 feet down the
side of the rock to reach the ground. Kids may enjoy looking for
puddingstone—a conglomerate rock that has white quartzite pebbles
imbedded in it, like marshmallows in a chocolate pudding.

After the second switchback, the trail winds right up through a
jumble of large boulders into a cave-like area where patches of snow
and ice may last until June. Do not camp here, although others have.
There are better places to camp up ahead where the scars of camping
have less impact. Watch the blazes in this area and follow the trail
up stone steps. At the top, a side trail bears right to the base of the
overlook, but continue left to the next side trail, which leads 25 feet
to the Minister Valley Overlook, about 1.2 miles from the trailhead.
The maples in the valley are bathed in brilliant color in the fall. This
is a good place to eat lunch or just soak in the view. Keep kids away
from the edges of the rock, because it drops off precipitously. Do not
be surprised to meet climbers or rappellers here on the weekends.
This is a possible turnaround point, for a 2.4-mile day hike.

After the overlook, the trail descends alongside big boulders, and
numerous side trails branch off to go around the boulders. Watch the
trail blazes. The trail goes through a wide fissure between huge, moss-
covered boulders. Children might enjoy imagining that they are
underwater, as this area once was. This is a great place to explore,

but if it is icy you might want to take the side trail to the right to go around the lower side of the fissure. This is also a good turnaround point for weary hikers, at 1.6 miles.

Make your way downhill, past the other end of the side trail that goes around the fissure, and continue down into the valley. Cross a branch of Minister Creek, then go through mountain laurels and pass two more small creeks. Watch for the blazes here, because at the second small creek there is an easy-to-miss junction at 2.3 miles, at which a side trail heads downhill on an old roadbed to Deer Lick Camp; bear left on the Minister Creek Trail along the sloping hillside, gently ascending. Watch for stinging nettles in this area. You will know why they are named that if you accidentally brush against one. Next head downhill and cross two small creeks before reaching Minister Creek, which you follow along on a flat grade for a while.

Reach a branch of the creek that used to have a bridge that is now washed out. Cross the creek, either by wading or crossing on fallen logs. Use caution here in the spring when high waters can make this crossing a bit tricky. Continue through a more open, sunny area and hop across several wet areas.

The trail goes uphill in the shade again for a short while before you reach a junction with the blue-blazed North Country National Scenic Trail that comes in from the left at 3.6 miles. Go right, following the North Country Trail for a few tenths of a mile; the Minister Creek Trail is now blue- and white-blazed. Cross Minister Creek on a wooden bridge which is currently in disrepair. This area, known as Triple Fork Camp, has no outhouse but plenty of water and flat tent sites.

A backpacking family enjoys lunch along Minister Creek.

Leaving Triple Fork Camp, head uphill until you come to a trail junction after 4.2 miles, where the North Country Trail leaves and goes left. Continue right on the white-blazed Minister Creek Trail. Amble through rolling hills and begin to see more boulders again, crossing several seasonal creeks. At 5.4 miles, reach a yellow-blazed side trail on the right that leads to Deer Lick Camp. Stay to the left and continue downhill on the Minister Creek Trail, and soon begin to see

Minister Creek below on the right. Hop across several seasonal creeks and bear right where the trail crosses Minister Creek on a large, newer, wooden bridge. Cross a smaller creek on a bridge and come to a junction. A side trail follows an old railroad grade back to the campground on your left. The trail heads uphill and at 6.1 miles comes to the Y junction where you began. Make a left and head downhill on the trail as it follows an old road back to the trailhead.

65. Reservoir Loop Trail

Type: Day hike
Difficulty: Easy–moderate (uneven footing)
Distance: 2.8-mile loop
Hiking time: 2.5 hours
Elevation gain: 100 feet
Hikable: Spring–fall
Map: Deer Lick Cross-Country Ski Area Map
Rest rooms: No toilets or water
Fee: None

The Reservoir Loop Trail in the Deer Lick area is primarily a cross-country ski trail, but it also makes a very pleasant day hike along an old railroad grade as it follows attractive Deer Lick Run up to the small and secluded Deer Lick Reservoir, which is perfect for a picnic lunch. The trail loops back through the lush forest, mostly on an old road. It is best hiked after early spring, when it can be muddy. The area is rich in wildlife. Watch for wild turkeys and ruffed grouse (the state bird) along Deer Lick Run, and look for white-tailed deer anywhere along the trail. The barred owl may greet you if you hike in early morning or late afternoon. During winter, this is a fine ungroomed cross-country ski trail, with three loops for all skill levels.

To reach the trailhead, take US 6 east from Warren, taking note of where PA 666 branches off into Sheffield. A few tenths of a mile past this intersection, you will see signs for the Allegheny National Forest office. Turn left onto (dirt) Toll Gate Road immediately before the office. About 0.2 mile up the road there is a small parking area to the right of the road. Park here.

Begin at the parking lot and walk 0.3 mile up the road, past a camp on the right, and bear right over a bridge that crosses over Deer

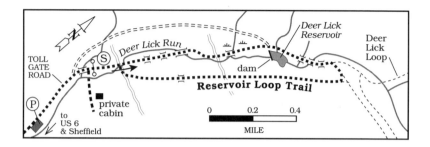

Lick Run by a cabin. Go around the gate straight ahead and proceed on the wide, grassy pathway. The trail is blazed with bluish green diamonds. The hemlock-lined creek is on the left and soon you cross a small wooden bridge over a brook, then soon after another one. At nearly 0.5 mile, reach a junction by some blue natural gas pipes where a trail up the pipeline goes right. This is where you will end up when you return at the end of your loop.

Continuing straight ahead past the blue pipes, the trail becomes quite grassy. The footing becomes bumpy as you walk on an old "corduroy" road. Logs were placed one after another across the road to keep vehicle wheels out of the mud in spring. Soon cross a small bridge, which is slippery when wet, and then come to another bridge and cross that. Note the lush moss by the bridges. How many different kinds of moss can your kids spot here?

Cross three culvert-type bridges, afterward noting that the creek is now on your right. Reach a pipeline cut at 0.9 mile and continue gradually uphill through a grassy, more open area. Cattails grow along the trail here, as it is very moist. At 1.1 miles reach the Deer Lick Reservoir, a peaceful place to take a break and relax or have a picnic along the grassy banks. This area is especially nice in the fall when the maples are at their peak of color. An old road veers off heading back to the trailhead, but follow a fairly flat old road along the left (northern) edge of the reservoir. You are back in among the hemlocks and beeches now, in deep shade. See if children can feel cold spots along the trail, where pockets of air are much colder than the surrounding air.

Cross three more small bridges as you go gradually uphill through some patches that may be a bit muddy. Look for animal tracks. Watch the trail markers here and at a Y intersection make a right uphill a short distance, crossing a bridge. Make two more right turns very soon afterward at 1.6 miles. You are now on another old road that will take you gradually back downhill. Soon see glimpses of the reservoir through the trees on your right. As you continue your easy stroll downhill, look for woodpeckers in the dead snags that are scattered through the forest here. You may be lucky enough to spot a pileated woodpecker, the granddaddy of woodpeckers in size and drilling power.

Cross a pipeline that comes in at an angle from the left at 2 miles. Deer Lick Creek is visible below as you continue your steady downhill stroll. Pass some natural gas pipeline markers. Natural gas and oil are plentiful in the Allegheny National Forest, and sometimes you can smell their fumes as you walk through the forest. Oil was first discovered in Pennsylvania in Titusville, southwest of here, and is still an important industry in the area's economy.

Cross a wooden bridge and go briefly uphill, then downhill again past more feathery hemlocks. Look for places by the tree trunks where the squirrels and chipmunks have stashed pine cones and then returned later to dig them up. At the next trail junction, at 2.4 miles, bear right downhill following the natural gas pipeline, then turn left to rejoin the trail you came in on.

After the rain this artists' conch fungus grows a new skin.

Northcentral Pennsylvania

Listen to the breeze whisper through these pines.

66. Aspen Trail

Type: Day hike
Difficulty: Easy (just bridge)–moderate (hiking loop)
Distance: 2-mile loop
Hiking time: 2 hours
Elevation gain: 301 feet
Hikable: Spring–fall
Map: Kinzua Bridge State Park map
Rest rooms: Toilets, water at trailhead
Fee: None

Take a hike across one of the highest railroad bridges in the world for a bird's-eye view of Kinzua Valley. The Kinzua Bridge, or Viaduct, was built in 1882 and at that time was the highest and longest railroad bridge in the world. It transported coal and logs from the riches of McKean County to Buffalo, New York, and beyond in the late 1800s. This bridge saw no railroad traffic after 1959 until a tourist train began running in 1987. The hike described here takes you on a flat hike across the bridge, then loops back through the Kinzua Valley and back to an overlook of the bridge. Though a hike across the bridge is not for those who are afraid of heights, parents will be comforted to know that the bridge has wooden walkways on both sides of the tracks, handrails, and fencing to make it safe for youngsters. The area can also be enjoyed by hiking the Aspen Trail, which offers a good view of the bridge from beneath. Short hikes up and back along the

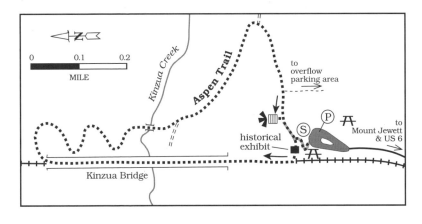

A view of Kinzua Bridge from the overlook

bridge are also possible, but stay off the bridge between 12:00 and 1:00 P.M., when the tourist train is on it. (For information on the train, which leaves from Marienville or Kane, call the Knox & Kane Railroad at (814) 927-6621.)

To reach Kinzua Bridge, take US 6 east from Kane to Mount Jewett. In Mount Jewett, turn left onto Bridge Street, SR 3011. Follow this road 3.2 miles and turn left over the railroad tracks into the park's driveway road. The parking lot is at the end of the driveway.

The trail begins at the north corner of the parking lot. A paved path takes you to a historical exhibit area under some steel railroad beams. The exhibit shows interesting photographs of the construction of the bridge and tells how the bridge was built in 1882 in ninety-four work days by a crew of forty men, then rebuilt in 1900 to accommodate heavier trains. Though at 2,053 feet it is not the longest bridge anymore, it is still considered the fourth highest, towering a dizzying 301 feet above the valley floor. Amazingly enough, this was considered the better option than going around the valley and constructing many more miles of track over rocky terrain.

After viewing the exhibit, bear left to the railroad tracks, then turn right and go alongside the tracks to the beginning of the bridge. Wooden walkways on each side allow plenty of room for many hikers to cross. It is also possible to cross on the tracks because the railroad ties are very close together, but this may be frightening to most people; the view between the cracks is straight down. If you or your charges get the willies halfway across, take a few deep breaths, fix your eyes on the far end of the bridge, and do not look down.

Children may notice that it can be quite windy on the bridge. When freight cars rode this track, the speed limit was 5 miles per hour and sometimes even then logs would get blown off the cars from the stiff wind. Like most large steel structures, this bridge sways slightly, though hikers will not notice. Midway across the bridge, pause to take in the view of Kinzua Creek below and the vast, green Kinzua Valley. To the west, Kinzua Creek flows into the Allegheny River at the Allegheny Reservoir in Warren County.

Once across the bridge, just after 0.5 mile, make a hairpin right turn onto the blazed Aspen Trail. It descends past luscious red raspberry bushes, switchbacking seven times before it reaches Kinzua Creek. Remind children not to cut the switchbacks. This has been done a lot here and the trail is suffering erosion because of it. Pay attention to the blazes and you will be on the easiest and best path down. At the creek's edge, bear left and cross on the metal beam bridge at 1.1 miles. It flexes because it is laid flat. Had it been laid on its end, this I-beam would feel much sturdier.

Continue up a steep hill now, and soon reach an old road. Turn left onto the old road and cross two seeps that run across the path. Climb gradually at first, then more steeply. Soon you get a brief breather as the trail grade eases up, then you climb steeply again. At 1.5 miles, reach a junction with a grassy old road on your left, but continue on the main path curving right. The climb eases and then levels off. Pass a side trail to the overflow parking lot, but continue ahead a short distance and turn right onto a bark-chipped path leading to the overlook deck. The view from the deck is perhaps the best view of the bridge from anywhere in the park. The upper level of the deck is handicapped-accessible. The trail, now a paved path, bears left back to the historical exhibit and the parking area.

67. Beaver Dam Trail

Type:	Day hike
Difficulty:	Easy
Distance:	2.5-mile loop
Hiking time:	2.5 hours
Elevation gain:	80 feet
Hikable:	Spring–fall
Map:	Parker Dam State Park Hiking and Nature Trail Map
Rest rooms:	Toilets, water at beachhouse across from trailhead
Fee:	None

This trail follows at a distance an area set aside for beavers. It stays mostly in deep shade, first through hemlocks and a plantation of pines, then comes out to the meadows where beavers are active and evident. The trail then heads into the woods again and loops back across Mud Run by a pond on Mud Run, which is a popular fishing spot. There are many places along this trail and at other areas throughout the park to spot beavers or beaver activity. The state park here has a campground, cabins, a lifeguarded swimming area, and numerous other trails.

To reach Parker Dam State Park, take Interstate 80 to the PA 153/ Penfield exit (exit 18) and head north on PA 153. Drive about 5 miles, and turn right into the park driveway, Mud Run Road. Go 2.5 miles to the park office drive on the right, then go 0.1 mile further and park on the left side of the road in a large lot just before the dam.

The Beaver Dam Trail begins at the parking area and proceeds southwest on a bark-chipped path through open woods, with grassy undergrowth. Cross a wet area on a boardwalk, and notice the small bog on the right. Thick sphagnum moss saturated with water covers the area in which few trees are growing. Pass under some hemlock trees, cross another boardwalk, and head into a tunnel of thick hemlocks. Notice the pine plantation behind the hemlocks. This area is pretty, quiet, and almost mysterious. Strong winds in the summer of 1995 uprooted some hemlocks and the trail passes under them. In the evening listen for the flute-like song of the wood thrush or listen for owls calling.

Cross more wet areas, go through a small meadow, and then reach an old logging railroad grade, left over from the Central Penn Lumber Company. Turn right onto the woods road, which parallels Mud Run

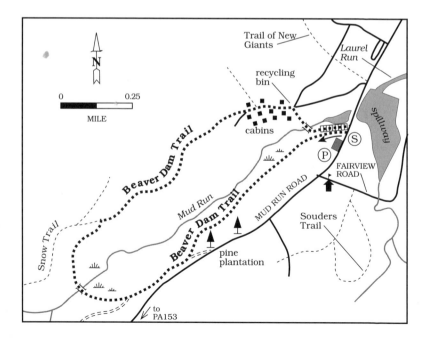

A busy beaver gnaws on a tree in Parker Dam State Park.

Road for a few tenths of a mile. Here walk through the pine plantation and notice the delicious piney smell and soft needles underfoot. As you begin to leave the pines, you also leave the old road, bearing right through the hemlocks. Arrive at a meadow and cross Mud Run on a bridge at 1.2 miles. Many wildflowers grow in the meadow from spring through fall, and butterflies and bees take full advantage of them.

The trail curves right. Hikers can see a beaver dam and a wetland area created by their dam. Beavers are nocturnal, so the best chance of seeing one is at dusk. They make regular rounds checking on their dams, repairing them as needed with fresh sticks and mud. Do not be surprised if you hear a loud slap on the water if the beaver detects your presence. The slap appears to be the beaver's way of signifying annoyance at the intrusion, and perhaps to scare intruders off. Binoculars might be helpful here, as the trail stays far enough way from the dam to not disturb the beavers.

Next curve left, away from the wetland area, and head into the woods again. This may be a good time to discuss the history of beavers in this area. Beavers were plentiful at one time, but they were heavily trapped for their soft, warm fur, which was made into hats and coats. By the early 1900s beavers had become eradicated in Pennsylvania. In 1917 the state of Wisconsin presented a pair of beavers to the Pennsylvania Game Commission. The beavers were released north of here in Sizerville State Park. Others were released there, too, and now Pennsylvania has a healthy beaver population again, especially in this area.

Cross two seeps and see the beaver pond off to the right. Climb gently and at 1.5 miles reach a junction with the Snow Trail. Bear right at the junction, continuing on the Beaver Dam Trail, through the forest, whose floor is covered with ferns. You might spook a white-tailed deer. Watch for the white "flag" of their tail, which flips up to warn those that follow of danger.

Arrive at the road by the cabins at 2.25 miles and turn left. Look for the recycling pavilion on the left. At the recycling bin, turn right and head down between the cabins to reach a shortcut trail, which crosses Mud Run Creek on a bridge and bears left on a boardwalk along the south bank of the creek, ending at Mud Run Road. The parking lot is on the right.

Other trails of interest: The Souders Trail is an easy 0.75-mile self-guided nature loop that focuses on making children aware of what often goes unnoticed as they walk along the trail. Ask for a booklet at the park office. Access is behind the park office.

The 1-mile Trail of New Giants leads hikers through the wreckage of a tornado that roared through in 1985, leveling a stand of old-growth hardwood trees. The trail focuses on the regeneration of the forest here. Access the trail from Mud Run Road 0.25 north of the Beaver Dam trailhead.

---

68. Old Sinnemahoning Road

Type: Day hike
Difficulty: Easy
Distance: 1 mile (or more) one way
Hiking time: 45 minutes (or more) one way
Elevation gain: 50 feet
Hikable: Spring–fall
Map: S. B. Elliott State Park map
Rest rooms: Toilets, water at campground
Fee: None

An easy walk that begins in S. B. Elliott State Park can be as short as 1 mile one way, or as long as 4.5 miles one way, on this old road that was one of the original routes between Sinnemahoning and Clearfield. The portion of the trail in the park is described here. The trail meanders through pretty second-growth forest, with lush ferns all around. Deer, wild turkey, grouse, and other forest creatures may be spotted along this route. The route is grassy and almost flat. If you desire a longer hike, simply continue outside the park boundaries—the road is on public land for another 1.5 miles. It continues on private land still further. The park has camping and cabins.

To reach S. B. Elliott State Park, take Interstate 80 to exit 18, the Penfield/PA 153 exit. Take PA 153 north less than 1 mile and turn right, bearing right onto old PA 153, which leads 0.8 mile into the park. Park at the lot on the left in front of the park office.

To reach the trailhead, walk by the park office and turn left up the dirt road leading to the cabins. Bear right at the first Y junction and in about 0.1 mile look for a grassy old road which bears diagonally left off the dirt road. This is the official starting point of this hike (from which subsequent mileages are calculated). Follow the grassy old road till it comes to the dirt road again, and cross it to reach the trail sign. Continue ahead on the old road, which is the trail, Old Sinnemahoning Road.

Cross the Old Horse Trail about 0.1 mile from the starting point. Stroll through the forest of young trees, mostly oak and maples. This area was logged completely about 100 years ago, so none of the trees here are older than that. This forest has changed from a pine-hemlock

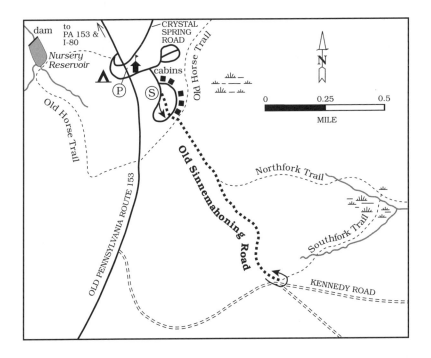

The white-tailed deer is a common sight along most Pennsylvania trails.

forest to a hardwood forest since then. S. B. Elliott, the conservationist for whom the park is named, promoted the idea of beginning a nursery to raise trees for the surrounding forest. You passed a portion of the nursery on the way into the park. It is no longer operating as it once was, but it still supplies seeds to other nurseries. Some of the trees along the route were planted from this nursery.

Reach a junction at 0.5 miles, where the Northfork Trail heads left. (This would make a good loop with the Southfork Trail and back to Old Sinnemahoning Road, but recent logging activity has obscured junctions and blazes, and the trail is difficult to follow. Once the logging is completed, this trail will be reblazed.) Continue to the right on the Old Sinnemahoning Road, walking uphill past some fairly old trees, some of the first to sprout after the logging was finished. Notice several different kinds of ferns, and see that they grow leaning toward the sunny patches. Pass a small meadow on the left. Look for white-tailed deer browsing on the edges. They prefer these areas for browsing, so they can dart back into the cover of the forest if danger approaches.

If you are hiking in the fall, notice the acorns, which are important food for squirrels, chipmunks, and other forest creatures. Arrive at a junction with (gravel) Kennedy Road after 1 mile. Turn around here (it is also possible to continue on the old road after crossing Kennedy Road). Backtrack on Old Sinnemahoning Road to return to the trailhead.

Other trails of interest: The Old Horse Trail, a 2-mile trail, leaves behind the campground and heads back toward a wet area along Stoney Run, crosses old PA 153, then ends on Crystal Spring Road.

69. Pine Tree Trail

Type: Day hike
Difficulty: Moderate
Distance: 2.25-mile loop
Hiking time: 2 hours
Elevation gain: 500 feet
Hikable: Spring–fall
Map: Pine Tree Trail interpretive brochure and map
Rest rooms: Toilets at Hicks Run Camping Area; no water
Fee: None

Pine Tree Trail Natural Area was named for the many white pines that have established themselves on the top of a hill where a homestead once stood. Though the pines are not virgin timber, they are pretty, as are the many other species of trees that line the old road you walk on. An observant hiker may notice remains of the old homestead—especially in the spring or fall when the ferns are not out. Part of the trail is an interpretive trail, with numbers on trees that correspond to tree species. (No interpretive brochures are available at the trailhead. To send for a brochure, write to Bureau of Forestry, Elk State Forest, P.O.Box 327, Emporium, PA 15834 (814) 486-3353. The booklet is hard to follow in terms of following the route in numerical order. Get the guide and refer to it, but do not try to duplicate its route.) The trailhead is across the road from the rustic Hicks Run Camping Area.

To reach the trailhead, take PA 120 south from Emporium and in Driftwood make a right on PA 555. Pick up an interpretive brochure at the Elk State Forest district office in Emporium at the PA 120/PA 155 intersection. Go 8.2 miles past Driftwood and turn right on (dirt) Hicks Run Road. After 2.2 miles, make a left at the Y junction onto West Branch Hicks Run Road. Go 0.1 mile to the Hicks Run Camping Area, where you can park.

The trail begins across the road from the camping area. Begin on an old road behind a sign for Pine Tree Trail Natural Area. Start

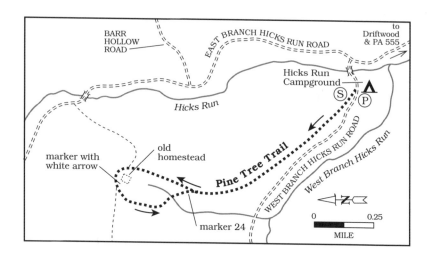

a steady but well-graded climb on the road built as a driveway by the former homesteader. As you climb you can look left and see the opposite ridge and the road below. White pines grow here, mixed in with oak, aspen, birch, maple, and other species. Grapevines drop down from the tree branches onto the grassy old road. Watch for white-tailed deer; they use this path, too. Judging from the steepness of the slopes on either side of the trail, you can understand why the path is attractive to them.

As you near the top of the hill, chestnut oaks drop their acorns on the path, which is spongy-soft from the thick moss underfoot. Would children like to have a moss carpet in their house?

Almost at the top, come to a Y junction at 0.75 mile; you will return to this spot. Though the interpretive brochure is numbered for you to go left, it is easier to follow if you bear right. Notice more white pines of various sizes. The homesteader had cleared this area in the 1800s but the homestead was abandoned by 1900. Since that time the pines have grown up in the former field, as have some other tree species.

Soon reach the top of the hill and the trail flattens. A sea of ferns covers the forest floor here. Come to a trail junction at 1 mile, where the right fork goes down to East Branch Hicks Run Road. Take the left fork, though please note that from here to the other end of the loop at the Y junction, the trail is blazed but the tread is indistinct. Hikers can follow it by walking from blaze to blaze, but the treadway is not well defined. The other option is to backtrack from here.

Going left to stay on the loop, look for a marker of a red circle with a white arrow on it. This points in the direction where the homestead stood. Look for signs of the remains of old foundations. How would you like to live here?

Reach another trail junction and bear left; the right fork goes up to a hill and beyond. Follow the blazes downhill, watching for double blazes, which signify turns and changes in direction. Bear left at the double blazes and continue through ferny areas, which have islands of no ferns among them. The trail curves left at another set of double blazes, and becomes

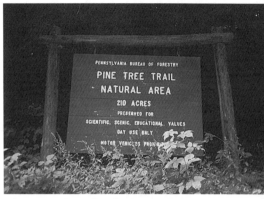

The Pine Tree Trail National Area is named for the white pines growing on the site of an old homestead.

more distinct. Soon after passing marker number 24, rejoin the path you came in on at 1.5 miles. Bear right and continue downhill on the old road back to the trailhead.

70. Fred Woods Trail

Type:	Day hike
Difficulty:	Moderate (distance, some rocks)
Distance:	4-mile loop
Hiking time:	4 hours
Elevation gain:	125 feet
Hikable:	Spring–fall
Map:	Fred Woods Trail Map, Elk State Forest
Rest rooms:	Toilets, water in Driftwood
Fee:	None

Though this is one of the longer hikes in this book, it is not the most difficult and is well worth making a day of. The trail loops around the summit of Mason Hill, a wide, fairly flat-topped mountain. Fred Woods, a forest foreman in Elk State Forest for whom this trail was named, would be proud to lend his name to this exciting trail.

The trail follows the contours of the side of the mountain around and through some of the most interesting rock formations I have seen on short trails in Pennsylvania, right through the 3-foot-wide fissures between the boulders, offering endless possibilities for children's exploration. Add to this the yummy blueberry and huckleberry patches along the trail, and the two scenic vistas of the surrounding deep valleys, and you have one of the best hikes in this book.

To reach the trailhead, take PA 120 south from Emporium on the Bucktail Scenic Drive (a state park), and in Driftwood turn right on PA 555 west. Go 0.6 mile past Driftwood and turn right onto (dirt) Mason Hill Road, which is also known as Castle Garden Road. Go 3.9 miles and park in the small parking area on the right, opposite a large sign for the trail on the left.

Begin across the road from the parking area, where the sign tells about Fred Woods, who was killed on the job in 1975. Head into the woods here, well shaded by hemlocks. In about 0.1 mile cross an old logging road and then a small seep. The trail is fairly flat here, and remains so for most of the hike. Reach an area thick with ferns and descend gently through a more open area. Children may enjoy looking for evidence of animal beds here, places where the grass has been flattened out by resting deer.

Notice an old stone wall on the left. This area was once cleared of trees and the stone walls were the most efficient fences, because there were plenty of rocks around. The trail curves left and comes

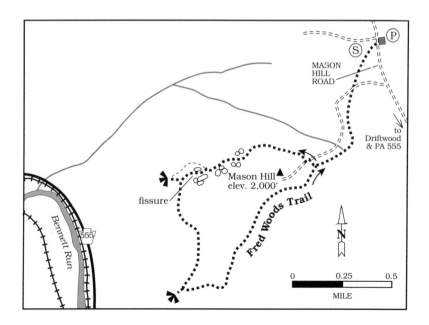

Trees cling to the sides of boulders along the Fred Woods Trail.

upon another old stone wall, this one almost concealed by the ferns. At 0.75 mile reach a ʏ junction. Bear right here, noting that you will return to this spot on the way back. Cross the old logging road again, and bear left on it momentarily, then bear right into the woods again. Pass the first of many ever more intriguing rock formations, this one a large boulder on the left. Notice the fairly large hemlock trees growing on the rock—how do they stay put?

Blueberry bushes line the path now, and you will see many more of these, as well as some taller huckleberry bushes. Curve left and notice you are on the edge of the ridge. Look for a spring that comes from beneath one of the boulders on the left. The trail gets somewhat rocky here. Watch for ruffed grouse; we spooked one as we walked here. Reach an area of taller boulders. The trail passes among the wonderfully mossy, sculpted rocks, with many places to explore. Come to a ʏ junction at just past 1.25 miles, where you can take the lefthand loop and walk through a fissure in the rocks, a really fun experience for both kids and grown-ups. Touch the mossy rocks as you pass through and feel how cool it is here. Snow and ice remain in these cracks longer than in most other spots in this area, even until spring. (If you opt to take the righthand loop, you do not go through the boulders, but come out at the vista visited by the main route, described below.) The lefthand loop climbs to the top of the boulders, which is a great place to munch blueberries; they seem to be quite healthy here. Look for signs of bears, who also love to eat the berries. It is unlikely you will see one, and if you do, it will probably be headed in the other direction to get away from you. Signs include blackberry-filled scat, scratches on trees, and dug-up areas along the trail.

The trail drops back down, soon reaching a "CAUTION" sign alerting hikers to the dropoff to the right. Curve left and arrive at a trail junction—this is where the righthand loop rejoins the main trail. Bear right a short distance to take in the view from some exposed rocks. There is a good view of curving Bennett Run far below. Note that there is no guardrail along the rocks, so exercise caution near the edges. This is an excellent place for a lunch or a snack. If your charges have had enough for a day, this is a possible turnaround point at 1.5 miles. To continue ahead, turn right as you face the trail and return to the main trail. Bear right and continue ahead through more blueberry and huckleberry patches.

The trail climbs gently for a while. Watch the blazes and look for a turn by a boulder, which is easy to miss. Turn right and continue straight, at about 2.1 miles coming to a trail junction which you will return to momentarily. Take the short side trail to the right to reach another vista by some exposed rocks, with a view similar to the one before. Backtrack from here to the trail junction you passed, and turn right onto the main trail, walking along the edge of the ridge.

Cross a small seep. The trail becomes rocky and stays this way for a while. There are some views on your right, though they are not as good as the first two vistas. Children may be alerted to look for signs of a past forest fire in this area. Blackened soil and charring on the lower parts of tree trunks are some of the clues. Walk along the flat, grassy ridge; then the trail becomes rocky again. Curve left, away from the ridge edge, and soon reach an open ferny area where the trail becomes less rocky. Look for puffball mushrooms, which when full-blown erupt in a cloud of black dust when they are stepped upon.

As you continue back toward the loop trail junction, tiring children may be interested in being told about the elk. Pennsylvania used to have a healthy elk herd, but by the 1800s the only ones left were in nearby Elk County. By 1867 they were wiped out. In the early 1900s the Pennsylvania Game Commission reintroduced the elk in this part of the state. They have been protected from hunting since 1932. About fifty elk live in Elk and Cameron Counties, where this hike is located. The elk are large and weigh between 500 and 1,000 pounds, are dark brown, and have a buff-colored rump. Though they are rarely seen, the elk sometimes can be heard bugling in September during mating season.

Return to the beginning of the Fred Woods Trail loop at 3.4 miles and bear right, retracing your way back to the trailhead.

71. Turkey Path

Type: Day hike
Difficulty: Challenging (elevation gain)
Distance: 2.1 miles round trip
Hiking time: 1.5 hours
Elevation gain: 833 feet
Hikable: Spring–fall
Map: Leonard Harrison and Colton Point State Parks map
Rest rooms: Toilets, water at trailhead
Fee: None

The Pine Creek Gorge, known as the Grand Canyon of Pennsylvania, holds a particular fascination for many residents. There is nothing else like it in the state, where Pine Creek cuts a narrow gorge into the now steep sided plateau that surrounds it. The overlook area has an interesting environmental education center and a short looping overlook trail with good views of the gorge. A hike on the Turkey Path, though steep, is rewarding. It takes you down through the forest on a well-graded trail to a cascading waterfall, along Little Fourmile Run, which it follows to Pine Creek, whose shallow waters are great for wading in summer. Do not take your toddler on the Turkey Path unless you plan to carry him or her. Toddlers will better enjoy the Overlook Trail (see "Other trails of interest," below.) The park has a family campground and a playground.

To reach Leonard Harrison State Park, take US 6 to Wellsboro and turn onto PA 660 south, following it until it ends at Leonard Harrison State Park. Park along the parking loop.

The trail begins through the breezeway between an environmental education center on the right and the visitor center on the other side. Just beyond the breezeway, turn right onto the beginning of the Turkey Path. The trail makes numerous switchbacks and has boardwalks over some too-worn and wet areas. It also has many benches, which may be of no interest on the way down, but which will be gratefully accepted on the way up. Remind everyone to stay on the main path and not cut switchbacks as some others have done.

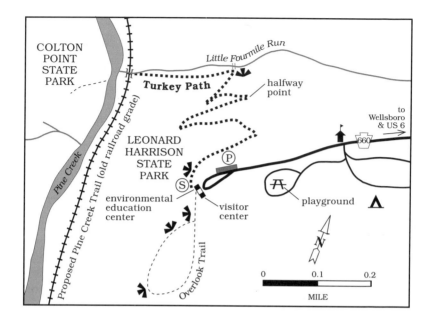

Staying on the trail protects endangered plant species growing along the trail.

Make four switchbacks and watch the chipmunks and squirrels scatter. A spring crosses the path, the first of several. After one more switchback begin to see Little Fourmile Run on the right below. Cross several boardwalks over wet areas and reach some interesting overhanging rock ledges on your left. Children might enjoy guessing who might live in some of these fissures . . . deer, mice, voles, garter snakes? Pass the sixth switchback and at the seventh there is a view of the waterfall below. This is at 0.5 mile, the halfway point to the end of the trail at Pine Creek. If youngsters are tired, this is a good place to turn around.

Continue on and at the next switchback reach another view of the waterfall and a lower trail that leads to a closer view of the falls. Do not go down to the falls, as the trail is slippery and the water is unsafe for swimming.

Go down the last long set of steps and reach the railroad grade at the bottom of the canyon at just over 1 mile. To reach Pine Creek, cross the railroad grade and head downhill on the left side of the railroad bridge. In the spring the creek is cold and fast; at other times of the year it is lower, and in the summer it is warm enough for wading and play.

On your return trip, estimate that it will take about twice as long to get up as it took to get down. Take it slow and it will seem easier. Tell young hikers about how Pine Creek used to flow northeast, but when the glaciers came through, they formed a natural dam that forced the creek to reverse itself and flow south to form the gorge.

Other trails of interest: The Overlook Trail is a loop alongside the edge of the gorge that has numerous overlooks and binoculars for viewing the gorge. The entire loop is 0.6 mile and is accessed from the breezeway by the visitor center; take the path straight ahead.

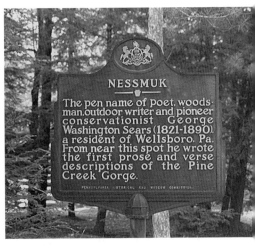

The Grand Canyon of Pennsylvania continues to be an inspiration to many people.

72. Pine Creek Trail (Proposed)

Type:	Day hike
Difficulty:	Easy
Distance:	4.5 miles one way
Hiking time:	4.5 hours one way
Elevation gain:	None
Hikable:	Spring–fall
Maps:	Tioga State Forest public use map; Tiadaghton State Forest public use map
Rest rooms:	Toilets, water in Colton Point State Park
Fee:	None

This railroad grade through the spectacular Pine Creek Gorge, the Grand Canyon of Pennsylvania, is being developed as a Rails to Trails multi-use trail and when finished will begin at the intersection of US 6 and PA 287 north of Wellsboro and go to the intersection of PA 44 and 220 just west of Jersey Shore, a distance of over 60 miles.

The grade is currently on the original ballast and is hikable, especially from Ansonia south to Blackwell. The grade is flat and follows quite closely to Pine Creek, along which many species of birds, including great blue heron and bald eagle, can be seen, as well as animals such as beavers, muskrats, and, if you are lucky, river otters. In the spring rafts and canoes float down the creek; the rest of the year it is virtually empty. In winter, the trail is maintained with a cross-country ski track setter when there is enough snow.

The trail is due to be constructed beginning in August 1995 and the trail will be closed during the construction, so check with the District Forester office for the current situation: (northern end) Tioga

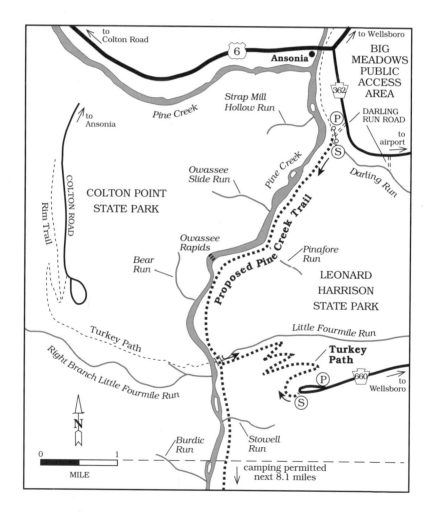

Wide, inviting Pine Creek

District Forester, P.O. Box 94, Route 287 South, Wellsboro, PA 16901, (717) 724-2868; (southern end) Tiadaghton District Forester, 423 East Central Avenue, South Willamsport, PA 17701, (717) 327-3450.

The day hike suggested here travels along the gorge through the area of Colton Point and Leonard Harrison State Parks. For this hike you will need two cars; leave one at the Darling Run Road trailhead described below, and take the other vehicle to the trailhead for hike 71, Turkey Path, in Leonard Harrison State Park. Hike the Turkey Path 1 mile down to the proposed Pine Creek trailhead (described in hike 71, Turkey Path), then head north on the proposed Pine Creek Trail for 3.5 miles to the gate at Darling Run Road, for a total hike of about 4.5 miles.

There is no camping permitted between Darling Run Road and the state parks. Camping is currently allowed 6 miles south of the Big Meadows public access area (north of Darling Run Road access area) or about 5 miles south of the Darling Run Road access. Check with the District Forester office (see addresses above) for a detailed map of the permitted camping areas if you are interested in making a backpack trip.

To take your shuttle vehicle to the Darling Run Road access point, from Wellsboro on US 6 take PA 660 west for 3 miles to where it intersects with PA 362. Take PA 362 west 3.4 miles, passing the Grand Canyon State Airport on the way, and make a left on the second (dirt) Darling Run Road (there are two roads of the same name here). Go 0.2 mile and park your shuttle vehicle at the end of the road near the gate.

Take your second vehicle to the Turkey Path trailhead; to reach it from the Darling Run access point, take PA 362 east for 3.4 miles, turn right onto SR 3029, continue for 0.8 mile, then turn right again onto PA 660, which ends at the parking area for the Turkey Path.

Beginning at Leonard Harrison State Park, descend the Turkey Path (described in hike 71), and once you reach the proposed Pine Creek Trail at the bottom of the gorge at 1 mile, turn north at the railroad bridge. The trail is virtually flat and easy to walk on from here until the gate at Darling Run Road. Children will enjoy being so close to the creek. There are plenty of places to walk to the water's edge to practice skipping stones, look for water dogs, or just cool off. Use caution in the spring when the water is running fast and deep. During the rest of the year, the creek is generally shallow.

After just over 2 miles, watch for the Owassee Rapids. Explain to the children that rapids are created by the water moving over large rocks and deep drops in the creekbed. In the spring these rapids give canoeists and rafters a thrill. In about 3 miles pass Pinafore Run on the right. As you continue north, children will notice numerous small islands in the middle of the creek. Their size depends entirely on the current water level.

After nearly 4.5 miles, watch for Darling Run, which descends to Pine Creek on the right. Just past Darling Run, look for the gate at the end of Darling Run Road on the right, visible from the proposed Pine Creek Trail.

For a shorter hike, begin at the Darling Run Road trailhead with just one vehicle. Walk past the gate and turn south on the proposed Pine Creek Trail. Walk as far as you like; retrace your steps on the return. Another option is to head north on the proposed Pine Creek Trail from the Darling Run Road trailhead; it is 2 miles round trip to the Big Meadows Public Access Area in Ansonia and back.

For a longer day hike or overnight, begin at Darling Run Road trailhead and hike south on the proposed Pine Creek Trail. Camping is permitted between miles 6 and 14.1. Hike as far as you like, and retrace your route on the return. Longer hikes on the proposed Pine Creek Trail can be as long as you want—up to 60 miles!

Other trails of interest: The Rim Trail hugs the edge of the Pine Creek gorge in Colton Point State Park, opposite the gorge from Leonard Harrison State Park. The 0.5-mile Rim Trail connects with the other end of the Turkey Path, which leads about 1 mile down into the canyon to the shore of Pine Creek, opposite the end point of hike 71, Turkey Path, Leonard Harrison State Park. To reach Colton Point State Park, take PA 362 past Darling Run Road, described above, to the town of Ansonia. Make a left onto US 6 west, then a left again in about 0.1 mile on Colton Road between a gas station and a tavern, following signs to Colton Point State Park.

73. Stephenhouse Run Trail

Type: Day hike
Difficulty: Easy
Distance: 1.4-mile loop
Hiking time: 1.25 hours
Elevation gain: 100 feet
Hikable: Spring–fall
Map: Stephenhouse Run Trail Map, US Army Corps of Engineers Ives Run Recreation Area
Rest rooms: Toilets, water at administration building
Fee: None

There is something about a pine plantation that appeals to kids of all ages. It might be the piney smell as the sun warms the trees, or it may be the soft feel of the needles underfoot, or the deep shade these trees provide. Whatever it is, the pine plantation through which part of this trail runs has all those pleasing qualities. This short loop is a rolling path in the Ives Run Recreation Area adjacent to Hammond Reservoir.

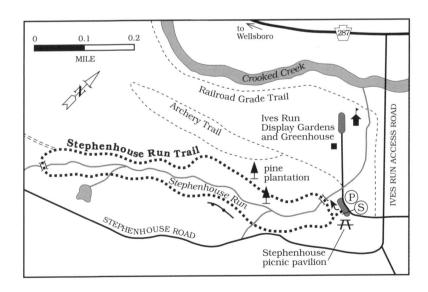

The trail is on an old road part of the way as it follows Stephenhouse Run, a tributary of Crooked Creek, which empties into the large reservoir. There is a camping area nearby, as well as several other trails suitable for family hikes. Not to be missed are the paths through the Ives Run Display Gardens, which have a figure-eight–looped tree walk, a wildflower and fern walk, and a greenhouse and nursery, all of which should be of interest to children and parents. The Stephenhouse loop is described here, and a brochure of the display gardens is available at the administration building, just up the road from the trailhead. The display gardens are across from the administration building. To get to the display gardens, turn left from the picnic pavilion and park by the administration building. The greenhouse is open during normal business hours.

To reach the Ives Run Recreation Area, take PA 287 north from Wellsboro for 12 miles, and turn right onto the Ives Run Access Road, which is well signed. Go 0.2 mile and turn right onto the first road on the right, which has signs pointing to the park administration building, and go 0.1 mile. Park on the left by the Stephenhouse picnic pavilion.

The trail begins at the picnic pavilion and you go through it to the bulletin board at the trailhead. Bear right immediately on a bridge over Stephenhouse Run. Stroll through a white pine plantation now, on soft pine needles. Pass through a tiny meadow and continue in the pine plantation.

Soon join an old road as the path heads gently uphill. Near the end of the plantation, children may want to look for a very old white pine

A young hiker pauses for a closer look at the water.

on the left that was here long before the rest of the pines were planted. Have them listen to squeaking, creaking trees in this area if there is a breeze. This happens when one of the trees falls against another and rubs together as they sway in the breeze. It sounds a little like Halloween.

Look for an old ash tree. Trees like this one have hollows that provide nesting for birds like owls or raccoons. Leave the pine plantation as the trail curves left. You are now in a mixed forest of deciduous and hemlock trees. Kids might look for dug-up areas in the trail, where squirrels have been rooting for pine cones and acorns. Listen to hear the creek below. At a trail junction by a paper birch, bear left, downhill, leaving the old roadbed. Reach Stephenhouse Run and cross it on a bridge at 0.7 mile.

Bear left and walk briefly through a sunny meadow where wildflowers and blackberries grow. Soon head into the woods again, on a path that bobs up and down through the forest, alongside the creek.

Cross two tributaries, which are good areas to look for animal tracks in the mud. Soon walk through a small meadow and see an old stone wall on your right, which you follow briefly. The trail leaves the creekside and weaves in and out of a young hardwood forest. Cross another tributary. Now on a small ridge, you can look down toward the creek. Watch for ancient oaks that used to provide shade in a formerly open field. Walk downhill steeply from here and reach the trailhead.

Other trails of interest: C. Lynn Keller Trail is a 9-mile network that has several access locations, two off Ives Run Access Road and one off Camp Access Road. Numerous loops of varying difficulty can be made:

Archery Trail—a 1-mile beginner archery loop—begins along the west side of the park road that leads to the park administration building.

Railroad Grade Trail is an easy 2.6-mile trail along Crooked Creek. It begins by the park road near the Stephenhouse picnic pavilion and ends near the northern end of SR 4039 off PA 287 south of Hammond Lake.

Lambs Creek Hike and Bike Trail—a 3-mile paved multi-use trail that follows the former Erie Lackawanna Railroad bed along Lambs Creek—can be accessed in Mansfield behind Bi-Lo grocery market on PA 660 east of Wellsboro.

At Cowanesque Lake, the U.S. Army Corps of Engineers project north of Stephenhouse Run Trail, the 0.5-mile Tompkins Pond Nature Trail leaves from Tompkins Campground and has an interpretive brochure. Take PA 287 to US 15 north, then go west on Bliss Road to the campground.

74. Pitch Pine Loop

Type: Day hike
Difficulty: Easy–moderate (brushy)
Distance: 2-mile loop
Hiking time: 2 hours
Elevation gain: 50 feet
Hikable: Spring–fall
Map: USGS 7½′ Jersey Mills, Glen Union public use map, Tiadaghton State Forest
Rest rooms: Toilets, water in Hyner Run State Park a few miles northwest
Fee: None

This hike on a broad, flat hilltop just south of Miller Run Natural Area is a pleasant stroll through blueberry patches in an open forest of primarily maples and scrub oak, with some mountain laurel and pitch pines. At about the halfway point there is a great view of the deep valley through which Miller Run cuts. The trail is well blazed but not overused so the chances for viewing wildlife, such as wild turkey, hawks (by the vista), and white-tailed deer are excellent. The ferns are thick and can obscure the trail in spots, so I recommend hiking this trail in spring before the ferns are out, or in the fall after they have died back somewhat. In summer, the trail is still hikable, but wear long pants—and take a bucket for collecting blueberries.

To reach the trail take US 220 west from Williamsport to PA 44 north, and continue on PA 44 north, past the intersection of PA 44 and PA 664 in Haneyville. Go 2.6 miles to a small pulloff parking area on the right and a trail sign.

The trail begins behind the trail sign, where you can see both ends of the loop coming together. Start by taking the

Looking into the Miller Run Natural Area

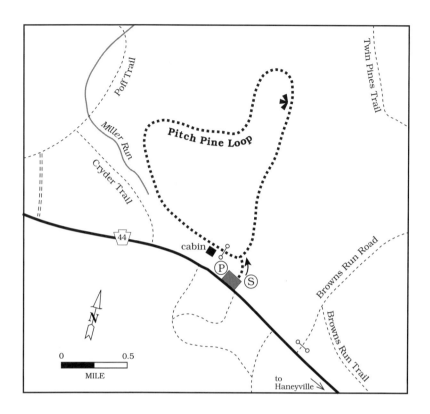

right fork and walk on a grassy path. This area burned in the past and its soil is poor. Walk through an open sunny forest, where mostly red maples and scrub oak grow, and of course, blueberries and ferns, which seem to be everywhere along the path.

Following the light blue dot blazes, you wade through the ferns and might be lucky enough to surprise a flock of wild turkeys, as we did on our hike here. Head down a hill so gentle it is barely noticeable. Mountain laurels line the path. The trail gets slightly rocky and soon comes to a vista on your right at about 0.75 mile, with a fine view of the Miller Run Natural Area. This is a good place to get out the binoculars and look for hawks. We happened upon a small hawk perched on a snag on the edge of the gorge here.

The trail then turns left and follows an old road for a good distance. Amble along the path, which is lined with bracken ferns, sweet fern, and mountain laurel. The trail gradually curves left, then gradually right, and heads downhill slightly. Pass through thick ferns, then curve left again. Notice a ridge in Miller Run Natural Area on your right, through the trees. After about 1.75 miles, reach an open meadow with tall grasses. Look for deer beds here, flattened areas where deer have bedded down during the day. You might be lucky enough to rouse a sleeping white-tailed deer, as we did on our hike.

Back in the open forest again, walk uphill easily and pass a gate just past a hunting cabin. The beginning of the loop is just beyond the gate; turn right to return to the parking area.

75. Carsontown Trail

Type:	Day hike
Difficulty:	Easy
Distance:	0.9-mile round trip
Hiking time:	30 minutes
Elevation gain:	None
Hikable:	Year-round
Map:	Little Pine State Park map
Rest rooms:	Toilets, water at campground
Fee:	None

This little loop along the shore of Little Pine Creek takes hikers through a red and white pine stand to the shore of the wide, shallow creek. The creek is great for tubing, wading, or just exploring, and it is usually shallow enough that even young children can stand in it safely. The trail loops back through the pines on a mowed path.

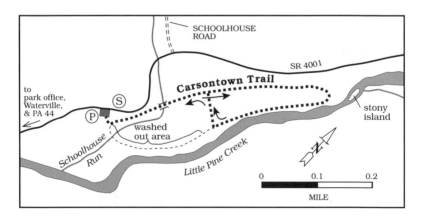

Little Pine Creek is a great place to spend time exploring, especially on a hot summer day.

This loop is currently being developed as an interpretive trail, so mileage markers and interpretive signs will be installed here in the future. A list of wildflowers will be posted along the trail. Ask at the park office for an update on this trail's status as an interpretive trail. The trail is in pretty Little Pine State Park, which is off the wide southern end of the 50-mile-long Pine Creek Valley, known at its northern end as the Grand Canyon of Pennsylvania. Camping, a swimming beach, and picnicking are available at the park.

To reach the trail, take US 220 west from Williamsport to PA 44 north to Waterville. Turn right in Waterville on SR 4001 and go 3.3 miles to the park entrance. Continue 0.9 mile past the park entrance to the park office, and continue another 2.4 miles north of the park office to the trailhead, located where there is a small parking lot on the right by the trail sign.

The trail begins at the left corner of the parking lot, and you walk only a few feet before you come to a γ junction. Take the lefthand fork on the mowed path and soon enter the shade. Milkweed, a favorite butterfly food, can be found along the path. Young sycamores and red maples are growing here also, making it pretty in the fall once their leaves have turned.

Cross Schoolhouse Run on a bridge—in midsummer it may be completely dry. Soon you are surrounded by red and white pines. Children may enjoy looking for pine cones here. Some shagbarked hickory trees are also making a start here. Notice the soft, light-green grass under the trees—it is called fox grass.

At 0.2 mile is a junction to which you will return; pass the old road on the right, continuing straight ahead. Stroll through more pines, and at 0.4 mile the trail curves right, toward Little Pine Creek. The creek's edge is a good place to spend some time. If you cross the narrow part of the creek here, there is an island of flat, round stones that is fun to explore. Tubing is popular here and the water is very warm in the summer.

The trail parallels the creek a short distance and passes a huge, ancient sycamore tree. Just past the sycamore, at just over 0.6 mile, is the other end of the old road you passed earlier. Hikers used to be able to bear left here and follow the loop all the way around to the trailhead, but the trail and a bridge recently washed out. It is not the first time this area has experienced flooding. In 1972 the park was ruined by the St. Agnes flooding and has been rebuilt. Flood waters have not risen above the dam since. Both the trail and bridge here are due to be reconstructed in spring of '97. When they are, you will be able to pass the shortcut on the old road and follow the trail along Little Pine Creek, crossing the bridge at Schoolhouse Run. Children may be interested in looking for fish near the bridge, as water and fish from the larger creek enter here. The mileage for the reconstructed trail will be 0.9 mile for the entire loop

For now, you must bear right on the old road at 0.7 mile, heading through the forest to the trail you came in on. Make a left onto the trail and retrace your route back to the beginning of the trail.

Other trails of interest: Lakeshore Trail, which begins on the dam at Little Pine Lake in the southern part of Little Pine State Park, is an easy 5-mile-long trail that follows the southeastern lakeshore and ends on SR 4001. Park at the dam, located about 0.25 mile north of the park office.

For more of a challenge, try a 2.25-mile loop that goes up gated Love Run Road (across the road from the beach area at Little Pine Lake) for about 1 mile to where it intersects with a connector trail on the right, and then turns right and follows Love Run Trail downhill back to the beach area. The route goes through pretty forest along Love Run Creek. Park at the beach parking lot, about 1 mile north of the park office on SR 4001.

Index

About the Author and Photographer

Sally Trepanowski is an elementary school guidance counselor and avid hiker who has put in many miles hiking with children. She is also a former camp counselor and outdoor instructor who has led groups of children on hikes, backpacks, and canoe trips of one week to one month. A Pennsylvania native, Sally has hiked extensively all over the East Coast and in the West. She met her husband Marty while backpacking the Appalachian Trail, which they have both completed end to end. They are working on finishing the Pacific Crest Trail, of which they have hiked 2,000 miles. Sally is a contributing editor for *American Hiker* magazine and has published articles in *Backpacker, Guideposts,* and other publications.

Marty Trepanowski is a carpenter and cabinetmaker who studied photography at Rochester Institute of Technology. He has published photographs in *Backpacker* and *American Hiker* magazines. This is the Trepanowskis' first book.

Other titles you may enjoy from The Mountaineers:

Best Hikes With Children Series
Guides to day hikes and overnighters for families, including tips on hiking with kids, safety, points of interest, information on flora and fauna, and more.
> ***The Catskills and Hudson River Valley,***
> Cynthia Lewis & Thomas Lewis
> ***Connecticut, Massachusetts, and Rhode Island,***
> Cynthia Lewis & Thomas Lewis
> ***New Jersey,*** Arline & Joel Zatz
> ***Vermont, New Hampshire, and Maine,***
> Cynthia Lewis & Thomas Lewis

Kids in the Wild: A Family Guide to Outdoor Recreation,
Cindy Ross & Todd Gladfelter
A family-tested handbook of advice on sharing outdoor adventures with children of all ages and skill levels.

A Hiker's Companion: 12,000 Miles of Trail-Tested Wisdom,
Cindy Ross & Todd Gladfelter
Entertainingly written real-life guide to surviving and thriving in the outdoors.

Are We Having Fun Yet? Enjoying the Outdoors with Partners, Families, and Groups, Brian Baird
Unique outdoor handbook focuses on solutions to the interpersonal conflicts that arise during group activities and provides advice on how to get the most out of trips with groups of all sizes.

An Outdoor Family Guide to Yellowstone & Grand Teton ***National Parks,*** Lisa Gollin Evans
Part of popular *Outdoor Family Guide* Series. Features 50 family-friendly outings, including biking, hiking, canoeing, cross-country skiing, and kayaking.

THE MOUNTAINEERS, founded in 1906, is a nonprofit outdoor activity and conservation club, whose mission is "to explore, study, preserve, and enjoy the natural beauty of the outdoors...." Based in Seattle, Washington, the club is now the third-largest such organization in the United States, with 15,000 members and five branches throughout Washington State.

The Mountaineers sponsors both classes and year-round outdoor activities in the Pacific Northwest, which include hiking, mountain climbing, ski-touring, snowshoeing, bicycling, camping, kayaking and canoeing, nature study, sailing, and adventure travel. The club's conservation division supports environmental causes through educational activities, sponsoring legislation, and presenting informational programs. All club activities are led by skilled, experienced volunteers, who are dedicated to promoting safe and responsible enjoyment and preservation of the outdoors.

If you would like to participate in these organized outdoor activities or the club's programs, consider a membership in The Mountaineers. For information and an application, write or call The Mountaineers, Club Headquarters, 300 Third Avenue West, Seattle, WA 98119; phone: (206) 284-6310.

The Mountaineers Books, an active, nonprofit publishing program of the club, produces guidebooks, instructional texts, historical works, natural history guides, and works on environmental conservation. All books produced by The Mountaineers are aimed at fulfilling the club's mission.

Send or call for our catalog of more than 300 outdoor titles:

The Mountaineers Books
1001 SW Klickitat Way, Suite 201
Seattle, WA 98134
1-800-553-4453